Male Homosexuality in
21st-Century Thailand

Male Homosexuality in 21st-Century Thailand

A Longitudinal Study of Young, Rural, Same-Sex-Attracted Men Coming of Age

Jan Willem de Lind van Wijngaarden

ANTHEM PRESS

Anthem Press
An imprint of Wimbledon Publishing Company
www.anthempress.com

This edition first published in UK and USA 2023
by ANTHEM PRESS
75–76 Blackfriars Road, London SE1 8HA, UK
or PO Box 9779, London SW19 7ZG, UK
and
244 Madison Ave #116, New York, NY 10016, USA

First published in the UK and USA by Anthem Press in 2021

British Library Cataloguing-in-Publication Data
A catalogue record for this book is available from the British Library.

Library of Congress Control Number: 2023936374

ISBN-13: 978-1-83998-923-0 (Pbk)
ISBN-10: 1-83998-923-8 (Pbk)

Cover image: Pongsak14\shutterstock.com

Disclaimer: The young man in the cover image has nothing to
do with this study and is not a participant

This title is also available as an e-book.

This book is dedicated to my parents,
Gerhard and Leny de Lind van Wijngaarden, and my sister Anneke,
the most loving, supportive, caring and understanding family
a young gay man could ever wish for.

CONTENTS

PREFACE

On 2 July 1989, I set foot on Thai soil for the first time. I felt miserable and had thrown up several times after the last meal served during my 27-hour, four stop-over flight from Amsterdam to Bangkok on Biman Bangladesh Airlines. My Dutch companion dragged me along from Don Meuang International Airport to Bangkok's Southern Bus Terminal, where we took the cheapest possible bus to the famous river town of Kanchanaburi. Seeing how pale I looked, the young male bus employee vacated the last seat in the bus, next to a window, so I could throw up if needed. Despite my sense of misery I could not help noticing how beautiful he was, and I smiled at him gratefully. When the bus started moving and the wind blew through the open windows, I felt better. I tried to sleep a little, but woke up when I felt a hand on my leg. The bus employee had taken the seat next to me and smiled at me broadly when I looked his way. I was in shock. How had he picked me out? How did he know I was gay? I had hidden my homosexuality from everybody I knew in The Netherlands for the past five years or so – including from my travel companion who, I worried, might be upset if he found out; I quickly glanced at him, but he was fast asleep in the other corner of the bus. Half a minute later, the young man removed his hand from my leg and jumped up to help an elderly passenger disembark. My heart was beating fast – was this country, indeed, the tolerant paradise I had heard about?

Later I discovered that physicality between Thai men has, more often than not, nothing to do with homosexual desire. This first Thai 'erotic moment' I had experienced in the bus to Kanchanaburi was most likely not a shared one. The young man's hand on my leg and his broad beaming smile were signs of his solidarity with my miserable state – they were not an acknowledgement of any erotic interest or 'spark', let alone an invitation for sex or a long and happy relationship.

This incident was the first in many that came to trigger my interest in Thai masculinity and homosexuality. Within a few years after my first holiday, I managed to learn Thai, and in 1990, I lost my virginity and embarked on my first relationship with a Thai man. To my disappointment, cracking the language code appeared not quite enough to gain an understanding of Thai (homo)sexual culture, let alone to establish a stable relationship. I discovered that many things worked differently in relationships between Thai men – besides the cultural and age differences that often characterize relationships between Thai men and Caucasian men. I experienced many of these things first-hand over the following 25 years. Sometimes my relationships mimicked relationships between married Thai men and women; others mimicked a nurturing support situation. Some were about pleasure and sex; others about longer-term expectations, security and stability; yet others were like 'friendships with benefits'.

In the mid-1990s, my fascination with and interest in Thai homosexuality became not only of personal but also of public health interest. Thailand was in the grip of a rapidly expanding HIV epidemic. When I started losing Thai friends and colleagues to AIDS, I wanted to make a contribution by making strategies for HIV prevention, care and support more relevant and appropriate for young Thai homosexual men. This meant I had to make homosexuality in Thailand a serious topic of investigation.

This book is based on a study I conducted in 2010–14 to understand Thai homosexuality in depth, partly because I wanted to make sense of the experiences I had had with a series of Thai boyfriends, and partly because I wanted to understand the vulnerability to HIV that I observed in so many young Thai gay men. It was a scientific study but, as is often the case in social science, personal experiences and insights played a major role in it – not only in the way the questions were asked and in the focus of the interviews, but also in the interpretation of the results.

I hope this book will be of use to people wishing to understand Thai homosexuality better – and in doing so, I hope it can help people and organizations fighting to reduce the impact of HIV on Thai homosexual men design more appropriate and effective HIV service interventions by better understanding the social-cultural contexts in which HIV transmission occurs.

I am indebted to many people who contributed to my thinking, to the design and conduct of this study, to the process of making sense of the data I collected, and to the development of this book. First of all, my professor and supervisor Gary Dowsett at the Australian Research Centre in Sex, Health and Society (ARCSHS) has been a wise, inspiring and constructive teacher along the way. Other people – both staff and students – at ARCSHS contributed to the study as well, especially Stephen McNally, Duane Duncan, Jo Grzelinska, Emerich Daroya and Gillian Fletcher. Chris Lyttleton of Macquarie University in Sydney kindly reviewed parts of earlier versions of this book and provided invaluable advice and support during many stimulating and exciting discussions before I even started the project. I gratefully acknowledge the hard work and excellent support of my research assistant, Mr Ekkaluck Champarsi (Aum). I would also like to thank Pimpawan Boonmongkhon, Peter Aggleton, Peter A. Jackson, Nareupon Duangwises, Timo Ojanen, Frits van Griensven, Joe Carrier, Scott Berry, the late Len Unterberger, Sheldon Shaeffer, Alessio Panza, Matt Yoxall, Louis Gooren and Setthabut Ittithumwinit (Ake) for their input, feedback and wisdom. Megan Sinnott, Graham Fordham and Gilbert Herdt reviewed a previous version of this book, and provided important input into the final version.

And finally, without the friendship, love and moral support provided by my friends and family I would have been unable to complete this work. First of all, I wish to thank my parents, Leny and the late Gerhard de Lind van Wijngaarden, and my sister, Anneke de Lind van Wijngaarden, to whom I dedicate this work. I also wish to thank my friends (some of whom were listed above), including Kriangkrai Prajuabpol (Rick), John Ellis, Kangwan Fongkaew (JoJoe), Maurits van Pelt, Bas van Loon, Philippe Girault, Bettina Schunter, Jetske Bijdendijk and Ruben Helmers, Twan Nooitmeer, Bruce Parnell, David Clark, Atiphan Chanthipma (Sam), Narin Wongchak (Rin), Decha Noymaleewan Boonmee (Ui), Pooyai Porang (Poon), Chaiwat Muangthong (Bon), Chaiyut Iampasit (Oad), Robert Bennoun, Paul Janssen, Paul Jager, Paul Jansen, Frans Mom and Christine Prast.

Bangsaen, Thailand
5 September 2020

Chapter 1

INTRODUCTION

This book analyses how 25 same-sex-attracted men who grew up in rural northeastern and southern Thailand came of age. I interviewed each of the young men three times in a period of 20 months in 2011–12. The first of the three interviews was timed to coincide with the period when they were aged 18, graduating from high school, and were about to move on to the next phase of their lives. The second interview occurred about 6–8 months later, and by the time of the third and last interview, another 6–8 months after the second, most participants were around 19–20 years of age.

I explored the young men's sexual life histories and how they became aware of and created an understanding of their sexuality and gender. Most of them continued their studies in a bigger city; hence I was keen to look for changes between the first and the second, and the second and the third interviews, looking at the impact of the transition many of the men made from a rural to an urban area on the way they viewed their sexuality and gender. I also tried to understand their lives in the context of wider processes of globalization, especially influences that reached them via the Internet and social media, including the growing importance of social media in dating and romance as well as in maintaining friendships.

This book emerged from my fascination with the fluidity and variety in how sexuality and gender are expressed in Thailand. Because I followed each study participant over many months, it became possible to view this fluidity and variety not only between participants in the study but also within the same individual over time. If this book has produced one important insight, it is that it has confirmed that sexual/gender identities, and the linguistic terms to describe them, are not static. Individuals often try on different identities over the course of their life, and even in the limited time frame of this study this became abundantly clear.

The study focused on transition at several levels. I followed the young men during an important transition in their lives: the end of their high school years and the end (in most cases) of their life as a child with parents or extended family at a rural home. There was a transition from the teen years to life as an adult, often meaning a shift from being a passive and dependent actor in the household to a more active (but often still financially dependent) one. Nearly all of the men in the study moved to a city to continue their education; others left to find a job. Several also had stints of sex work in one of Thailand's well-known centres for prostitution, which is also discussed in this book. This transition, combined with increased access to and use of the Internet, brought nearly all the men into contact with new ideas about gender and sexuality. Some participants transitioned from a public presentation as non-sexual (or assumed heterosexual) to a more or less disclosed homosexual or 'gay' presentation of themselves. Having moved out of the heavily supervised sphere of their parental homes, most participants also moved from a virtually non-existent or less active sex life to a more active one: many experienced an abrupt increase in their opportunities to have sex, often leading to radical changes in the way they understood and valued themselves as sexual beings. The book therefore provides significant new insights about Thai gender and sexuality, and particularly how it is affected by processes of globalization, including the ascent of the Internet and social media.

An important purpose of the study was to better understand why and how young Thai homosexual men are so severely affected by the HIV epidemic. Severe HIV epidemics have been reported among men who have sex with men across Southeast Asia (De Lind van Wijngaarden et al. 2009), in line with global trends (Beyrer et al. 2012; van Griensven et al. 2009). In Bangkok, the HIV prevalence (defined as the proportion of a population that has HIV at a given moment in time) among homosexually active men rose from 17.3 per cent in 2003 to 30.8 per cent in 2007 among large samples of men enrolled from entertainment venues such as saunas and bars, and has since plateaued around that level. The HIV prevalence among 18- to 22-year-old men was 12.9 per cent in 2003 and had risen to 22.2 per cent in 2007 (Van Griensven et al. 2010).

The basic premise of this book was that a better understanding of the culture and other social structures in which young Thai same-sex-attracted men live and act, and of their ideas and conceptions about sexuality and gender, are pivotal to obtain insight into their vulnerability to HIV. More appropriate and effective HIV prevention and treatment programmes can be only designed if we deeply understand the young men we are trying to reach. Different ideas and understandings about what it means to be gay/non-heterosexual (including the ways these young men interacted with their family, friends and boyfriends) are explored and placed in the overall context of the moral values that parents and the education system try to instil, aimed at guiding how a Thai person should live their gender and sexuality.

Purpose and Outline of This Book

This book will present the very first analysis of male homosexuality in modern Thailand based on sociological research that was conducted directly with young men. It is unique in that it explores changes in the way these men viewed and described their sexuality during a period in which their lives were rapidly changing because most of them moved from a rural family home to a new, more independent urban context.

This book uses the term 'sexual subjectivity' to help understand and ana-lyse how the young men in this book are formed by society, family, friends and the Internet, and in response also form their own meanings when it comes to sex and sexuality. Sexual subjectivity is defined as a set of ideas, desires, fantasies, practices, experiences, relationships and interpretations related to sex and sexuality that emerge, are learned and change in practice and in per-formance in relation to others, in reaction to different social, cultural, polit-ical and religious symbols and discourses, as well as resulting from a person's bodily experiences and sensations. Sexual subjectivity is not static but fluid; it is in constant flux, especially during the teen years, in which sex and sexu-ality start to become more important aspects of the conscious self and of life. Sexual subjectivity can be expressed in multiple and contradictory ways, often depending on the situation or context. It cannot be seen in isolation from societal and class-related expectations and roles related to gender. Sexual subjectivity encompasses the mind/psyche and the body, the spoken and the unspoken, the pleasurable and the shameful, the social and the private, the novel and the routine.

The term 'sexual fluidity' refers to the fact that sexual responsiveness and desire are often situation dependent, regardless of (and often in direct contradiction to) someone's professed sexual orientation or identity (Diamond 2008). Lisa Diamond (2016, 249) has defined sexual fluidity as 'a capacity for situation-dependent flexibility in sexual responsiveness, which allows individ-uals to experience changes in same-sex or other-sex desire across both short-term and long-term time periods'. This study will demonstrate the confusion that can arise when a sexual experience one has had does not fit the repertoire of sexual acts and experiences that belong under the label of one's chosen or presumed sexual or gender identity.

The book aims to answer three broad questions. First, I wanted to under-stand how sexual subjectivity emerges among young, rural, same-sex-attracted Thai men. How do they start to understand about sex, sexuality and gender, and how do they relate this knowledge and their bodily experiences with sex to this understanding? Second, I was interested to find out how sexual sub-jectivity varied among the young men in the study, as well as over time, and how these variations and fluidity could be explained. And finally, as explained earlier, I was interested to learn whether and how the transition from a rural secondary school to a new life phase affected the young men's sexual subjectivity and their HIV vulnerability, in the hope that such findings would provide new insights and ideas for providing HIV prevention, testing and treatment services to young Thai homosexual men.

The research participants will be introduced briefly in Chapter 2. It is impossible to understand the lives of the young men in this book without having a basic understanding of the Thai context in which they grew up. Therefore, in Chapter 3, the focus will be on introducing certain cultural aspects of Thai society and Thai identity or personhood, and how this makes Thai people different in certain ways from people in the West. Buddhist beliefs played an important role in most of the young men's initial understandings about homosexuality and their hopes and aspirations about same-sex relations. This will be discussed in Chapter 4. The men's first awareness of being 'different' and how they (re)acted to this will be described in Chapter 5. Chapter 6 will show how mainstream Thai ideas about masculine and feminine gender roles played an important role in their interpretation of their homosexuality. Culturally determined characteristics of (good) personhood and forms of culturally appropriate communication, introduced in Chapter 3, help explain how the young men dealt with disclosure of their sexual preferences to their families and others. This is explained in Chapter 7. While the men initially used concepts of gender to conceptually divide homosexual people into feminine 'bottoms' and masculine 'tops', sexual experiences with fellow-minded friends gradually weakened the conceptual links between gendered identity and sexual behaviour. This will be explored in Chapter 8. Object choice (a man rather than a woman) gradually gained importance in their understanding of homosexuality to the detriment of heteronormative gender roles, which led to a greater valuation of masculine demeanours and behaviours and a gradually growing desire to have less clear gender differences between male–male lovers. The Internet played a key role in this. Internet imagery and pornography promotes masculinity as an aesthetic ideal, and for these young men, the Internet also served as a platform for increasingly masculine presentations of the self, as will be discussed in Chapter 9. Many of the young men in this study saw their sexuality as having value – especially those who considered themselves to be more or less feminine in nature. Several of the study participants described in this book – especially those coming from poor families – engaged in sex work and also tried to use their youth and beauty to find a wealthy long-term partner who could support their education and pull their families out of poverty. This is the topic of Chapter 10, which tells the stories of three young men who had experiences working in Thailand's sex industry. In the final chapter, a summary of the findings and some conclusions are presented, as well as some recommendations for further research and for reducing the HIV vulnerability of young Thai homosexual men.

Methods

The Thailand National Research Council gave formal permission for this study. The study participants were all recruited via the Internet, mainly via Facebook but also via the gay dating platforms GayRomeo, Grindr and chatrooms in the webcam app CamFrog. Criteria for inclusion in the study were that the participant had to be born male, be sexually attracted to men, be at least 18 years of age when interviewed for the first time, be of Thai nationality and be studying in the final year of either *Mathayom* (high school) or *Po Wo Cho* (vocational training school). Because the study sought to zoom in on the shock of the transition from a rural to a more urban life and how this affected ideas about gender and sexuality, it made sense to focus on young rural men who were about to embark on such a transition because of their age and the fact that they were finishing high school.

Geographically, the participants had to be based in the northeast or the south of Thailand and live in a rural area, where 'rural' was defined as living at least 30 kilometres from Thai cities (of >100,000 inhabitants). These two regions were chosen to ensure sufficient diversity in the religion and socioeconomic background of the study participants (see Chapter 2).

Each participant gave written informed consent for participation in the study, and was made aware that the (anonymized) data and findings of the study would be used in consequent publications and in this book. The interviews – a total of 87 hours – were conducted, digitally recorded, transcribed, translated and analysed by me, and the transcripts then carefully checked and corrected by a native Thai-speaking research assistant. Out of the 25 participants, 23 completed all three interviews; the other two were interviewed only once and then could not be contacted for follow-up interviews. An overview with short biographies of all 25 participants is provided in the next chapter.

Some Remarks on Language, Terminology and Formatting

The book is based on interviews that were conducted in the Thai language and then translated into English for analysis. There are some challenges and problems that come into play when doing this. First, translations from one language to another do not always 'fit' and some creativity is required to make proper translations. More importantly, when analysing texts based on spoken words and stories, the contexts in which these stories were told can easily get lost. Unspoken communication, such as facial expressions, bodily posture and movements of the body or hands, cannot be recorded on a tape recorder. For this reason I conducted a brief report after each interview was completed, commenting on and describing the setting and my impressions about how the interview went. Where needed, comments derived from these informal interview notes were used in analysing the interviews.

Gay / Homosexual / Same-Sex-Attracted

The word 'gay' has been introduced to the Thai language in recent decades as an alternative identity label to the pre-existing effeminate/transgender category of *kathoey*. Despite this, in describing the young men in this study, the term 'homosexual' or 'same-sex-attracted' is preferred because of the potential for multiple interpretations of the word 'gay'. The terms 'same-sex-attracted' or 'homosexual' take desire or sexual attraction as their starting point, without predetermining what this may mean for how research participants view themselves or their sexual partners in terms of their gender or sexual identity.

Men: Phu Chaai

The use of the word 'men' (in Thai: *phu chaai* [ผู้ชาย]) is a bit complicated in the Thai context, as will also become clear in this book. The word *phu chaai* is usually used in relation to heterosexually oriented men; however, Thai *phu chaai* can (and do) have sex with other men or with *kathoey* (feminized men) as well. They do not see this as necessarily threatening to their masculinity or status as heterosexual men, especially if the sex with men happens in private settings. Throughout the text, when referring to supposedly 'straight' men, the Thai word *phu chaai* is used.

Phet: Gender, Sex, Sexuality

Another difficulty in using English to describe Thai sexual subjectivity (see definition on page 3) is the lack of separate words for 'gender', 'sex' and 'sexuality' or, more correctly, the existence of only one word (*phet* [เพศ]) to refer to gender, sex and sexuality in colloquial Thai. For that reason, where participants talk about *phet* this is often translated as 'sex/gender' or 'sexuality/gender'. Recently, new Thai terms have been coined to distinguish between the two – *phet phawa* [เพศภาวะ] for gender and *phet withi* [เพศวิถี] for sexuality – but these terms are not widely understood outside a small group of academics and activists, and for this reason I have avoided using these terms in this study. As will become clear in Chapters 3 and 6, it is impossible to understand Thai sexuality (including homosexuality) without understanding and applying concepts of gender. Indeed, the growing awareness among the young men in this study of the conceptual difference between 'gender' and 'sexuality' over time, and the contradictions and confusion this entails – partly because of the lack of a linguistic distinction between the concepts in colloquial Thai – is a key theme of this book. In this study, the terms 'gender identity' and 'sexual identity' are narrowly defined as labels describing the social categories that the research participants drew on to refer to themselves, as part of the wider set of fluid and changing ideas and concepts referring to masculinity and femininity and those comprising their overall sexual subjectivity.

Loan Words

Whenever the participants used a word in English, I have capitalized it in the text and have added [Eng] after it. I did this because the use of English words where Thai language equivalents exist often has social meaning: sometimes the use of English words indicates a desire on the part of the speaker to appear worldly, well-educated or modern. Loan words for which no Thai equivalent exist (such as 'computer' or 'internet') have not been capitalized.

Use of Thai Words and Phrases in This Book

Thai words that are used in the text have been Anglicized and put in italic script. Non-Anglicized Thai words or phrases have sometimes been added to quotations taken from interview transcripts. Translation from one language to another is seldom 100 per cent accurate and rarely straightforward; the occasional inclusion of the original Thai word or phrase will allow readers who are able to read Thai to verify the quality of my translation. A glossary of Thai terms used in this document can be found in appendix 1.

Chapter 2

INTRODUCING THE RESEARCH PARTICIPANTS

In this chapter, the participants are briefly introduced and described, including their first sexual experiences. The chapter will end with a brief description of the two regions from which the participants were recruited in the study: the northeast and the south of Thailand.

The Participants

The 25 participants in this study were all between 18 and 19 years of age at the first interview. They all had had (or tried to have) anal sex, except one, who remained a (proud) virgin even at the final interview, nearly two years later. One of the first things to note is the young age at which the men in this study first had sex: almost all of them were under 18 years at the time. Disregarding the two men who had had some early sexual experiences with girls, and not counting the rape of one of the participants as a boy, the average age of first sex with another male among the 24 who had had sex was a little over 15 years. It is interesting to note that this is not too different from the average age of sexual debut of 14.7 found in a randomly sampled population of same-sex-attracted vocational students in northern Thailand (van Griensven et al. 2004).

The participants in the study were given pseudonymous names starting from A to Y in the order that they were first interviewed; each will be briefly discussed next.

Ake grew up in a small village in rural Phuket province in southern Thailand and moved to high school in Phuket town. His family were Muslims but not strict, and were accepting of Ake's adoption of feminine gender traits, which started during childhood. Ake went through a process of masculinization during the research period: between the first and second interviews he abruptly shed his initial gender identity of *sao praphet song* ('second type of woman', loosely translatable as 'transgender') according to which he had long hair and wore women's clothing occasionally, and moved to a gay concept of self with shorter hair, less make-up, men's clothes and a new Facebook page. Ake met a (younger) *phu chaai* ('real man') boyfriend who lived in his neighbourhood when he was 15 years of age, with whom he had anal sex regularly. Following that he had no sexual partners, but this changed after he left home to study in Bangkok, where he became popular in his more masculine presentation of self and, consequently, much more sexually active.

Bon was a masculine-looking, slightly gruff-looking fellow who was not a good talker. He was originally from Phuket town (southern Thailand), but his family, which was well-off, moved to the province of Nakhon Sri Thammarat to work there. Bon moved back to Phuket town with his elder sister when he was 15 to complete his senior high school, and he was continuing his studies there. Bon was sexually abused by an older man when he was 14 or 15. Compared to other research participants, he changed little during the period of the study.

Chai was one of two participants who was lost to follow-up after the first interview. He was effeminate and very talkative. He was from a middle-class family in the southern city of Trang. He moved to Bangkok to study management. Chai had had a one-year-older *phu chaai* boyfriend from the age of 15. After some months his boyfriend took a girlfriend, leaving Chai heartbroken. Chai saw a psychologist for a while to deal with this, the only research participant to seek mental health support.

Dee was from a lower-class Muslim family and the second participant who was lost to follow-up after the first interview. He was born in the southern province of Surat Thani and was an only child. After his birth, his mother remarried and moved to the southern town of Pattalung when he was in fifth grade. Dee had a conflicted relationship with his stepfather, who disapproved of Dee's homosexuality. Dee planned to move away to study in Songkhla. His first sexual experience was with a girlfriend at the age of 15. He met his first male sexual partner at a party when he was 16. His partner was his age, and Dee was receptive in anal intercourse. After this experience he had his first boyfriend, which relationship lasted three months.

Ed was born in the southern province of Nakhon Sri Thammarat and was Buddhist. He had lived in the southern town of Pattalung since he was a child. He had one older brother. His family life was harmonious. Both his parents were teachers. Ed was diagnosed and treated for anorexia nervosa during the study period, an experience that helped him choose to study psychology and move away from his parental home. He had strong moral (conservative) convictions and was well-read. He met his first (non-sexual) boyfriend when he was 16; his boyfriend was 28 and they broke up following Ed's refusal to have sex. Ed was an avid user of the Internet for anonymous cybersex. His first mutual orgasm with somebody else came with his fourth boyfriend, between the second and third interviews.

Ek was Buddhist. He was born in the southern town of Trang but moved to Phuket soon after. He had been raised by his grandmother since he was six months old as his parents were unable to look after him. When his grand-mother died a few years ago, Ek went to live with an aunt not far from Phuket town. After the first interview he unexpectedly decided to move to Nakhon Pathom (near Bangkok) to study. Ek changed considerably, presenting himself in a more and more masculine way during the research period. Ek met a 30-year-old man via the Internet when he was 13 years old; the man picked Ek up in his car in front of his house, and they drove to a quiet spot and had oral and masturbation sex. He started having anal sex only after leaving high school, trying both roles and not finding much pleasure in either.

Fluk was Buddhist and had one older brother. He lived with an aunt in a district close to the southern town of Trang. His mother was a rubber tapper in a rural area of Trang, where the family moved after his father died following an accident when Fluk was about 15 years old. Fluk enrolled at a university in Bangkok but then dropped out. He planned to re-enrol the year after. Fluk's first sex was with men he met in a pub in Had Yai when he was 15 years old; also he sometimes received money for sex at that time. For a while he had two longer-term boyfriends at the same time.

Gop was the younger of two children and was from the northeastern town of Mahasarakham, living in an extended family. Gop fought with his family to be allowed to study in Chonburi, but he disliked it and came back after just a week to enrol at a university close to home. Gop was around 16 when he visited a university student in his dormitory room, and was talked into having sex to 'prove his love'. He dated several boyfriends via the Internet after this, sometimes simultaneously, but most of these people Gop never met in person. He had been actively searching for a foreign boyfriend via the dating website GayRomeo and other cyber platforms.

Hong lived in a small rural village outside the northeastern city of Buriram. He was the younger child and had an older sister. His parents separated when Hong was 7 months old. After finishing high school, he enrolled to study at a university close to his mother's home to become a teacher. He went to the seaside tourist resort of Pattaya a number of times for short periods to work as a sex worker in a gay bar and was interested in finding a foreign boyfriend. He transformed from a shy, skinny, unkempt schoolboy during the first interview into a sophisticated, self-confident and well-coiffed metrosexual young man during the research period. Hong had his first sex with a *phu chaai* school friend starting when he was 13–14 years old. At age 16 he met a 27-year-old Thai man who became his first 'real' boyfriend, moving into Hong's mother's house; they dated for more than a year with the approval of his mother.

Ives changed from *kathoey* to gay in his late teens. He grew up in a relatively poor family in rural Buriram. After finishing school, Ives moved to Bangkok for a few months to work and then moved to live with his sister who worked in a factory in Nakhon Pathom. Between the second and the third interview, Ives worked as a go-go boy in a gay bar in Phuket for two months. Ives had sex for the first time at age 17. This happened after he had stopped dressing and behaving as a *kathoey* and started posting a masculine-looking picture of himself on a gay website. He met his first partner, who was 11 years his senior, in a motel and lost his virginity there after much persuasion; they were 'boyfriends' for a brief period after this.

Joe's family was poor and both his parents worked in the fields in rural Buriram in the northeast. His mother had remarried and Joe had been under the impression that his stepfather was his real father until he was 15. Joe found a job at a pig farm a few hundred kilometres from home after graduating from high school. A friend invited him to move to the seaside tourist resort of Pattaya for sex work, with the aim of finding a foreign boyfriend. This did not work out. Joe's first sexual experience occurred in Bangkok at age 16–17, where he went during his school holidays to meet a man in his late twenties, whom he had met via the Internet. Joe went on to have many sexual encounters and was worried about HIV infection.

Kit was from a middle-class family and was the elder of two sons. He grew up in a rural northeastern district of Buriram. He was masculine looking and not open about his sexuality; his mother pressured him repeatedly to find a girlfriend. He studied junior high school at an all-boys boarding school. Kit was selected to enrol in a prestigious civil-service college not far from his hometown, but he dropped out because his grades were not high enough. He lost his scholarship and then enrolled at another university, in Bangkok, and moved to a third university during the same year. He felt bad because he was unable to meet his mother's expectations. Kit's first sex was at age 16, with a male student of his age whom he had met at a special studies camp in a different city. They later made arrangements to meet in a hotel and started a relationship. Kit also had sex with other people in between and he became sexually involved with a female student during his first year in university, but also continued to see his male partner who studied in another city.

Lert lived in a small and isolated village in Sisaket Province in the northeast of Thailand. His parents were farmers. He was the first of two children. His father died when Lert was 10 years old, and his mother remarried. Lert had been a *kathoey* until he moved to one of Bangkok's well-known red-light districts during his school holidays to work briefly in a gay bar when he was 16. He had another stint in sex work in Pattaya after finishing high school. He briefly had a French boyfriend whom he had met in Pattaya. By the final interview, he had embraced a more masculine identity. He had enrolled in the Air Force, strongly supported by his mother and other family members, and he appeared to have given up on gay life.

Mint was the first of two children in a well-to-do, middle-class, urban family in the northeastern town of Yasothon. He desperately wanted to have a foreign or mixed-race boyfriend. He moved to Bangkok to study to become a teacher. Initially he became immersed in the gay scene there, including gay saunas, going out and partying. He underwent an operation to enlarge his nose during the interviewing period and was very popular among his new friends. During the final interview he had settled down with an older Thai boyfriend who was very controlling, and Mint was no longer able to go out. He had sex for the first time with a same-age friend at age 15.

Nook was from a poor agricultural family from the northeastern province of Nong Bua Lamphu. He had been a *kathoey* until briefly before the first interview. Nook was the middle child of three; he had one older brother and a younger sister. Nook was small, good looking, talkative and emotional. He tried to enrol at university after completing high school, but he failed the entrance exams. He then worked for a year, after which he succeeded in enrolling at a university to study nursing. He was determined to do his parents proud. He said he would like to have a rich boyfriend, or even a foreign boyfriend if possible. Nook failed in his efforts to seduce his favourite high school teacher, when he was 16–17 years of age, and he was heartbroken. He then met his first partner, a 29-year-old Thai man, who seduced him. The relationship did not last and Nook felt betrayed. Since then, Nook has had several brief affairs.

Oad was from the northeastern province of Beung Kaan and had two younger sisters. His family was well-to-do. Oad was always first in, and representative for, his class and school. He was talkative, funny and self-confident. He went to study at a university in Bangkok. Oad expressed doubts about whether he was gay or bisexual, especially during the first interview. When he was 9 years old, Oad remembers that he tried to have sex with a girl of the same age as part of a game they were playing. He had a first, non-sexual boyfriend at age 16, and the second not long after that. He lost his virginity after meeting a 29-year-old man. He met a new boyfriend after the second interview, whom Oad brought home to introduce to his family. They had broken up just before the third interview. He says he is still interested in girls as well.

Pong lived in a rural district of Buriram Province in the northeast of Thailand. He was the youngest of six children. His parents worked as farmers. Pong moved to study accounting in Bangkok. None of his siblings had higher than secondary education; hence, his family had high expectations of him. Pong was another of the participants who set his sights on landing a foreign boy-friend. Pong was 15 when he had a sexual affair with a classmate. He had been in a relationship since coming to Bangkok, but he was pessimistic about his romantic prospects.

Quan was born and raised in the northeastern province of Kalasin, in a middle-class family. Both his parents were teachers at the secondary level. During the first and second interviews he was obsessed by his involvement in a direct marketing scheme selling health and slimming products. He was convinced he would be a multimillionaire in a few years' time, able to retire at the age of 21. After finishing high school he enrolled to study marketing at a university not far from home. Quan had only just discovered that he was gay, less than a year before the first interview. He was very much focused on studying and working to make his parents proud and improve their lives. Quan had sex for the first time when he was 17 with a male university student who was two years older and to whom he was introduced by friends. The relationship ended, and Quan had a wild period of many sexual contacts before meeting another boyfriend whom he was seeing at the time of the last interview.

Roj was born in an outer district of Kalasin Province in the northeast of Thailand. His father was a secondary school teacher and his mother was a housewife. He had one older sister. He moved to a dormitory for his high school studies at the age of 13, visiting his parents only on some weekends. Roj was effeminate, and referred to himself as '*toot*' (loosely translatable as 'fag') during his primary and junior high school years, but he gradually moved to a more masculine gay role. After completing high school he moved to study in Khon Kaen. Roj had his first sex at age 16 with a university student who pursued him to the extent that Roj said he felt 'pity' for him and agreed to have sex. He said he was 'wild' in 11th grade, having sex every week, mainly with university students he met online.

San lived outside the provincial capital of the northeastern province of Udon Thani with his adoptive parents. He was their only child, but he had an older brother and sister who stayed in another area. His adoptive parents ran a small restaurant. After completing high school, San moved to Khon Kaen to study nursing. When San was around 17 years old he was wooed by a 25- to 26-year-old male nurse who stole his telephone number from a hospital file when San showed up there for medical care. After many months of dating, San visited him at his house and they started a sexual relationship.

Tam lived in a northeastern province and was the first child of three with two younger brothers. His father worked abroad and his mother was working as a maid. He was an 'activity child' (*dek kitchakam*), representing his high school in competitions many times, and he was selected 'exemplary youth', competing for his province at the national level. He moved away from home to study law in another city in the northeast. He became a student representative and had plans to become a politician in the future. Tam was not forthcoming with information about his sex life. It appears he had had sex with a *phu chaai* classmate since the age of 13. His first 'love' was for a married *phu chaai* schoolteacher with whom he had a one-off drunken sexual encounter in the school.

Ud was from the southern town of Trang and had one younger sister. His father was a mechanic and his mother helped out in the restaurant of a family member. He was the only Christian (Protestant) in the sample. He had strict parents and had to go to church every Sunday. He moved to study at a university in Bangkok and had some exposure to gay life via the Internet and in gay saunas. Nearly all of his friends in Bangkok were also from Trang; via some family members, who also lived in Bangkok, he had joined a church in Bangkok. Ud met his first boyfriend, a schoolmate who was one year older, during a special study camp when he was 16. They had sex only once, but were boyfriends for a number of months.

Vee was Muslim and born as the last child of 11 in the family of a middle-class Muslim shopkeeper in southern Thailand. He was slightly effeminate in his demeanour. He moved to Surat at the age of 15–16 to stay with his older sister. Vee was open about his sexuality. He continued his studies in Surat Thani, close to home. During the second interview he had changed markedly, had become stronger looking and taller. He was the only participant who mentioned anything about drugs during the study period, admitting that he had been addicted to amphetamines. Vee had been interested in having a foreign boyfriend. Vee had a three-year sexual relationship with a one-year-older schoolmate, which started when Vee was 13 when he moved to a dormitory. It ended when this person moved to continue senior high school in Bangkok. Vee was still in touch with this person.

Win was Muslim and had a Malaysian father and a Thai mother. The family's home was in the southern Thai province of Krabi. His parents broke up when Win was young. He had two older siblings. His mother remarried and there are three younger stepsiblings (all girls) with his stepfather. Win was brutally raped at the age of 11 by a visiting Muslim cleric. Win ran away when he was in the final year of high school to a lover whom he had met online and who lived in the northeast. This did not work out, and the relationship ended within two months. As a result, Win dropped out of vocational school and had to move to work in Phuket. After those disruptions he had to re-do his final year of secondary school in Krabi, staying at home. He ended up postponing his studies for yet another year. His stepfather died in between the second and third interviews. His first consensual sex happened when he was 13, with a 26-year-old Thai man whom he met via the Internet.

Yud was slightly effeminate and the second of two sons. He lived close to the southern city of Nakhon Sri Thammarat in a lower-middle-class family. He was one of the best students in his class and school and was often asked to represent the school in competitions and activities. He described his home environment as 'very warm'. Yud was accepted into a university in Nakhon Pathom and moved there. Despite finding many friends who were gay or *kathoey*, something he never had before, Yud was and remained a virgin throughout the interviewing period and was very proud of this fact.

The Northeast of Thailand

The northeastern region of Thailand consists of 20 provinces and is called *Isaan* or *Isan*. Around 22 million people, or about a third of the Thai population lives here, and the region also covers around a third of Thailand's territory. The northeast of Thailand is culturally closer to Lao than to Central Thailand; indeed, the native language of people in *Isaan* is Lao, although they do not use the alphabet commonly used in Lao PDR. While the majority population of the Isan region is ethnically Lao, northeastern Thai do distinguish themselves from the Lao of Laos by calling themselves *khon Isan* or *Thai*

Isan in general. However, some refer to themselves as Lao. Prominent aspects of Isan culture include *mor lam*, an indigenous folk music performed by travelling dance troups, Thai boxing (*muai Thai*), cock fighting and celebratory processions. Isan food, in which glutinous ('sticky') rice, fresh herbs and chili peppers are prominent, is distinct from central Thai cuisine, though it is now found throughout the country.

Central Thais often stigmatize Lao people and Lao culture, associating the Lao (and, by extension, northeastern Thai) with being stupid, unfashionable and backward. Since education is seen as an important vehicle to foster Thai national identity (Mounier and Tangchuang 2010), the Thai government does not permit any other language in schools than central Thai. This means that children outside the central Thai region are at a structural disadvantage when entering primary school. The prohibition of learning and teaching in their own language, combined with a strongly Bangkok-centric history curriculum, has fostered feelings of inferiority regarding the northeastern Thai culture and language, even among *Isan* people themselves. The emergence of the Thai Rak Thai (and later Pheu Thai) parties under the populist leadership of Thaksin Shinawatra mobilized and fostered growing awareness that the disadvantaged position of Isan when compared to Bangkok has much to do with a chronic lack of investment in the region and with other policy choices made by the central government. The northeast remains Thailand's most rural and therefore poorest region; one-third of the Thai population living there contribute only around 10 per cent to Thailand's GDP, and many people from the northeast migrate to other parts of the country permanently or temporarily in order to make ends meet.

The South of Thailand

The southern region of Thailand consists of the entire peninsula south of Prajuab Khiri Khan Province down to the border with Malaysia; it consists of 14 provinces and has a population of around 9 million. Three languages are commonly spoken here: Pak Thai (or Taam Thro), Yawi (also referred to as Kelantan-Pattani Malay) and central Thai. The seven southernmost provinces of the southern region are predominantly Muslim, and this was a key reason why this region was included as an area for exploration in this study. The southern region has a varied economy in which agriculture and tourism are dominant.

Chapter 3

UNDERSTANDING THAI PERSONHOOD

Introduction

This chapter is meant as an introduction to the presentation of the findings of the study, and focuses on theories and ideas about what it means to be Thai. The focus is on how specific characteristics of Thai personhood affect the study of gender and sexuality.

Is Thai Society 'Loosely Structured' or Rigid and Hierarchical?

Foreigners who come to Thailand for the first time often wonder about the country. People seem different: the most clichéd observation is that Thais 'always smile'. Communication is often difficult as Thailand's terrible education system produces people who generally do not understand phrases such as 'What is your name?' despite having undergone more than 12 years of English-language education. The issue of how Thai society and identity 'work' has been at the fore of what has come to be called Thai studies since the 1950s and 1960s. John Embree (1950, 187) was struck by what he called the 'individualistic behaviour' of Thai people, and noted an 'almost determined lack of regularity, discipline, and regimentation in Thai life'. Embree concluded that Thai society was 'loosely structured' compared to what he called 'rigid societies' such as China, Japan and Vietnam. Embree credited the loose structure of Thai society with enabling the Thai to deal with change more flexibly and with fewer shocks to society than more rigid societies could endure.

Another American scholar, Lucien Hanks (1962), conducted studies on what he called the 'Thai moral order' by describing how the Buddhist principle of merit influences Thai personality. Thai people believe in reincarnation, with one's rebirth based on the balance of accumulated good and bad karma at the end of one's life determining the socio-economic position or form in which one is reborn. A second important aspect of Thai personality Hanks described was power, which provides for (in)stability and (in)security in the world, based on feeble alliances – this leads Thai people to rely strongly on their family and/or clan and to distrust outsiders. Hanks therefore disagreed with Embree: he did not see any 'looseness' in Thai society but came to the opposite conclusion, which was that Thai society is rigidly organized in a strongly hierarchical manner. Hanks noted the importance of the concepts of age and merit in determining one's place in Thai society, and he observed that rituals and norms for dealing with Thai people are connected to their position in this hierarchy, rather than to their personalities per se. Younger or less powerful people pay tribute to or support older or more powerful people and are rewarded with their care and protection. Similarly, within Thai families, a child is seen as morally indebted to its mother forever, and it is impossible ever to repay the goodness (*bunkhun*) of a mother (and, to a much lesser extent, a father) for having brought them to life (see also Mulder 1997, 2000).

These aspects of the Thai worldview make people understand that their position is not a given, and changes in position and fortune are common – in a way it makes Thai people see themselves first and foremost as nodes in a social structure, rather than as independent individuals. Just the process of aging will mean automatic promotion in the moral order (as well as in government and other bureaucracies); similarly, children, morally indebted to their mothers, will often at some stage become parents themselves and reach a higher moral status. People can climb even further up the ladder by embarking on careers aimed at increasing their merit and power, for example (at least in the days of Embree and Hanks) as monks or teachers. Hanks noted already in the 1950s and early 1960s that many changes were occurring in Thai society, but he concluded that 'the fundamental principles of merit and power still operate, and the new occupations are readily fitted to the hierarchy. Desire to rise and fear of falling remain the emphasis' (Hanks 1962, 1258).

The Australian scholar Nerida Cook (2002) conducted a study of Thai fortune tellers and the use and consumption of horoscopes by Thai people. She found that the consultations that Thai clients had with their fortune tellers were strongly focused on social relations and social issues. This was in contrast with the consultations by Western consumers of horoscopes, who were more focused on issues related to self-realization and self-knowledge. Related to this, Cook quoted a 1985 study by Suntari who found that Thai society fosters a relative lack of individual ambition, and that moving 'up' in society is linked to fostering good relations with significant others in one's social network, and less to individual ambition or hard work:

> To be successful and to 'achieve' in Thai society does not depend so much on one's competence as on one's ability to perceive and to choose the right means and opportunity that lead to success in the society [...]

In short, achievement in Thai society does not mean hard [work] or
task orientation. To quite an extent, it is more of a 'social achievement'.
(Suntari, quoted in Cook 2002, 198)

The observations of the scholars briefly introduced here point at a fundamental way Thai people make sense of themselves or their sense of personhood, which is seen more in the context of social relations with others and less
as an innate self that is or can be (or should be) separated from its context (ten
Brummelhuis, cited in Cook 2002). This is why I prefer the term 'personhood'
over the word 'identity', as I feel that the term personhood focuses more on
the way an individual conceives of him or herself through the eyes and in the
context of his or her social environment.

The Dutch anthropologist Niels Mulder (2000) has done decades of
anthropological research in Thailand, Indonesia and the Philippines drawing
comparisons between these societies. He also described the southeast Asian
sense of personhood as being fundamentally different from the way Western
societies define individual identity in that there is a strong(er) focus on
relationships with family and kin and with people in one's own community
and environment. Thai people feel more distance from and distrust of people
outside their own social circle, even those who are in a similar position or
situation, which can be easily observed by the way Thai people often avoid
each other while living abroad. Mulder notes that the moral debt of children
towards their parents (discussed above) explains the much closer ties many
Thai children maintain with their parents, even after they establish families
of their own.

Mulder's interpretations explain why unions and political movements and
activism based on common interests have been so weak in Thai society, and
why there has been, at least up until recently, very little consciousness of 'class'.
Instead, vertical 'patron–client' relationships, that is, linkages between more/
less powerful individuals, remain predominant in Thailand (Walker 2008) –
vote buying, in which politicians reward the support of an entire village or
neighbourhood, is an important manifestation of this. Mulder's insights also
help explain why most Thai same-sex-attracted men do not have a strong
sense of being part of a community based on their common sexual or gender
orientation, at least in rural areas (discussed in Chapter 7). In a later article,
Mulder (2011, 105) made some further observations on Thai personhood and
the importance of groups in defining the Thai identity:

This culture fosters people's abilities to find their identity in their group;
the person feels secure because he is accepted by his fellows and, in a wider
sense, because of his reputation. In other words, his points of reference

are primarily social, and typically not idealistic or self-centered. This is reinforced through a social game that emphasizes outward appearances that are not compensated by inner development.

This can be seen in the way Thai people often refer to themselves not as 'I', but in the third person, referring to their position in the group, using terms denoting a relationship: 'mother', 'uncle', 'older brother' or, for younger inferior females or young children, 'mouse' are linguistic manifestations of this. Another indication is that Thai people tend to use the word 'we' (*rao*) rather than 'I' when talking to hierarchical equals or friends. Mulder (2011, 105) contrasts this, with a certain sense of humour, to 'Western culture', where the emphasis is on the development of the individual personality:

> [In the West, o]ne has to be a person in one's own right, or, at least, one should endeavour to become one. Because of it, we have to fend off our parents whom we'll blame for everything we are and do not want to be.

In contrast to Embree, who wondered about the lack of rigidity in Thai society, Mulder (2011, 106), in line with Hanks, observed that rather than being participants in a loosely structured society, Thais do in fact strongly 'tend to rigidity':

> Their lives are laid out, ritualized, as it were; people are afraid of change and cannot rely on their individuality. Life is strictly organized, obsequiousness a virtue, and originality equal to social suicide. Life is a show, composed of ceremonies and ritual, in which obligations are taken very seriously. The exterior is more important than the interior, and often it appears as if the presentation of things is equivalent to their sum and substance.

It is important to realize that there is some truth in each of Mulder, Hanks and Embree's contrasting claims about the rigidity or looseness of Thai society. Embree is right that people tend to mind their own business when they are in an uncommon environment, which Mulder explains is because of fear and distrust of strangers. This makes it very easy to feel free and unencumbered as a foreigner in a new environment – an experience Embree, as an American outsider studying Thailand, must have experienced first-hand. No wonder so many foreign visitors and residents consider Thailand the 'land of the free'. But for Thai people themselves, this is very different. They do not live by themselves, but have family and close social entanglements and obligations. Mulder described how Thai individuals, as part of their home, family and community environment, are under a high level of pressure to conform to parental and community expectations and life trajectories, which include at the very least getting married, having children and taking financial care of parents and grandparents.

Feeling Exceptional: The Power of Thainess

Another important aspect of Thai personhood is nationalism, or being proud of being Thai. Successive Thai governments have continuously tried to define the word 'Thainess' (the word 'prescribe' is often more appropriate), focusing on how exceptional Thai people are in comparison to other nationalities. The Thai scholar Thongchai Winichakul (1997, 5) stated that 'although Thainess is never clearly defined, it is supposed that every Thai knows it is there'. Since the early twentieth century, the 'Nation, Religion, King' mantra defined Thainess at the national level: all Thai people love their country, respect their Buddhist religion as the guardian of morality and worship their wise and unifying king (Wyatt 2003). These concepts have been deeply ingrained in the curriculum of Thai schools, where they are (inaccurately) presented as if they were centuries-old traditional pillars of the Thai nation-state. The American scholar Craig Reynolds (2002, 311) observed that an important 'fabrication, commodification and consumption of Thainess' has occurred since the 1980s, paralleling the Thai economic miracle: 'Thainess was no longer something to be defended in the interest of national security, as it had been before the economic boom, but to be consumed in the interests of boosting the economy.' Reynolds noted that a stronger 'capacity to produce fabricated Thainess' (2002, 312) has emerged, as a result of advertising (including campaigns by the Tourism Authority of Thailand with the slogan 'Amazing Thailand'), the presence of Thai diasporas around the world, the increase of tourism and the popularity and worldwide availability of Thai food.

The American scholar Michael Connors (2005) studied the creation of the Thai Ministry of Culture and its efforts to defend Thainess from foreign pollution. He zoomed in on the ministry's fear of everything new and modern, including a worrying desire to control the Internet and social media. Connors saw this at least partly as an attempt by urban elites to retain their position of power over the poor rural hinterland. One could also regard the Ministry of Culture as a government-sanctioned marketing effort by 'Thailand Inc.' to guard and promote its unique brand. This unique brand, it should be added, is very singularly based on a middle-class, conservative, royalist, central-Thai, urban fantasy vision of Thainess, in which there is no room for diversity. Yawi-speaking southern Muslim Thais, northeastern Lao-speaking Thais, northern Thai-speaking Thais, Khmer-speaking northeastern Thais or Thai citizens who speak any of the several northern hill tribe languages are not represented in it; their languages and cultures are routinely ignored or dismissed as inferior and backward. The same goes for the languages, cultures and societies of neighbouring countries such as Laos, Cambodia, Malaysia and Myanmar, for which the Thai education curriculum (and, as a result of decades-long brainwashing, the majority of the Thai population) have nothing but disdain and disrespect.

The decades-long continuous migration of young Thais to cities for education and work has resulted in the gradual weakening of ties with family and village or community. This has led to the emergence of new mechanisms of belonging, in which being modern and urban is contrasted to being backward and rural. Reynolds quoted the Thai academic Kasian Tejapira, who observed 'tension and conflict between the desire to remain Thai [traditional, rural, "authentic"] and the desire to be "un-Thai" [read: modern, Western, urban]' (Tejapira, quoted in Reynolds 2002). Anjalee Cohen (2009) found that Chiang Mai teenagers aspired to be what they called *inter*, a word inspired by the English word 'international', meaning modern/Western, innovative, prosperous and fashionable. The opposite of *inter* was *lao*, the Thai word for Laotian, which the teenagers considered synonymous with backward, traditional, rural, poor and unfashionable. The young people in Cohen's study used consumption and style (of dress, talk and entertainment) as ways of expressing their belonging to modernity, which led Cohen to observe: 'One's sense of self no longer stems from "the village" but from "signs of desired identity" [...], which is increasingly being sought through consumerism and the construction of new symbolic communities' (2009, 167). Such 'symbolic communities', Cohen said, are a way for Thai youth to create a 'space of their own', as they negotiate the often significant difference between the life they led at home and the life they have created for themselves at their destinations, forging new understandings of what modern Thainess means.

In reaction to the growing importance of consumption and consumerism in defining lifestyles and creating a symbolic sense of belonging in recent decades, academics, both conservative and progressive, have stressed the importance of local knowledge and called for the preservation and promotion of local Thai lifestyles (Reynolds 2002; Sivaraksa 2002). Sometimes such statements are framed in the context of a romantic idealization of village life and of a purer Thai past, and a rejection of the anonymous lifestyle of Bangkok and other large cities that is the result of the enormous economic expansion in recent decades.

Despite the efforts of the Culture Ministry, there are distinct regional variations in Thai culture and in Thai personhood. Until the beginning of the twentieth century, the system of government in Thailand (then called 'Siam') was not yet centralized; instead, there were regional leaders who paid tribute to the Siamese king in Bangkok, and different parts of Thailand, with their distinct languages and cultures, enjoyed relative independence. Centralization started only after the neighbouring colonial empires, France and Great Britain, started to encroach on Siamese territory by pressuring and wooing these regional leaders from Bangkok's control, often with promises of lower tributes or taxes or military assistance (Wyatt 2003). The Bangkok elite started to embark on a decades-long campaign to erase cultural differences, for example, by forbidding the use of Lao or the language of the north, Muang, as languages of instruction in education. Despite these efforts, to this day, strong regional differences persist: people in the northeast still speak Lao; in the south, Yawi (a form of Malay) is widely spoken, and people adhere to Islam. Other, more subtle differences exist between northerners and central Thai, and even within each of Thailand's regions. Strong cultural and linguistic differences also existed between the tens of thousands of Chinese immigrants to Thailand and their Thai hosts; since then, the Thai Chinese, also called Sino-Thais, have mostly assimilated into the urban Thai mainstream, while in some cases maintaining a distinct Chinese identity (Bun and Kiong 1993). Ironically, this assimilation happened partly as a side effect of racist nationalist policies in the 1930s, which forced Chinese immigrants to take Thai surnames and which limited the immigration of Chinese women into Thailand as marriage partners for local Chinese men. This forced Chinese men to take Thai wives. Policies that discouraged Chinese-language education also indirectly contributed to the relatively successful assimilation of Chinese residents into the Thai mainstream (Wyatt 2003), part of the Bangkok-based government efforts to erase or at least downplay population differences, promoting their ideal of a more or less uniform Thai (and central-Thai-speaking) citizen. During the Shinawatra years, probably partly in response to the ongoing conflict in southern Thailand (McCargo 2009), the government expressed more tolerance for regional differences, and more autonomy was granted to provinces, for example, in the area of education (Mounier and Tangchuang 2010), although this process seems to have been wound back since the latest military coup d'état.

Next, I will introduce a number of key Thai concepts that can help interpret and understand the way Thai people function in their family and society.

The 'Fetishization' of the Surface/Outside Image

The Australian scholar Peter A. Jackson (2011b) discovered an important but little-known study conducted in 1974 by an anthropologist named Richard Davis. Davis found that the northern Thai rituals he documented and studied emphasized the determinative power of the 'surface' over the 'essence', or the inner self. In other words, the cultural logics that guide northern Thai ritual behaviour and forms of representation, which are unlikely to differ significantly from other regions in Thailand, reversed the order of the relationship between 'inner essence' and 'outer surface' that characterizes Western ways of looking at the world. In northern Thai folk theology it is the 'logos' (inner essence) that is inconstant, unknowable and unreliable while the material world of 'surface' ritual is steadfast and solid. This is in complete opposition to Western metaphysics, where it is the surface that is considered unsteady and impermanent, with the inner core steadfast and lasting. Jackson quoted Niels Mulder, who called this the 'fetishization of surface', in which presentation becomes 'the essence of reality':

> This appreciation of presentation as the essence of reality describes the phenomenon in which outside appearance is taken to be the essence of social life. It is the manipulation of form as content, or the equation of these two, in the sense that they are understood and taken as being one and the same thing [...] Presentation is therefore more than superficial reality: it is essential reality; this mental recognition is at the basis of the tendency to equate the manipulation of the symbols of social reality with its actual mastery. (Mulder 1985, 198–99, quoted in Jackson 2011b, 188)

The Principles of *Kala-Thetsa*

Several scholars have observed that Thai people tend to avoid, at almost all costs, the disruption of the outside appearance of calm, warm and stable social relations. In an effort to understand and describe this, the American sociologist/anthropologist Penny Van Esterik (2000) pointed at the importance of the Thai concept of *kala-thetsa* [กาลเทศะ], a noun that is close in meaning to the English words 'comportment' and 'circumstance'. *Kala-thetsa* can be seen as a set of mediating principles that govern communication in Thai society. Whereas the English word comportment is considered to be an individual virtue, usually linked to professionalism and social etiquette during particular occasions, the Thai term *kala-thetsa* is more encompassing and philosophical, more strongly linked to a person's circumstance in terms of their social position and relations towards other individuals in the social structure of their family, community and society. *Kala-thetsa* can be described as the way one deals with others, how appropriately one acts and speaks in relation to others in particular situations, and how well one dismisses one's personal emotions for the sake of social harmony. *Kala-thetsa* is about knowing one's place in the hierarchy by behaving (and dressing, speaking, conducting oneself) according to the norms linked to one's gender, age and family position in relation to the person one is dealing with.

Applying the principles of *kala-thetsa* successfully will help ensure that communication occurs in a harmonious and smooth manner, without disturbances, misunderstandings or conflict. This explains why Thai people who have just met each other start off by asking each other a number of questions that help them determine their position vis-à-vis one another, especially in relation to their age and social status. This will help them decide how they should refer to each other (for example, who should be called 'older brother' and who should be 'younger brother'). Doing this successfully avoids the loss of face (in Thai: *sia naa* [เสียหน้า]) either for the self or for the other, and fulfils other people's expectations by keeping the surface of smooth social interaction intact. At the basis of *kala-thetsa* is wisdom and insight into society and social hierarchy. Van Esterik (2000, 36) explained that *kala-thetsa* can be seen as a cultural interaction strategy: '*Kala-thetsa* [...] draws attention to the importance of understanding surfaces, appearance, face, masks and disguise as parts of important cultural strategies of interaction.'

Kala-thetsa is especially important to understand ways of communicating within unequal relationships, for instance, those between younger and elder people, including children and parents and relationships between men and women. It should be noted that *kala-thetsa* is strongly gendered; the principles instil and promote different rules for and expectations of females and males in particular social situations.

Barami and the Separation between the Public and the Private Self

Linked to the concept of *kala-thetsa* is the distinction between a person's private actions and ideas and the public performance of certain roles. Thai people are preoccupied with maintaining their prestige and keeping face (in Thai: *naa*), which is basically done by playing public roles in line with societal expectations of how these roles should be played. Rosalind Morris (1994) noted that there is not necessarily a link between who one is in private and the way one presents to the outside world. One's public presentation is therefore more or less learned from and practised in relation to the outside. Penny Van Esterik (2000, 203) explained that, despite the rigidity of having to enact one's *naa* in public, there is plenty of room for variety and flexibility, but only in private: 'Surfaces are transformable, temporary and aesthetically pleasing, while the self – who he/she really is – remains hidden and ultimately unknowable, a worldly accommodation to the Buddhist concepts of *anatta* [non-self] and *annica* [impermanence].'

Implementing the separation between private and public in a successful manner will guarantee one's *barami* (respect, prestige) in society. Niels Mulder (1997) conducted a study focusing on how 'Thainess' is defined and how it is presented and taught in the Thai education system. He calculated that around three quarters of school time goes to teaching about maintaining one's public role in the form of 'morality, good manners and conduct, and state ideology' (Mulder 1997, 56, quoted in Van Esterik 2000, 38). These are needed for children to learn to acquire and retain *barami* in society, and to act to avoid loss of face, according to the principles of *kala-thetsa*.

Rosalind Morris (1994, 20) constructed a Thai model of three genders and four sexualities. She defined the Thai gender system as consisting of *phu chaai* (man), *phu ying* (woman) and *kathoey* (transvestite/transsexual/hermaphrodite). The second system is a system of four sexualities: heterosexual male, heterosexual female, homosexual male and homosexual female, in which *kathoey* is construed as the most effeminate form of a homosexual male. She explained the importance of maintaining neatly compartmentalized private and public domains:

> The crucial element in the Thai system of three [genders] seems to be a division in which sexual and gender identity is conceived as a repertoire of public appearance and behaviours that is quite independent of the various subject positions and sexual practices available within the private realm.

Morris (1994, 32), similar to Van Esterik, suggested that, as long as people perform their public roles effectively, the private realm becomes irrelevant as long as there is no 'inappropriate self-disclosure':

> By the traditional Thai logic of visibility and invisibility [...] virtually any [sexual] act is acceptable if it neither injures another person nor offends others through inappropriate self-disclosure. As one of the country's most prominent *kathoey* [male-to-female transgenders] remarked about being gay in Thailand, 'there is no problem [...] providing you don't ripple the surface calm'.

Hence, the three gender roles are the available options for a public identity, whereas the (private) realm of one's sexuality is 'presumed heterosexual' for everybody. Again, the importance given to the surface (presentation) and its prominence over the inner essence is striking. Peter A. Jackson (2011b) noted that Thai people in power are expected to uphold proper and appropriate images. Thai officials therefore show 'an intense concern to monitor and police surface effects, images, public behaviours, and representations combined with a relative disinterest in controlling the private domain of life' (2011b, 181). This explains, to draw on a famous example, how a Thai interior minister, in a press conference with Western journalists in the early 1990s, managed to claim – without blinking or smirking – that 'prostitution does not exist in Thailand'. The idea is that the interior minister, in his role as a representative of all Thais towards a group of foreigners, is expected to project an image of Thailand that Thai people (or at least those in the conservative Bangkok elite) want to promote; it has nothing to do with the factual truth. The power of 'prestige' over factual truth also helps explain why ostensibly heterosexual men work in Thailand's gay bars in considerable numbers. The discrepancy of their sexual behaviours with male customers and their public presentation (towards girlfriends, wives, children, family, friends) as 'straight' men is socially acceptable, as long as they manage to perform each role in the right situation.

Peter A. Jackson (2011b) explained that prestige (*barami*) of image or self-presentation overrides the fundamental concept of knowledge or objective truth. As a result, the drive for surveillance and confessions to unearth knowledge and the 'truth' as the mechanism for exercising or being subjected to power, a process that the French philosopher Michel Foucault (1979) unearthed in Western countries, is absent from Thai society. Thai society allows multiple truths to coexist, separated by private–public boundaries, even though these truths may be factually contradictory. The image/*barami* is more important than the factual truth. This is important to remember while attempting to understand how Thai people communicate about their sexuality or sexual behaviours. When this is applied to the situation of same-sex-attracted men, as long as they can manage a public performance that is convincing enough to pass as a normal (read: heterosexual) man, they retain *barami* and are able to participate in society with no or few questions asked about what they do sexually, as long as that remains in private.

The importance of retaining *barami* has important consequences for Thai people's romantic and sexual relationships, as well as for their sexual health. This is mainly because of a reduced likelihood of truthfulness between partners when there are instances of infidelity. Boyfriends who have 'strayed' will normally choose to keep this information from their partners, preferring to maintain their (and their boyfriend's) prestige as 'faithful lovers', even if this may result in the risk of HIV exposure for the partner. This aspect of Thai communication may help explain the explosive HIV epidemic among Thai gay men, and HIV prevention campaigns should take into account that many, if not most Thai men, are 'naughty' (i.e. unfaithful to their partner) and culturally they are inclined to hide these sexual escapades; one could also say they are truly not able to discuss this openly because of this cultural baggage.

When it comes to living their sexual lives, Thai people therefore adhere to a concept of sexual subjectivity that has multiple truths and is situation-determined – indeed, appropriate in time and space. Thai homosexual men may act 'camp' or 'gay' but generally only in social surroundings where this causes no affront or disapproval, for example, in entertainment venues or during particular social events with friends. In family settings, they generally act as the exemplary son. Communication about the social (let alone sexual) life of the child is kept to a minimum and a regime of 'don't ask, don't tell' is in place, which suits all parties well (see Chapter 7). In an early study, Jackson described the resistance that exists in Thai society to integrating private lives with one's public role or appearance, making same-sex experience of little importance for 'a "man's" public performance of his civic duties' (Jackson 1997, 176).

Conclusion

In this chapter I have defined Thai personhood by linking the Thai individual first and foremost to his or her social context, including his or her place in the social hierarchy, and I have discussed how a Thai person's sense of self-worth is related to the ability to fulfil social obligations, uphold rules of *kala-thetsa*, maintain *barami* and play a part in rituals and ceremonies. Such a sense of personhood has important consequences for understanding Thai sexual subjectivity, which must be placed in a wider context linked to family and love for the nation, which means focusing on an individual's commonalities with mainstream society rather than zooming in on differences. This is in sharp contrast to the Western context, where acquiring a non-mainstream sexual identity often involves a painful struggle to eventually confess to being 'different', and attempting to bring one's differing sexuality into harmony with one's social world, even if this proves detrimental to the quality of relationships with family or friends.

In Thailand, an important source of self-worth and self-respect is being able to maintain face and prestige/*barami*, and self-worth is derived from the ability to fulfil parental and societal expectations in everyday life. In other words, one's self-worth is derived from how one looks and acts, rather than what one 'is' behind the surface. Having a discrepancy between one's private feelings, desires and sexual behaviours and one's public persona is seen as normal rather than exceptional, and there is not necessarily a sense of shame or guilt connected to these private sexualities. Therefore, Seidman's (2004) concept of homosexual pollution, and the result of this, homophobia, are not relevant to the Thai situation, as will be further discussed in Chapter 7. Indeed, there are several indigenous cultural explanations for the existence of homosexuality in Thailand, none of which are intrinsically homophobic in nature; one of these, derived from Buddhism, is discussed in Chapter 4.

In conclusion, while same-sex attraction is an important characteristic and attribute of the private sexual subjectivity of young homosexual men, it is less important in the public enactment of Thai personhood. As will become clear from the following chapters, Thai same-sex-attracted men, as a whole, appear to prefer to fit in with mainstream heteronormative society. As this chapter has made clear, sexuality, including homosexuality, is considered to be in the private realm, and there seems to be an overwhelming desire to keep it there.

Chapter 4

HOMOSEXUALITY: A MATTER OF KARMA?

Love is like a flower garden to be watered by tears.
— Buddhist-inspired proverb

Introduction

Around 95 per cent of Thailand's population is Buddhist. Of the 25 young men in this study 20 were Buddhist; 4 were Muslim and 1 was Christian. I had expected that including young men from the south and the northeast in the study would lead to a certain variety in terms of interpretations of homosexuality that could partly be derived from the young men's religion. However, the four Muslim men in the study seemed to be Muslim in name only; they hardly ever went to the mosque or attended other religious services or events. They were recruited from Phuket, Pattalung and Nakhon Sri Thammarat, which are provinces where only a small percentage of the population is Muslim. For security reasons, I was unable to recruit men in the four 'troubled provinces' in the south of the country, where Islam has a much stronger role in everyday life and where life for a young homosexual man is likely to be very different. The influence of Islam on the development of the sexual subjectivity of young same-sex-attracted men could therefore not be studied in sufficient depth and detail in this study.

This short chapter will look at the role that Buddhism and the concept of karma played in the young men's explanations of why they are homosexual.

Buddhist Theories about Love and Homosexuality

What does Buddhism have to say about sex and love? The Theravada Buddhist concept of love is called *metta*, meaning compassion, giving, caring, which lay Buddhists do by gaining merit in the form of giving alms or money to the monastery as well as to fellow laypeople in need. Apart from this term, there is a Thai word for love in the more worldly sense: *rak*. This form of love has multiple meanings, as it includes the loving ties between mothers and children (Mulder 2000), love for the nation, as well as romantic love (Klima 2004).

Buddhism generally does not have a lot to say about lay love or sexuality. In contrast to many other religions, sex per se is not considered a sin, except, of course, for Buddhist monks and nuns. Sex and love are considered as forms of attachment, similar to craving material possessions or craving food. Attachment leads to dependency and dependency leads to suffering when the thing one has become attached to ceases to be there. Hence, sex and love are not seen as intrinsically bad, or at least not worse than other attachments. In theory, Buddhists try to avoid attachment in order to avoid suffering. At the very least one should aim to reduce one's dependence on attachments as much as possible.

Buddhist thought about homosexuality is not entirely uniform. The Australian historian Peter A. Jackson (1995b) distinguished between what he called the traditional Buddhist view of homosexuality, which explains it as a result of karma (as described later), and a more modern and less tolerant view, which is that homosexuality derives from an individual's indulging in sexual excesses. This latter view also blames the rapid growth of HIV among men who have sex with men on increased promiscuity and less faithfulness among them. While HIV is not commonly viewed as a divine punishment for prom- iscuity in Thailand, in the way it has been in some Christian countries, it is sometimes seen as a logical consequence of the failure of same-sex-attracted men to have long, stable and committed love relationships – mainly because of the absence of children (see also Ojanen 2010). Paradoxically, it was reformist and supposedly progressive Buddhist thinkers who, in the mid-1990s, started to adopt this less tolerant position, placing less emphasis on karma and more on individual responsibility for life circumstances (Jackson 1995b).

Since Jackson's work, now more than two decades ago, no further investigations have been conducted about Buddhist viewpoints on homosexu- ality. It is therefore unknown how widely the anti-homosexuality stance of these thinkers is still adhered to. In any case, these thinkers are likely to have a limited, urban-based, more intellectual/middle-class appeal. Being from rural backgrounds, it is likely that the young men in this study have been influenced more by the traditional than by the modern interpretation.

What does traditional Buddhism have to say about homosexuality? Nothing specifically: Buddhist texts make no distinction between homosexual and het- erosexual sex or love; both are seen as forms of attachment and suffering (Van Esterik 2000). Thai interpretations of Buddhism view homosexuality as a punishment for sins committed in a previous life, or to be more precise, being born homosexual is seen as a form of heightened suffering. Indeed, in a survey among Thai male-to-female transgender people, just over 50 per cent mentioned 'karma' as the main or one of a series of perceived reasons for being transgender (Winter 2006a).

The Thai view on having a different gender or on being homosexual is therefore generally relatively accepting and tolerant, because these are not seen as a conscious or free choice or as 'illnesses' that are treatable or changeable. This does not mean that it is always easy for parents or siblings to accept a child who is 'different' – more on that in Chapter 7. But being different is part of one's karma or fate, and fate is, by definition, not changeable. Homosexuality could therefore even be seen as natural, as it occurs with a reason, and it has a function in that it allows persons who have committed immoral actions in a past life to bear the consequences during their current life, so that they can – it is hoped – be reborn a 'full man' in a next life, or in the case of most *kathoey*, as women. One study found that 75 per cent of transgender respondents wanted to be reborn as women, 15 per cent as *kathoey* and only 10 per cent as *phu chaai* (Winter 2006b).

Childlessness and Unfulfilling, Unstable Relationships

Why is homosexuality seen as a punishment, as something negative? Homosexuality, while not specifically mentioned in Buddhist teachings, is interpreted as being problematic and abnormal because homosexual relationships do not produce offspring, and are therefore not considered equal to heterosexual relationships. To illustrate this importance of childlessness as an indicator of heightened suffering, the Thai language also uses the word *kathoey* for fruit trees that fail to bear fruit. Without children, homosexual relationships are thought to be inherently unstable and doomed to fail, and homosexuals therefore face more suffering in life than heterosexuals. Jackson (1995b) notes that, contrary to beliefs in some other religions, homosexuality is basically seen as 'bad luck' that is deserved because of one's actions in a previous life rather than as inherently evil or sinful.

This means heterosexuality is implicitly seen as superior to homosexuality. This becomes clear when one considers that the sins that are committed and lead to a rebirth as homosexual are, without exception, related to heterosexual adultery, for example, 'stealing' somebody's wife or husband – which suggests that heterosexuality is the default mode for human sexuality in the Buddhist worldview (or at least in the most common interpretations of Buddhism). One of the participants, Ek,[1] explained:

---

[1] See Chapter 2 for a brief biography of each study participant.

EK: Like, in the past life, when we were a *phu chaai* or a girl, and we do
something wrong related to lust [กาม], like – one makes a mistake like
you sleep with the wrong wife – like you steal somebody else's partner
[แฟน], or like – you date, like, a girl and then you throw her away,
things like that. Yes. Like if you do wrong, or say something wrong
about issues related to sex, things like that, it will lead to consequences
like – do good, get good, do bad, get bad. In the end the result will
be presented to us, and in the next life one has to, like, stay hovering
between masculine and feminine. It is a kind of suffering.

INT: Do you believe in this?

EK: I secretly believe – I secretly believe in it, a little bit [แอบเชื่อนิดหน่อย].
But for me, if – in reality [ในหลักความเป็นจริง], [people may become homo-
sexual] because of things in their environment.

Ek mentioned that he believes that environmental factors can also 'make'
someone homosexual (see Chapter 5). It should be noted that the belief that
one is born homosexual as a punishment and the belief that homosexuality arises because of environmental factors do not contradict each other.
A Buddhist theorist may explain that the deserved punishment with homosexuality might lead someone to be born in a particular environment that
fosters and develops it further.

Another participant, Joe, from a poor rice-farming family in the northeastern province of Buriram, and one of the few participants who did not
continue his studies, was told by a fortune teller that he had 'stolen somebody's
husband' in a previous life, which was the reason why he became 'like this':

JOE: They said, 'Do you know?' They asked me, 'Do you know why, in
this life, you are like this?' They said, 'In your past life, you [ตัวเอง]
were a girl! You were a beautiful girl, very beautiful. And then, you
stole somebody's husband [แย่งผัวเขา]', something like that.

INT: They told you that?

JOE: Yes. That I stole somebody's husband. So this life, I was born like
this. Not as a 100 per cent *phu chaai* [man].

In line with both the traditional and the later Buddhist beliefs, many of the
young men thought that gays and *kathoey* suffer more in life than heterosexual
people, as Ek illustrated:

It is since one is born, it is like, one's existence is difficult [การดำรงชีวิตลำบาก].
General people watch us, something like that. And once you have, once
you have a boyfriend, gay people will like, not sincerely love you. [...]

They have only hopes to get – to get happiness, sexual happiness, for a short time. [...] They cannot find love like men and women. And, if it is a *kathoey*, it is difficult, how to behave as a woman.

This helps explain the overriding negativity about the possibility of finding love or romance that the young men in the study expressed, including Ek:

I have one friend who is *kathoey*, she has told me before that 'a *phu chaai* pairs up with a woman, a woman pairs up with a *phu chaai*, gays pair up with gays. And with whom does the *kathoey* pair up?' [...] The tomboy pairs up with the lesbian. But with whom will the *kathoey* pair up? Real *phu chaai*, they are hard to find, one that would really love [a *kathoey*].

Joe was the only participant in the study who linked a negative moral judgement of homosexuality to the issue of sexual excess, but he did not use Buddhism in his criticism as such, but the moral teachings of another important institution in Thai society, the monarchy:

JOE: Gay life, and *kathoey* life, they say, gay life, and *kathoey* life, it is never enough. [...] Even though they ask us to follow in the footsteps of the king [ในหลวง], the self-sufficiency economy. But for gays and *kathoey*, it is never ever enough. [laughs]

INT: But maybe being gay is not related to the economy, or is it?

JOE: [laughs] It is related. They use resources, like, too many human resources [ใช้ทรัพยากรมนุษย์มากเกินไป]! [laughs]

Most young men in the study found it difficult to imagine how to live their lives in any other way than in the context of a heterosexual family; they saw no credible alternative life path to having a family and children. Many of the participants saw children as the *raison d'être* of a household; why would you stay together if it was not because of a shared responsibility and love for one's children, who also happen to be your insurance policy for when you are old? Joe made a link between the durability of a relationship and the presence of children:

People who are like this, there is no way that they will stay together, something like that, that they will have a family together like normal men and women [ผู้ชายผู้หญิงทั่วไป], and have children together, it is not like that. Ehm, if one is like this, one has to be able to take care of oneself first. That you live together with someone [forever], that is unlikely. That doesn't exist in this world.

Lert, a talkative young man from a poor farming family in the northeastern province of Si Sa Ket, was similarly pessimistic about the possibility of a long-term relationship with the conscripted soldier, a 'real' *phu chaai*, whom he was dating at the time of the first interview:

> LERT: Really, it is not possible. Because we are not like men and women. [...] We cannot have children, or have something that lets us stay together forever. We cannot, right? Eh.
> INT: So you mean that people can stay together only if they have children?
> LERT: Now, I just want to [ขอ] stay together, look after each other [ไปเรื่อยๆ ดีกว่า] for as much as we can [พอที่เราจะทำได้]. I think like this.

Other reasons for this pessimism were the assumptions the young men held about the nature of Thai masculinity (discussed further in Chapter 6). Lert expressed it as follows:

> I think, I don't need anybody, that is the best. The love of gays, *phu chaai* together, I think, it – they cannot love, cannot go together. I think like this. Right? It – it is disappointing [ไม่สมหวัง] [...]. It is not the same like women and *phu chaai*. But women and *phu chaai*, when they love each other, they can get married, and even they can still break up. Eh. So sometimes, we like each other, a *phu chaai* and a *phu chaai*, right? I think it doesn't really fulfil our hope [ไม่ค่อยสมหวังเท่าไรหรอก].

The mainstream media play an important role in perpetuating such negative ideas about homosexuality and being transgender. Households portrayed in popular media and in the participants' environment include single mothers with children, grandmothers or parents with grandchildren (where mothers or both parents are off working somewhere else) or married men and women in households with children – but no gay male couples or lesbian couples, let alone successful families comprising a *phu chaai* and a *kathoey*. A recent study by UNDP Thailand, conducted by the social scientist Kangwan Fongkaew, confirmed the role of the Thai mainstream media in perpetuating stigma against LGBTI people (Fongkaew et al. 2017).

Partly as a result of this media influence, the participants were unable to imagine any living arrangement other than one modelled on the heterosexual family. Several of them said they would like to have children, but few had clear ideas on how to arrange this. For them marriage between a man and a woman was the only conceivable way to raise children, and this may be the reason why some of the participants did not support the idea of gay marriage. Fluk, a self-confident young man raised by his rubber-tapping mother in challenging circumstances in the southern province of Trang, thought that gays should not be allowed to legally get married:

> They will – fuck around, with [the boyfriends of their] friends, all the time. Better to do it like this: Nobody has to know. They don't have to announce [ประจาน] that they – like, I have dated with this person, I have just broken up, I have divorced, something like that. Or I am dating with a new person. No need to announce ourselves. We are people who – eh, are very quick when it comes to issues of love.

Rejection of Karma-Related Explanations

Some participants, however, rejected karma-related explanations for homosexuality, or at least they rejected the idea that being gay or *kathoey* was inevitably equivalent to a life full of misery. Despite agreeing that homosexuality was a punishment, Ek, introduced above, also saw some positive aspects:

> But even though we have only suffering, we also have – it is like God [พระเจ้า, means the Buddha in this context] gave us something like, people who are gay they usually have – have ideas; they are fun-loving people [มีความสนุกสนานในตัว], no matter how much suffering we face, we can still laugh every day. Because, it is like, it is like, He [God] gave us willpower [กำลังใจ].

Fluk even said he would like to be reborn 'like this' in a next life, if he had a choice (so said 15 per cent of the transgender women interviewed by Winter 2006b quoted above). Fluk, whose father had left him and his mother when he was very young, went further and turned the Buddhist argument on its head, claiming that heterosexual men and women may endure the same level of suffering in life as gay people:

> Suffering is there [anyway]. If you compare with a girl, if I am born like a girl in the next life, the suffering is that you have to be pregnant, you have to have menstruation, we are raped, yes. That is suffering. If you are a *phu chaai*, hmmm. That is suffering if, if you are born with the tendency to behave badly [เกเร], you will end up in jail [ต้องเข้าไปอยู่ในตาราง].

When asked to compare this with the suffering that gays face in society, Fluk suggested that gays have their life more in their own hands:

> Gay have suffering, yes. Everybody has. But […] if you look at the society who accepts us, it is not so much. […] The suffering of gays, we can solve it ourselves. […] [G]ays are not accepted in Thai society. This creates suffering because there is gossip [เสียงวิจารณ์] that we have to deal with, they will scold us, like, 'You were born a *phu chaai*, why don't you be a *phu chaai*?' That is suffering. But we can solve it by focusing on our friends. Inviting each other to go out together. So we can get rid of our depression [ความเครียด] like this.

Other participants also focused on individual behaviour and responsibility in the present life as predictors of suffering or happiness, and also dismissed the karmic predicament of suffering. Gop, a bright and talkative young man from a middle-class family in the northeastern province of Mahasarakham, said he would prefer to be reborn as gay in in his next life. Nook, an emotional and talkative young man from a poor rural family in the north-eastern province of Nong Bua Lamphu who considered becoming a girl when he was younger, also considered being 'like this' a blessing rather than bad luck or the result of bad karma.

Conclusion

Buddhism was an important explanatory framework that helped the young men in this study understand themselves as a key first stage in the formation of their sexual subjectivity. The Buddhist concepts of karma and suffering helped to frame how they viewed themselves and how they found a position for themselves in society during their childhood and secondary school years. Whereas karma and Buddhism provided some explanations for understanding sexuality to the participants, these explanations seemed particularly helpful when they felt pessimistic or sad, for example, when they had a broken heart. Apart from their answers on specific questions about the reasons for the existence or emergence of homosexuality, there was little reference to Buddhism in the stories of most of the young men.

In the eyes of the participants and influenced by Buddhist thought, the absence of children makes a family unviable and unsustainable. This made it hard for them to imagine how same-sex relationships could be possible in the longer term after the initial sexual attraction that brought the partners together wears off. There are simply no models for such same-sex relationships in Thai society. As will be explored in Chapter 6, traditional notions of masculinity have little room for monogamy. So-called open relationships, defined as relationships based on a mutual agreement about having sex with others outside the relationship, which are common in many Western gay relationships, were (still?) too far outside the moral compass of the young men in this study.

In the following chapter, the first sense of being 'different' that the young men felt is explored.

Chapter 5

IN THE BEGINNING ... EXPLORING EARLY AWARENESS OF BEING DIFFERENT

Introduction

This chapter examines the earliest awareness of being different of the young men in the study. Most young men described experiencing a sense of 'gender nonconformity', which often occurred long before they became aware of any same-sex attraction. A smaller group of men found out they were attracted to fellow males later in life, after reaching puberty; they did not encounter the same sense of gender nonconformity, but I will show that gender played an important role in their early understandings of their sexuality as well.

Kathoey, Thailand's 'Third Gender'

The third gender, *kathoey*, has often been described as having both feminine and masculine characteristics. The term has been translated into English in many different ways: transgender, transsexual, transvestite or the popular term 'ladyboy'. The definition used in this chapter includes all these terms. Ten Brummelhuis (1999) observed that, in the eyes of prospective sexual partners of *kathoey*, the feminine-sexual aspect and a homosocial aspect adds to their attraction. For example, unlike 'good' Thai women, *kathoey* often drink alcohol, smoke, like talking about sex and making naughty jokes, and like to go out, dance and have fun. The fact that *kathoey* cannot have children automatically disqualifies them as serious marriage partners in the eyes of 'traditional' Thai men, making them suitable for fun and casual sex only. *Kathoey*, because of their cross-dressing habits as well as specific social roles, are easily recognizable in Thai society. It is therefore not surprising that for the same-sex-attracted young men in this study, *kathoey* was either a role model or an example of how they did *not* want to be.

Many scholars have marvelled about the fact that Thailand has supposedly transcended the female–male binary by having a third gender category, *kathoey*, often defined either as 'neither male nor female' or as 'both male and female'. But are *kathoey* really a third, separate gender? One could also claim that *kathoey* is a type of woman and not a third gender category. Since Thai male bodies tend to be smaller, smoother and slimmer than Western bodies (at least before the mass introduction of Coca-Cola, Lay's and Western fast food), a degree of physical femaleness may be more attainable to them, provided they have the means, financially and medico-technically, to move in this direction. Besides this, Thai cultural notions of sex and gender tend to delink biological sex from socially performed gender roles, as will be further discussed later in this book. This means that playing a social role indicating one's gender is often enough to 'become' that gender, even though the biological body is of a different sex. This was also found among same-sex-attracted females (Sinnott 1999), where the *tom*, a masculinized female, can become male by playing particular masculine gender roles (including smoking, drinking, womanising and fighting). This would mean that *kathoey* are females rather than a 'third gender'. Indeed, linguistically, at least in urban circles, it seems the term most *kathoey* prefer to describe themselves is '*phu ying praphet song*' which translates as 'second type of woman' (ten Brummelhuis 1999, 123). This would indicate that most *kathoey* want to be seen, first and foremost, as women, and not as a third gender category; this is confirmed by Winter's (2006b) research, in which nearly half of the sampled *kathoey* prefer to be called women and slightly over a third second type of woman.

So, is there truly a third gender then, or is *kathoey* a mere manifestation of how performative and body-based gender in Thailand is in allowing, literally, for a relatively easy crossing of gender boundaries from male to female and vice versa? According to the Thai scholar Narupon Duangwises (personal communication), the answer to this question is partly determined by class. Urban, middle- and higher-class *kathoey* usually have a desire and the financial means to become 'real' women, including sex-change operations, fitting the consumer and popular culture of urban Bangkok. In contrast, rural, lower-class *kathoey* often refuse to be classified as either women or men, choosing to retain their masculine, muscular bodies as well as their penises, and embracing the *kathoey* label. According to this view, a real third gender *kathoey* may exist only for the lower classes, whereas in middle- and higher-class (urban) settings *kathoey* have become a 'second type of woman' who have become more or less assimilated into the cultural gender-scape occupied by urban cisgender women. The hyperfeminine urban *kathoey* (or *sao praphet song*) have become associated with material wealth, consumerism, urban life and modernity, whereas rural *kathoey* are linked with poverty, rural life and backwardness. This is manifested by the popular use of the Thai word *kathoey khwaai* ('buffalo *kathoey*') to scold a presumably ugly and masculine-looking *kathoey*; the buffalo is a symbol not only of the rural world and of brute (supposedly masculine) strength, but of the rural world before there were mechanical agricultural tools. Therefore *khwaai* refers to utter backwardness.

A Sense of Having Been Born the Wrong Gender

When looking at the age at which the young men first realized that they were different from other boys of their generation, two patterns were found. The first – and most prevalent – was that they felt they were born into the wrong gender, or in short 'gender nonconformity'. This was the case for the biggest group of young men in this study (19 participants out of 25). These 19 men said they started feeling different from their male peers at a very young age, often during kindergarten or early primary school (aged 4–9). Five of these 19 young men had experiences dressing and behaving as females during their childhood. They called themselves (or were called by friends or people in their surroundings) *kathoey* or *toot*. The word *toot* is a derogative or, in some contexts, teasing or playful term for *kathoey* and is most likely derived from the Hollywood movie *Tootsie* in which Dustin Hoffman performed in drag (Chonwilai 2012c). Ives, who had only recently decided to 'become' gay rather than *kathoey*, is an example of this:

> At the time, I had the feeling [that] I was born – I know I was born in the wrong sex. I was born in this life, I want to be [literally: to become] a woman. I will wear long hair in the future. I will change, have an operation, to change my sex. So – I wanted to become a woman [ต้องการเป็นผู้หญิง].

The cross-dressing of these five boys was not and could not be permanent, because dressing as a girl was not allowed at school. They did it in the company of friends outside school hours, and in one case it was done alone, at home.

The stories of these five young men in the study show that there was influence of other *kathoey* or gay friends, helping them recognize themselves as *kathoey*, at least temporarily. Lert, who was relatively late to adopt a *kathoey* identity at the age of 13, described how he watched in awe when older *kathoey* friends made up their faces, wanting to play along:

> My environment, it was like, I saw them do their eyebrows, they would whiten their faces with powder, something like that. '*Oei*! [เอ้ย] Come here, I will do it for you!' So, I said, 'Do it for me.' So then I was, it became my habit [นิสัย], it was like this, like that, so I tied my hair, I was like that ever since [laughs]. So it stuck to me.

Ives also mentioned the presence of *kathoey* friends, whom he (she, at the time) admired and wanted to emulate: 'Because first, [for] example, there were many [*kathoey*] who woke me up [ปลุกเรา]. [I thought,] "They can be beautiful, I can do that too."' Note that in using the words 'waking up', Ives indicated that he thought something was already present inside him beforehand, something that was dormant and that could be and was ready to be awakened. Nook, who only started cross-dressing in ninth grade when he was 15, wanted to try out new things after he discovered that he wanted to be a woman, including participating in *kathoey* beauty contests:

> I was a girl, I dressed like a girl. Like, when there was a ceremony, a party, I would, like in Thailand you have the rocket festival, in Isaan, the rocket festival. There would be *kathoey* beauty contests [ประกวดนางงาม], I went everywhere! I wanted to try out, when I dressed like a girl, would I be pretty? I have a picture, have a look!

Fourteen other boys in the study never felt the need or never had the opportunity to dress up or behave as a girl, but they nevertheless felt they were different during kindergarten and primary school in terms of their gender. They realized that, because most of their friends were girls and they played 'girls games', they were different from the other boys in their villages. Hong, an introverted young man who was raised by his mother in a distant rural district of the poor northeastern province of Buriram, explained:

> HONG: [W]hen I was a child, I liked to – sometimes my older sister was bought a new toy, and I liked to fight with my sister over her toys, I mean, so [my mother] could see already that I didn't play with *phu chaai* toys, something like that.
> INT: Oh. You played with dolls?
> HONG: Yes [laughs].

Joe, who calls himself gay these days, mentioned the role of his social surroundings in understanding himself while growing up, and noted that his identity has changed since he was a child:

> In the past, when I was very young, I didn't think that I was gay. I thought I was a *kathoey* more. Because around my home, around that zone, the children who were born in my generation, there would be more girls. And it made that I was, like – what a person will be, it has to develop according to one's society, right? [พัฒนาไปตามสังคม] When a society is like this, one has to develop according to that society. Am I correct? That is

it. I think there were many girls. And another thing, at my home, there were a lot of girls. That gave me girly habits [นิสัยตุ้งติ้ง], to be like a woman [เป็นผู้หญิงไปเลย].

These fourteen young men described themselves as tidy and neat or *riab roi* [เรียบร้อย] and often were good students. As a result, they were generally well liked by their teachers and other elders in their communities. They would stay away from the fights or rough games that the other boys would engage in, instead preferring the gentler games that girls played. Bon, a masculine-looking young man who lived with his working elder sister in the southern province of Phuket for his senior high school years, disliked the roughness that he saw in the games his brother and father played:

> They use violence [or roughness], they play, kick [soccer], beat each other, and I feel I get hurt, and I don't like it [...]. And I would avoid [it] and [...] escaped to be with – to be the gender that is gentle, soft [or slight], without pain, it gave me a better feeling, better.

Although these young men did not dress or behave as women in public, they still explained their sexuality largely in terms of their gender nonconformity and less in terms of an innate sexual attraction to other men, as Ek illustrated:

> I liked to play with girls [...], I played and stayed with girls. Something like that. So I knew for sure, like, I thought I was not the same as others [ไม่เหมือนชาวบ้านเขาแล้ว], at that time. They also thought, and knew [เค้าก็คิด ก็รู้]. It was not like, all of a sudden I would think and know, it was not like that.

Many of these young men saw their feminine company or the feminine games they played as the reason they gradually took over 'feminine habits' [นิสัยของผู้หญิง] and thus became gay or even *kathoey*. Oad, a confident and talkative young man from an upper-middle-class family in the northeastern province of Beung Kaan, explained how he used to be a 'real man' (in Thai: *phu chaai tem tua* or *phu chaai 100 per cent*) when he was younger:

> In the past I was a *phu chaai*, when I was a child I liked to tease/bully my friends, I once made a friend fall from the swing, he had a wound on his head. My 'gang' was naughty [ซน]. [...] We were a gang that was not afraid of anything. We liked to tease people. Because the leader of the gang was the child of the deputy director of the school, we were not afraid of anything.

Note the arguments that Oad used to convince me of his masculinity at that time: he liked to tease and bully friends; he was rough and violent (making a friend fall from the swing); he was closely allied to a group of fellow rough mates and he was fearless. But then his exposure to the girl next door began, and rather than falling in love with her, that is when he started to like men. Note how Oad saw the development of his same-sex attraction as a result of activities, of practice, and how he firmly placed the blame for it on too much femininity in his environment:

> But after that – there was a girl living near my house. She was a friend, I liked to play with her, we played together often, so I felt, like, I habitually played like, played father, played mother, I played father and mother and played like I was cooking, things like that. Because the children around my house, there were only girls, I was the only boy. So I absorbed feminine habits. When I was a child I never thought that I would like men. If I remember correctly, it was during [fifth grade], I liked men, so – I knew myself.

Ek, who was attempting to develop a more masculine identity over the course of the three interviews, mentioned an even more distant environmental factor – watching Thai soap operas – as the factor that led him to gradually begin absorbing feminine habits.

How can 'too much femininity' have such an impact on Thai men? In the Thai worldview, feminine power is well represented. It is traditionally and spiritually grounded in the spirits of earth, water and rice, which are all basic to survival (Hanks 1964). Feminine power is in fact so strong that Thailand has a long tradition of men fearing 'pollution' by women – pollution that would sap them of their masculine strength. This fear is most clearly articulated in the strict rules that exist for women's conduct, dress and behaviour in temples and around monks (Keyes 1984). Thai people also tend to believe that contact with female underwear, being exposed to menstrual blood (Manderson 1992) or performing oral sex on a woman can sap a man's strength (Fuller et al. 1993). It therefore does not take much imagination to stretch such beliefs a bit further and explain 'feminine influences' as the reason for decreased masculinity in the form of either reduced sexual desire for women or the emergence of sexual desire for men in the way that Oad and Ek do above.

At face value, of course, this argument contains contradictions. Most importantly, many of the young men in the study had brothers who grew up in exactly the same circumstances but did not end up being gay or *kathoey*. Second, the exact effect of having so many females in the home environment is unclear in the men's stories; whereas Ives used it as an explanation for why he started to cross-dress and embark on a process of becoming female, Oad, Joe and Ek used it to explain their sexual preference for men, but they did not take the step of actually wanting to change into women.

The young men in this study also saw the composition of their family and the way they were raised as explanations for their gender nonconformity or their homosexuality. Both were also indirectly linked to gender, and indicative of the power of gender as an explanatory framework for homosexuality. An absent father or a lack of brothers was a recurring explanation, for example, by Ake, a talkative and frank former *kathoey* from a middle-class family in the southern province of Phuket: 'I stayed with my mother since I was born. My father never really took care of us. I stayed with my mother, and with my older sister.'

Bon mentioned that he, being the youngest child, was kept inside the house all the time; he blamed a lack of activities with other (masculine) family members for becoming gay: 'If you have brothers, your father, or your grand-father, or uncles [they] will take you to do masculine things.'

Again, these beliefs are easily dismissed if one considers the composition of modern Thai households, as single-parent households (usually headed by a mother) are very common, and most boys and girls growing up in these households turn out heterosexual. Be that as it may, both of these ideas – an 'overdose' of feminine influence or an underwhelming presence of masculine caregivers (many of the boys had no or distant fathers) – give an indication of the importance gender plays in how the young men in this study made sense of the cause of their same-sex attraction.

In summary, a large majority of men in this study used gender-related explanations to explain their own same-sex attraction, seeing their sexual pref-erence as caused by a lack of masculinity or a surplus of femininity because of an unbalanced social or family environment. Such explanations tend to be widely accepted and understood in Thai society, including by heterosexuals. Therefore, using such explanations, the men did not go against the way main-stream Thai society sees and understands gender. The young men did not speak about or imagine a separation or an escape from mainstream society in the way many rural homosexuals in Western countries often do – Western gay men often talk about moving to a big city as an act of personal liberation from a situation of oppression, secrecy and frustration in their rural family envir-onments. The Thai men in this study, in contrast, explained themselves using concepts that are universally understood to be part of the heteronormative gender regime. In doing this, the Thai young men naturalized their sexual preferences while at the same time remaining firmly embedded in mainstream Thai society.

Sense of Sexual Attraction to Other Men

The second pattern of discovering same-sex attraction was found among a much smaller group of five participants who realized that they were different from their peers at a much later age than the young men discussed above. These five young men found out after entering puberty (usually around 14–17) that they lacked the sexual feelings for girls that their male peers experienced. Fluk, for example, had mainly male friends when he was in high school (unlike most of the boys discussed above), but he realized that his male friends were talking about girls all the time – a topic he found utterly uninteresting:

> So there was this sports tournament between schools [กีฬาสี], right? So there was a school with girls there too. And I realized, my friends, they like girls, and I didn't like them. I felt nothing, I felt nothing [about girls]. So I thought, I probably am [gay].

Ud, a serious young man from a strict Christian family in the southern city of Trang, mentioned having girlfriends in junior high school, but then, at the age of 15, he fell in love with a male student at his school, who was one year his senior:

> I saw him and – he was a *phu chaai*. [...] I saw him at first, I was like: Wow! [เฮ้ย] He is cute! [น่ารัก]. I was speechless [อึ้ง], very happy [ปลื้ม], at first, I just thought, I like this older brother, he is cool [เท่ห์], he is handsome, something like that. At first, I started to feel like, a little bit shaken [หวั่นไหวนิดนึง]. [chuckles] [...] But later, I felt strange, I felt I did not want to look at girls [anymore], like, I wanted to look at boys.

In contrast to the first group discussed above, the young men in this category focused not on their overly feminine environment or the lack of masculinity in their upbringing to explain their homosexuality. Instead, they explained these feelings as emanating from inside themselves. Kit, a self-confident and normatively masculine-acting only child from a well-to-do family in an outer district of Buriram, illustrated this:

> I think, this is because – it comes from the heart [or mind]. And – I think – some people say, some – my friends, they say: You are good looking, why aren't you a [real] man? I said, If one doesn't like [girls], one doesn't like. Something like that. I think, you cannot choose how you are born in this regard [มันเลือกที่จะเป็นอะไรตรงนี้ไม่ได้].

Note how Kit – despite not having experienced a sense of gender noncon-formity in the same way as the first group of participants reported – still also used gender as a way to make sense of his feelings, referring to himself as 'not a [real] man'.

Such beliefs, however, were sometimes subject to change. Ives, introduced above, strongly focused on his environment and upbringing to explain his desire to be a girl, focusing on his exposure to girls and lack of masculine guidance during the first interview. During the third interview – nearly two years later – he had started to believe that same-sex attraction is innate rather than caused by one's environment or childhood experiences. Ives went a step further by claiming that the potential for liking or loving men is intrinsically embedded in the genes of every man, regardless of the environment they are raised in:

> But in reality, people who are gay – it is inside every *phu chaai* anyway. It is just that he hasn't tried it [yet], he hasn't touched it [yet], that person – if it happens, he tries it, he touches [sex with men/*kathoey*], he will know immediately, 'This. I like this!' Yes. Because [...] the GENES [Eng] of a *phu chaai*, there is X and Y. They have liking for both *phu chaai* and women. But – they haven't come across it [yet]. So they don't know, so they don't like it. But once they touch it, they do it, something like that, they will, like, be curious, want to try [more]. And when they have tried it already, they will like it.

Ives had taken on the belief that every man is potentially available for sex; it just needs a particular event or experience for it to be triggered. Note how he also used a reference to 'genes' to bolster the argument that this feature of Thai masculinity was 'natural'. Believing this makes the act of sex with a man in and of itself an unreliable marker of being non-manly and, likewise, having sex with a *kathoey* or homosexual person does not necessarily affect a 'real' man's masculine status. This may help explain the large number of 'heterosexual' men working in Thailand's male sex industry (De Lind van Wijngaarden 1999). The American anthropologist Penny Van Esterik (2000, 216) has also pointed out that 'Thai definitions of masculinity do not pre-clude homoerotic behaviour and practice', which is in line with her important statement that gender in Thailand is 'body-based' and not necessarily linked to sexuality, sexual behaviour or stated sexual expressions.

In line with what was discussed in Chapter 3, it is the outside surface that counts, not what really happens behind the scenes. In other words, having a body that looks masculine enough to be identified as a man by society is, in principle, enough to maintain one's sense of being a *phu chaai*; what one does with this body in private settings does not affect this status. How one *feels* about sex with men remains important, but is a private matter. This explains why Kit, who described some passionate sexual relationships with men, despite his masculine demeanour, still did not consider himself a 'real man'. Kit made a clear distinction between men who love men and *kathoey*. Ives was more 'traditional': by saying the ability to have sex with men is 'inside every man anyway' it became clear that Ives did not see *phu chaai* who love or like men as a different species from those who do not, which is in line with his childhood worldview in which there are only females (who include 'real' women and girls and *kathoey*, also referred to as 'second type of women') and their natural sex partners: men.

Quan, an only child from a middle-class family in the northeastern province of Kalasin, used a line of thinking that was similar to Ives's to explain why and how he 'became gay', mentioning the experience of having his heart broken by a girlfriend during secondary school as a reason for him to experiment with male-to-male sex. Then he got 'hooked' on it:

> It was like – I was dating women, and I was thinking already, 'If I date a girl, and if I am broken hearted with a woman, like this, would it be better to try to be gay?' [ลองไปเป็นเกย์ดีกว่าไหม] [...] So I was like, 'Shall I try to change?' So – So I changed and tried it [เปลี่ยนดู], and when I changed, it made me, like, it made me think in another direction, like, 'Eh, it is better!' Something like that. He TAKES CARE [Eng] of me well, I felt that he knew my heart [รู้ใจเรา] [better] [...]. So I changed.

Contrary to my expectations when I started the study, unexpected, wanted or unwanted sexual experiences with men or sexual games with other boys or men had only a small role in the explanatory narratives about the emerging gender identity and sexual subjectivity of most young men in this study. Bon and Kit both talked about masturbation games with other boys during high school, but they did not say that these triggered sexual feelings for men in them. Bon said it was normal for boys to play such games; Kit also implied this, saying that he and his friends would watch (straight) porn together and masturbate in a group when he was at an all-boys high school. When asked if he was looking at or interested in the bodies of his friends while masturbating, Kit said he was not:

> KIT: No. I mean, at that time, it was just fun. It was like mutual encouragement [การชู], like this.
> INT: You didn't look, like, you were not curious?

KIT: Eh … We would compare, who was big and who was not, like this. And we would talk about that inside our group, something like that.

INT: But you didn't have [sexual] feelings [for your friends].

KIT: I didn't.

Kit and Bon confirmed Penny Van Esterik's point that gender is firmly body based, that is, doing sexual things with other men does not lead people to feel guilty or fear that they must be 'intrinsically gay' because of these actions. Despite what Ives said about there being a potential for every man to have same-sex experiences, these experiences do not 'condemn' these men to become 'gays' or 'homosexuals'. Homosexuality is not seen as something that is transmissible by being confronted or engaging in it, a belief that is seen as an important source of homophobia in Western countries (Murray 2009).

At the same time, however, homosexual experiences or relationships can trigger the realization that one prefers these to heterosexual experiences or relationships. Kit only became interested in men when he was slightly older, and had experienced 'disappointment' with girls – again, here is a similarity with Quan, who gave a similar reason for switching from liking women to liking men. Both Quan and Kit also talked about how their male partners 'take care' of them and their feelings better than girls do, which would be a rather pragmatic and non-sexual reason for explaining their switch from dating women to dating men; the importance of 'taking care' in the definition of a good boyfriend is further discussed in Chapter 10.

Conclusion

Two distinct patterns were discovered when looking at how the young men in this study first realized that they were not like normal *phu chaai*. First, there was a group of young men who talked about experiencing a sense of gender nonconformity, mainly in their everyday actions and habits. Often these men said they felt they were not like normal boys from the time they were in kin-dergarten or early in primary school. Some young men discovered at a young age that they did not like the physicality and roughness of boys' games. Two of these young men (Ake and Ives) reported a sense of feeling trapped in the wrong body, and thought they should have been born female, although both eventually learned to live and feel content with(in) their male bodies. For same-sex-attracted young men in rural areas, growing up in a social environment where three genders have traditionally been the norm, the emergence of being and feeling different was initially often expressed by dressing, acting, walking, dancing and talking like a female. Their family and friends would have noticed a lack of masculinity in the young child, and would have easily categorized it as *kathoey*, which is a gender category families and communities understand and of which they can make social sense. While there may be disappointment for parents (especially the father) that their child is not a 'normal' boy, there is no loss of face involved here because the child is not held responsible for his being and his actions. As was discussed in Chapter 4, being a *kathoey* is not seen as sinful in itself and is not usually seen as a choice, but as the effect of karma. The participants in this category mostly discovered that they were different as very young children, long before they started to have sexual feelings or desires. Most in this group mentioned they felt they were different from other boys for as long as they could remember. This is in line with a study that describes the very early awareness of being different in Thai gender-nonconforming children (Winter 2006b). A larger group of participants developed their sexual subjectivity in ways that did not involve a rejection of their male bodies, but they nevertheless drew heavily on mainstream stereotypes of masculinity and femininity. They saw themselves as having either a surplus of femininity or a lack of masculinity, and sought to complement this in their romantic partners.

The second, much smaller, group of young men realized they were different at a later age, when they started to develop sexual feelings. They either found out they lacked a sexual attraction to women, often while comparing themselves with 'straight' friends and the things they talked and joked about, or they fell in love with another man.

In Chapter 6, the importance of gender in making sense of homosexuality and of one's early romantic and sexual experiences is further explored.

Chapter 6

THE IMPORTANT ROLE OF GENDER IN UNDERSTANDING HOMOSEXUALITY IN THAILAND

This chapter focuses on the importance of gender in how the young men in the study explained their sexuality and their early sexual experiences. Gender is defined here simply as common (some might say 'stereotypical') notions about masculinity and femininity that exist and are learned and taught in a society.

The first part of the chapter will briefly summarize some of the studies on gender and sexuality that have been conducted in Thailand. After this I will describe how the young men in this study used stereotypical notions of femininity and masculinity to frame and interpret their early romantic experiences and expectations, and discuss the implications of this.

Gender and Sexuality in Thailand

The Australian historian and Thai scholar Peter A. Jackson (2000) remarked that there are no separate words for 'gender', 'sex' or 'sexuality' in the Thai language. All three terms are denoted by the term *phet*. The word *phet* therefore sometimes refers to the English term gender, sometimes to sex and sometimes to sexuality, and sometimes to something in between. This linguistic fact indicates how important gender is for understanding sexuality in Thailand, and suggests that it may be difficult to draw clear boundaries between genders and sexualities. The American anthropologist Penny Van Esterik (2000, 202) noted that considerable flexibility and fluidity exists in how gender is expressed and lived in Thailand, even within the same individual over time:

> Thai gender can best be represented as a continuum with permeable boundaries, a system that is in essence non-binary but in conventional language provides conceptual space for a third gender [...] what is stressed in the Thai system is the ability of people to move in and

out of the categories. It is the Thai sensitivity to context – expressed as *kalatesa*, knowing how time, locations and relationships intersect to create appropriate contexts – that allows for the flow of multiple gender identities.

Morris (1994) argues that Thailand has three distinct genders: the man (*phu chaai*), woman (*phu ying*) and the third gender *kathoey*. The sexualities of the male and female genders are considered to be fundamentally different in Thai sexual culture, with 'normal' women being considered to have fewer sexual urges than men and being more in control of them. Women are stereotypically divided into two: 'good' women – whose sexual life is aimed at reproduction in the context of marriage and who play the role of mothers/nurturers – and 'bad' women – who are defined as having sex for fun (or money) and with multiple partners. For men there are at least three stereotypical gender roles: that of the monk (denouncing their sexuality and to an extent also their gender), the father/provider for the household and the playboy. It is important to note that these stereotypes are partly situational and fleeting, and are not irrevocably linked to individual character. These stereotypes rather function as indicators of direction for individuals on a moral compass indicating different gradations of 'goodness' and 'badness'.

Where did these ideas about 'good' and 'bad' femininity and masculinity come from? To an important extent, they had to do with marriage. Thailand used to have a system of arranged marriages in which two families agreed that their children would get married, often many years before the children reached maturity, although it rarely happened that the prospective marriage partners had no input or disagreed with their parents' choice (Van Esterik 2000). Marriage was, first and foremost, aimed at forming an economic unit, as well as an investment in the future, when offspring were supposed to take care of their parents during their old age (Rabibhadana 1984). Sex without reproductive purpose (i.e. oral and anal sex or any sex for the sake of pleasure) was not part of this concept: respectable married women would never indulge in such acts, or at least they would never admit to it. Similar to other countries, from the beginning of the twentieth century Thailand started to embrace the ideology of romantic love – marriages based on romantic preferences by men and women, as described by Anthony Giddens (1992) and, for Bangkok/Thailand, by Scott Barmé (2006).

Remnants of the arranged marriage system remain in the persistence of marriage-related gender stereotypes about men and women, and their respective good or bad sexualities. For example, the 'good woman' stereotype included the expectation on both sides that a married woman would be a virgin or at least be sexually inexperienced and restrained. One study, admittedly dated, reported on focus group discussions with Thai factory workers of both genders (Ford and Kittisuksathit 1994). It found that both young men and women in the study perceived sexual desire to be solely in the masculine domain. Young men could openly talk about their sexual feelings and experiences, but women felt ashamed of their sexual curiosity and thought women should wait until they were older and married before they found out about sex. They definitely did not conceive of a feminine need for sex for the sake of pleasure in the same way as they justify sexual behaviours (and transgressions) of Thai men. Most Thai men still do not expect their wives to be sexually experienced or skilled (Tangchonlathip 1995, quoted in Van Esterik 2000), although in recent decades many changes have occurred in the sexual freedom of unmarried Thai women.

Past Studies of Male Homosexuality in Thailand

The Australian historian Peter A. Jackson (1995a) was the first to publish an English-language book about male homosexuality in Thailand. It was based on an analysis of letters written by Thai homosexually active men to an 'agony aunt' (who was in fact a man) in a popular magazine. Since then, Jackson has analysed written sources and media reports and he tried to describe the connections he saw between the emergence and growth of the market economy and the first signs of what he calls 'emerging modern Thai queer identities' (Jackson 2009a). Jackson has undertaken a number of investigations of Thai homosexuality since then, including a history of the emergence of homosexual identity labels in the media and, more recently, what he sees as the 'queering' of Thai notions of gender and sexuality in the context of modernization and globalization (Jackson 1997, 2000, 2004, 2009b). Because Jackson is a historian, his sources are archives, written articles, movies and magazines. This has biased his findings, since many of these sources were written by and for a well-educated, middle- or upper-class minority of gay men and 'queer' activists, who were mainly Bangkok-based. The findings of Jackson's work cannot easily be generalized to same-sex-attracted men in Thailand as a whole, as this book will show.

In social and anthropological research on Thai same-sex cultures, two early scholars focused on processes of self-identification and notions of male homosexuality and gender among transgender women and homosexually active men in Bangkok and Chiang Mai (De Lind van Wijngaarden 1995; ten Brummelhuis 1999). My own (1995, 86) study in Chiang Mai described the importance of gender in explaining and framing male homosexual relations, and how important a person's level of femininity or masculinity were in predicting and explaining their sexual behaviours, norms and values:

> Sexual affairs between men are more often than not constructed in terms of [a] traditional gender-model. It is not the object choice (a man instead of a woman) that shapes one's identity, but one's preferred sexual act or role and one's social appearance.

Han ten Brummelhuis, who was my academic supervisor and mentor at the time, also described this gender model for the feminine-identified *kathoey*. He observed that *kathoey* do not see themselves as homosexuals, and that their sexual partners do not see themselves as homosexuals either. The sexual partners of the *kathoey* see their partners as women, not as men. Therefore it is inappropriate to lump *kathoey* under the same banner as homosexuals or gays, as health care providers as well as the Thai media still tend to do (ten Brummelhuis 1999). Research on Thai *kathoey* has continued, mainly by Sam Winter, with a strong focus on sexual behaviour and sexual health in the context of the HIV epidemic (Winter 2006a, 2006b). Other work related to homosexuality in Thailand has focused on male sex work, and has also had a strong focus on HIV risk and vulnerability (De Lind van Wijngaarden 1999; Gallagher 2005; McCamish et al. 2000; Shulich 2006; Storer 1999a, 1999b).

A Thai masters student, Thawatchai Pachun (2008), conducted a study on what he called 'identity conflict management' among a small sample of male homosexual medical students in Bangkok. He found that the students in his study lived in two distinct social worlds, one professional and one personal. In the former, they 'usually managed their identity by not deviating visibly from their heterosexual classmates' (Pachun 2008, iv). While the students mentioned that there was more openness about sexual diversity in their university, 'heterosexual norms still predominate' (92). The important point that Pachun made is that the men in his study, rather than separating themselves from mainstream society into gay communities, chose to remain part of mainstream society. In order to do so, they had to 'manage' their homosexual 'needs' on the margins of it. As will be shown in Chapter 7, this was very much the case among the men in the study presented in this book.

As briefly discussed in Chapter 3, Rosalind Morris tried to develop a model or theory of Thai gender and sexuality in the 1990s. She proposed a distinction between three genders and four sexualities. Morris identified the gender system as consisting of *phu chaai* (man), *phu ying* (woman) and *kathoey* (transvestite/transsexual/hermaphrodite). The second system is a system of four sexualities: heterosexual male, heterosexual female, homosexual male and homosexual female, in which the *kathoey* is construed as the most effeminate form of a homosexual male. These two systems, Morris said, are two 'different and mutually irreconcilable systems [that] cohabit in a single social field' (1994, 19). Morris observed that the sexualities system conflates sexual practice with social identity, but noted that the 'three gender' system remains visible throughout. Morris said that although 'sexuality' and 'sexual identity' emerged later in the history of Thai sexuality and gender than gender identities did, there is no logical sequence: 'Both exist in the present and vie for hegemony in a society that is deeply influenced but not fully determined by transnational forces and ideologies' (1994, 17).

Penny Van Esterik (2000) used the concept of the *palimpsest* as a heuristic tool to explain how this works. When text is written over an existing text without fully erasing what was already written, the previous text that remains visible through the new is a palimpsest. She quoted Fabian, who stated that palimpsests allow us to see 'cracks through which the past creeps up on modern society' (Fabian 1991: 223, quoted in Van Esterik 2000). In the context of Morris's theory, this means that a system of three genders was already present and that a second system, based on sexual identities and emerging in the context of an increasingly consumerist and globalizing society, is partly overwriting the previous system, resulting in a hybrid that contains elements of both the former and the latter.

As an example of this, Jackson (1997) explored the historical process of the adoption of the word 'gay' in the Thai language. Jackson found that the word 'gay' was rapidly adopted in Thai vernacular, as it helped to resolve what he called 'tensions within the structure of [Thai] masculinity' (1997, 167). Indeed, before the term 'gay' became popular, there was no linguistic term or label to describe homosexuality beyond the terms referring to the effeminate *kathoey* and her partner, the masculine *phu chaai*.

Jackson noted that the growing use and popularity of the term gay in recent decades suggests the following:

Gay male identity in Thailand represents the emergence of a ternary term in the previously binary structure of Thai male sex/gender categories, and that gayness renders explicit a previously unlexicalized domain between the poles of the Thai 'complete man' and the demasculinized *kathoey*. (1997, 167)

Does this mean that the modern concept of 'gay' sexuality based on object choice is gradually sweeping aside the traditional idea that homosexuality requires a feminine *kathoey* and her masculine *phu chaai* partner? The answer is no. The situation should be perceived as a continuous tension between two coexisting systems of meaning from which individuals learn and to which individuals can contribute, and between which they navigate depending on their needs and on particular situations. This will become abundantly clear in the stories of the young men in this book.

Kunlasatree: Using Stereotypical Notions of Being a 'Good Woman' to Frame Early Romantic and Sexual Experiences

As discussed briefly above, according to Thai gender stereotypes, women can be divided into good and bad women, linked to their role in the family and their (lack of) desire for or engagement in sex (Fordham 2006). Good women are called *kunlasatree* ('virtuous woman'), defined as 'proficient and sophisticated in household duties; graceful, pleasant, yet unassuming in her appearance and social manners; and conservative in her sexuality' (Taywaditep et al. 2003: 1023). Many (especially middle class) Thai women endorse the *kunlasatree* notion, regarding it as a sign of dignity and honour (Fongkaew 2002) and even national pride. The role of a good woman is firmly linked to the family; she is a nurturer/mother, and she is a faithful and servile wife whose sexuality is confined by marriage. Both in the setting of the family as well as in school, girls are taught how to be a *kunlasatree*, and they learn that the highest achievable goal in life for a woman is to be a mother. Boys are taught the importance of choosing a good woman as a wife. Celebrity figures and politicians often praise the value of the *kunlasatree* in the media (Taywaditep et al. 2003).

The sharpest possible opposite to the *kunlasatree* is the loose woman, the prostitute, or the 'carefree woman' [ผู้หญิงรักสนุก]. The Thai phrase literally translates as 'a woman who loves fun', whom Taywaditep et al. (2003, 1031) describe as follows:

> A 'carefree woman,' or an unmarried woman who seeks sexual pleasure from casual partners, is stereotyped as shallow, emotionally disturbed, and self-destructive. She presumably has lost her virginity because she was amoral, careless, gullible, or blindly following the Western code of sexual behavior. Needless to say, sex before marriage for women is the key criterion that distinguishes a 'bad woman' from a 'good woman'.

The caricature of the loose woman is often depicted as an evil character in Thai novels, films and soap operas, where she tries to destabilize the life of good women, aiming to steal away their husbands (Harrison 1999). What is striking is that if she succeeds in seducing her target, the full blame always falls on the loose woman. The straying husband is generally depicted as a helpless victim; those poor men cannot help themselves, is the underlying message.

This message links with traditional Thai ideas about feminine power against which a man cannot defend himself, discussed in Chapter 5.

The Thai scholar Chulanee Thianthai (2004) confirmed the continued importance of the dichotomy good woman–bad woman in her research among Bangkok-based youth. The danger of 'bad women' as potential mates for married men is such that, traditionally, Thai wives would find it less objectionable for their husbands to visit sex workers, seeing them as no competition, in contrast to the threat of a husband having a *mia noi* (minor wife) who might end up rivalling the wife for her position (Saengtienchai et al. 1999).

The 5 participants in this study who identified as *kathoey* for a while, and the additional 14 participants who initially felt they had feminine traits and habits, all tended to use imagery of the good women in their narratives, especially during the first round of interviews. When discussing their first and consequent sexual experiences, they highlighted their passive and innocent attitude towards sex, framing their stories in an 'it happened to me' narrative. They provided excuses for the sex they had engaged in. Sex, sexual desire and the need for sex were downplayed in their stories. For example, Chai talked about staying at home and never going anywhere, while his *phu chaai* boyfriend went outside to socialize. Graham Fordham describes how both men and women see men having sex with minor wives (*mia noi*) or prostitutes as 'natural', as men need a 'change of flavour' (Fordham 1995, 171). Men also have the opportunity for such a change of flavour, since they operate outside of the household, where they can meet people easily, as Chai, a talkative, effeminate and emotional young man from the southern town of Trang who was interviewed only once illustrated:

I, I mean, I was not bored with him because I loved him. But he had to encounter something, many things outside, because I am a person who stays at home, I hardly ever go anywhere. And he was a person who liked to socialize, meet many people, he had to meet many people.

Chai clearly positioned himself as the feminine entity in this relationship, claiming the domestic sphere as his own and leaving the outside world to his man.

In expressing his aspirations, Ives also dreamt of being the 'mother' of a household; this is what attracted him when the person he was dating at the time promised to take him as his 'wife':

He said he didn't have a partner [แฟน]. He said, 'Younger brother [or sister], you are mine now' [น้องก็เป็นของพี่แล้วนะ]. [...] Like I was going to be his wife [เมีย], something like that. It was like, I believed him, he may really want to date me, he may be really honest with me.

The innocence Ives professed ('I believed him' and 'he may really be honest with me') is another aspect of this stereotypical good woman femininity: being uninformed and unprepared for the worldly and supposedly unknown pleasures of sex. Ives described his first sexual encounter with a 28-year-old man whom he met via the Internet after posting a picture of himself on a gay website. This was a big deal: Ives had just decided to abandon his *kathoey* identity and become gay. He cut his hair, removed his make-up, struck a more masculine pose and set up a new social media profile. He had never seen a picture of his date while chatting on the Internet; it was a blind date. Ives described this first sexual experience with a focus on how he kept resisting, saying 'no, no', and on describing how the man kept pressuring him to have sex. An example of the 'saying no' follows below, when the man started French kissing him, which was the first time Ives had ever kissed anybody:

> I pushed him away, normally, and I said, 'Don't!' I told him, 'You promised me that we wouldn't have sex', something like that. We were supposed to talk only. But – because of his habits and that he is already old, and he had lots of [sexual] experience, he used his words [ใช้คำพูด], the tricks [เล่ห์เหลี่ยม] that he had used before, and he, he said, 'There is nothing to worry about [ไม่มีอะไรหรอกนะ]'. And I believed him. I trusted him.

Eventually his clothes came off; Ives's 'no, don't' response and his partner's 'please, just a little bit more' pleas continued:

> He was going to penetrate [เสียบ] me, you know? And I said, 'No, can you not do that?' [อย่าได้ไหม]. And I pushed him away. And he said, 'Uncle will not penetrate you, just rub it outside [แค่ถูๆข้างนอกเอง]. I just want to touch your flesh [สัมผัสเนื้อ]', something like that. And I trusted him, and I thought, he probably won't dare to penetrate me, go that far. But – he was like, he penetrated like, like he was rubbing it against the skin around my bottom.
>
> INT: Did you not want it?
>
> IVES: Eh – I was in the mood, but I was afraid. I was afraid it would hurt. I was afraid it would hurt. And in my heart I thought, let us be together, lay down together, lay down and talk, lay down and hug each other, that should be enough. It should not be necessary that we have sex [เพศสัมพันธ์] in a very intimate way [ลึกซึ้ง] […].

While initially hesitant, Ives briefly admitted that he was 'in the mood', but he quickly jumped to another aspect of the story, the aspect that enhanced him as a good woman. What Ives said about losing his virginity zooms in on the pain and suffering he felt. As expected of a good woman, there was no mention of any pleasure he may have had, even though he later admitted that he and his sexual partner both reached orgasm, and that they had sex an additional three or four times over the next month.

Another way the participants used stereotypical imagery about good womanhood was in the way they described sex with their boyfriend as a duty they had to fulfil. According to this narrative, they had to give themselves to their boyfriends in order to establish, cement or maintain their relationship, in line with a good *kunlasatree* wife. Again, they downplayed personal sexual desire and pleasure and, when asked about that, they said very little about it. San, raised as an only child by adoptive parents in a rural district of the north-eastern province of Udon Thani, was an example of this:

SAN: It hurt. My feeling was, I was suffering. I didn't want to have [sex]. This, this was the first time. The first time has to hurt, right, but I didn't know it would be like this. And – it had been a long time, eh, I thought, older brother, [the] older brother who dated me, he should taste [have sex with] me [น่าจะลองผมแล้ว]. So if I was afraid to have pain, I was afraid that older brother would be unhappy [with me] [กลัวพี่ไม่มีความสุข]. So I didn't say anything, so I …

INT: Let him [ให้เขาเลย].

SAN: Let him.

Gop had been dating a university student via the Internet, and dropped by to see him 'because I happened to be in the neighbourhood' – of course it was not because he wanted to have sex. This boyfriend pressured Gop into allowing sex, using their status as boyfriends as the key argument:

He didn't force me. It was like, he was asking, asking. If I wouldn't let him do [it], he would say 'Don't you love me?', I don't know. […] It was, before, I didn't think, if I don't let him, he won't love me, or not? Until, maybe I thought, to do like this, it is a sign of my love. […]. But later I thought, it is not necessary that I, that we should have sex.

San and Gop both felt that they had to give themselves in order to make their boyfriend understand that they were serious about their relationship, and that they wanted to maintain it. Some participants managed to withstand such pressure, leaving their respectable female demeanour intact, or even strengthening it, as Ud indicated:

> He said, 'Can I ask you for something [ขออะไรซักอย่างได้ไหม]?' And I said, 'What do you want to ask for?' He said, 'Let's go upstairs to my room, then you will know what I want to ask for!' Then I already knew what he wanted. I told him, eh, 'We just met for the first time, why do you have to hurry?' [chuckles]. [...] At first he wouldn't agree. [But] I said, 'If you don't agree, I won't talk to you again!' So he agreed [not to have sex].

Ed, a studious, serious young man who grew up in a harmonious family in the southern town of Pattalung, expressed a strong dislike of sex, which is also a *kunlasatree* notion. Ed had a boyfriend by the second interview and he said that he was obliged to 'help' his boyfriend, which he did once by masturbating him and giving him oral sex very briefly, as he said he did not like doing that. Ed said he had no sexual desire during this brief sexual episode, no erection, and he even kept his clothes on. Despite Ed bringing his boyfriend to orgasm, the boyfriend wanted more:

> Hmmm. What to say, older brother [referring to the interviewer] – it was like, I was like, I was still new, too, older brother, like, I am not like we date and then we have something [sex] [immediately]. Eh – it was because, we were incompatible, more like that, older brother, it was like he wanted that thing with me. But I, I couldn't give that to him. Hmmm. So we broke up.

Despite this, Ed entertained an active cybersex life, regularly masturbating in front of the webcam, without showing his face, with anonymous men in one-on-one chatrooms. It is likely that Ed did not consider masturbation to be sex and hence, he did not morally disapprove of this behaviour, although he was shy to talk about it, and did so only during the final interview.

A related element of good womanhood is being uninterested in a partner's looks, just in his character and status. Ives had mentioned the fact that he had never seen a picture of his 'boyfriend' because a good woman, after all, should only be interested in finding a good and responsible husband, and not pay attention to something as insignificant and banal as a partner's physical looks. Nook, similar to Ives, also had never seen a picture of his boyfriend when he ventured out of his home village to meet him for the first time in the city. Nook described his first sexual partner as not good looking. He focused his story on his true love for this man, rather than physical attributes, let alone sexual attraction. In explaining his interest in his partner, Nook emphasized that he was a serious and good person, reliable and able to provide for him. In other words, Ives and Nook gave the impression that they did not squander the value of their young and beautiful bodies and the sexual pleasure the body could provide for nothing, but they intended to give it to somebody who seemed, at the time, a serious and marriage-worthy partner. Nook was clearly aware of the value of his virginity:

> He, he wanted to have someone who was – I was a virgin [จิง]. I had never experienced anything before. So we met, and we had sex, that was the first time. I loved – I loved, loved him. I loved him. If you ask me, was he good looking? No. Not good. But it was like, we knew each other via the Internet. I had never seen his looks. But I loved him, and I could accept him. I could accept him, like, he is not good looking, but I loved him, felt close to his heart [รักแบบสนิทใจ]. I loved him a lot.

In his story, Nook jumped over the sex quickly, not providing any details. Similar to Ives and Gop, Nook explained the loss of his virginity because of his innocence and his lack of knowledge about sex:

> I was like a child. I didn't think I would have sex with him. I didn't think that he would think like, he wants to [have sex] with me. I didn't think, I didn't know. I just thought, we have a date to meet, maybe to have a meal, watch a movie.

In summary, especially during the first round of interviews, many of the young men in this study downplayed their sexual experiences and pleasure, drawing on cultural narratives of proper women who do not desire or need sex. However, there were changes in the way some participants spoke about sex over time, and during subsequent interviews more and more contradictions appeared. Several of the young men kept drawing from the good woman stereotype, but added more and more masculine rationalizations while explaining and interpreting their sexual lives, which often evolved between interviews in terms of pleasure experienced and number of partners (see below). Ake, for example, after initially saying that he preferred to maintain his virginity, disclosed an enormous pride in his newly found ability to provide sexual pleasure to men during the second interview, and Ek, while being less negative about sex than Ake during the first interview, abandoned his more effeminate demeanour between interviews and found pleasure in a more masculine role, describing his joy at being fellated. These changes will be discussed further in Chapter 9.

Nak Leng and *Chaai Chatri*: Using Stereotypical Notions about Being a Man to Frame Early Romantic and Sexual Experiences

As briefly discussed above, for Thai men, as is the case for women, a number of stereotypical gender role models exist. John Van Esterik (1982) made a useful distinction between three masculine social gender roles. The first exemplifies the monk, a role reserved for men, who, through monastic discipline and practice of the Buddhist scripts, strives to eschew worldly attachments. This includes distancing himself from sexuality (particularly from women) and from his male sex characteristics, by shaving his hair and eyebrows and wearing special orange attire. Strict rules exist for monks, who, for example, are not allowed to walk next to women, sit next to women on buses or in other situations, or receive alms or goods directly from a woman's hands. These rules indicate how strong the belief is that masculine sexuality needs to be contained or it is unstoppable. These beliefs are also linked to ideas about certain aspects of femininity being a form of pollution against which men need to be protected in order to preserve their masculinity, as discussed above. These beliefs about feminine pollution are linked to men's powerlessness in the face of the seductive powers of feminine sexuality. Mary Beth Mills (1995, 251), in her study of beliefs in deadly 'widow ghosts' roaming the countryside of northeastern Thailand during the night looking for husbands, noted:

> Both Thai and Lao gender systems attribute potentially harmful powers to female sexuality when not contained within the marital relationship and circumscribed by appropriate displays of physical modesty and/or maternal solicitude. By contrast, male sexual powers pose little danger to the social fabric and phallic representations can be employed to preserve or restore spiritual strength, and physical and social health.

A second male role is the secular male, called the *chaai chatri* (ชายชาตรี), who embodies typical masculine features such as 'authority, courage, self-assurance, physical and emotional strength, and sexual prowess' (Taywaditep et al. 2003, 1023). Whereas having strong sexual desire is considered to be a sign of maleness (Knodel et al. 1996), the *chaai chatri* would under normal circumstances control his sexuality as much as possible and be loyal to his family.

A lower-middle-class role has emerged from the *chaai chatri* called the *nak leng* (นักเลง), symbolizing a man who is brave, daring, risk-taking but also fair. The popular meaning of *nak leng* has evolved to be more of a gangster in recent decades: a man who is tough, loyal to allies and a playboy with numerous sexual affairs with women. Megan Sinnott (2004, 88), in her study on same-sex erotics among Thai women, found that tomboys (masculine-oriented lesbian women) often aspired to such traits and would 'smoke, drink, play pool, and be flirtatious'.

The 'bad' masculinity of the *nak leng* and the 'good' masculinity of the *chaai chatri* can at times coexist within the same individual. In order to explain this, it is useful to apply Niels Mulder's sociological model of Thai society. He described femininity and masculinity as being tied to two distinct geographic domains: the domestic domain and the outside world, respectively. The domain of the home and, linked to it, the domain of safety and moral goodness, is the full-time domain of the woman, the mother or nurturer, and only the part-time domain of the father or provider. The outside world, characterized by potential danger, struggle and amorality, is, in Mulder's interpretation, the domain of the man, where the father/provider goes to earn money for his household, but where he can also let off steam, including in extramarital affairs. A different set of moral rules applies to both worlds, which Mulder used to explain the existence of sexual double standards (as well as why corruption remains pervasive in Thai society and why so few people seem to object to it). Sexual double standards and corruption are morally possible because of this compartmentalization into domestic and outside spheres, Mulder said. Thai men usually stand with one leg in the domain of the home as providers for their families and with the other leg in the world outside, where 'expectations about his virility should be proven' (Mulder 2000, 71), using minor wives or 'loose women' (prostitutes). These two spheres can coexist, provided they remain separate.

Women belong either to the domestic sphere (good women) or the outside sphere (bad women), whereas men are by definition part of both – at least, this was the way it used to be in the 1980s and 1990s when Mulder made his observations. In practice, however, women also have room to manoeuvre from one sphere into the other by reinventing themselves, moving from the bad woman into a good woman role, for example, a woman who has worked as a sex worker in Pattaya may return home to become a married housewife, simply because her past life is unknown to (or politely ignored by) the villagers she rejoins. The Internet is an important force breaking down the separation between the domestic and the outside moral spheres, with strong effects, in particular, on feminine sexual morals, as will be discussed further in Chapter 9.

As noted, masculinity is linked to strong sexual desire. Therefore, masculine traits also include being promiscuous. Thai words describing this trait include the word *jao choo* [เจ้าชู้], literally 'the owner of multiple lovers', and *lan-laa* [ลั้นลา], which means sexually playful or flirtatious. There are several variations of *jao choo*, for example, *jao choo yak* [เจ้าชู้ยักษ์], meaning a giant *jao choo* and the less well-known *jao choo kai jae* [เจ้าชู้ไก่แจ้], referring to a man who is intentionally showing his *jao choo*-ness like a strutting rooster. Chonwilai (2012b, 46) notes that these terms 'only describe, rather than condemn different types of *jao choo*, implicitly accepting that being a man and being a *jao choo* belong together'. She suggests that these traits are accepted and expected characteristics of a healthy *phu chaai*. The link of masculinity and promiscuity was confirmed in a study by Danthamrongkul and Posayajinda (2004), who found that four out of six *kathoey* and nearly two-thirds of gay queens in their study said they wanted a male long-term partner, compared with just 44.4 per cent of 'gay both', 34.0 per cent of 'gay kings' and 36.0 per cent of those who labelled themselves as 'bi (sexual)'. These figures suggest that the more feminine same-sex-attracted men regarded themselves to be, the stronger their desire to have a long-term partner was. Participants in Ojanen's (2010, 174) study thought that the more masculine male partner left the more feminine male partner more often than the other way around, although he added that 'viewing this as an absolute rule is an exaggeration'.

The belief in men's natural sex drive also provides a convenient explanation for why young, unmarried males indulge in sex with other men or with *kathoey*. It is a popular Thai belief that men's sexuality is boundless and, once provoked, a man cannot be blamed for being unable to stop (Taywaditep et al. 2003). Ives made a remark explaining his first sex partner's behaviour, invoking the 'men can't help themselves' notion: 'But – but he was in the mood [มีอารมณ์], and you cannot forbid it, right? [มันก็ห้ามไม่ได้เนาะ].' This belief reinforces the idea that men cannot be trusted or relied upon, and above all, that they cannot be blamed for this. Chai understood the playfulness of his first boyfriend in similar terms. He described this boyfriend as a 'real' *phu chaai*; they were the same age. Chai was hurt when his lover dumped him for a girl, leading him to seek psychiatric help for a while. Despite his broken heart, he did not blame his boyfriend:

> He thought he didn't want to have a serious [relationship] with me [ไม่ได้จะจริงจังอะไรกับเรา]. He wanted to woo me for fun [จีบเล่นๆ]. But because of many things, like, I was concerned about him, and I would ask him things, and I would give him advice, things like that. So then he became impressed by me.

Ake and Chai both said that they were aware that their boyfriends were not serious. Despite this, the fact that he dated a real *phu chaai* was a source of pride for Chai: 'I never thought that in this life, there would be a real, real *phu chaai* who would like me.' Win, the third child out of six, from a Muslim lower-middle-class family in southern Thailand and who was brutally raped by a Muslim cleric at the age of 9, did not open up about his homosexuality towards his friends and was one of the more closeted participants. He said that he thought that having sex with a real man was more pleasurable than sex with another gay person:

> The feeling, the [sexual] mood of both – I am gay, and I have something with a real *phu chaai*, the feeling is, if I speak frankly, it is more fun [มันกว่า] […]. It is better, and – it makes me feel, 'Eh, I have something with a real man, really' [ผู้ชายแท้ๆ จริงๆ นะ] who, eh, has something [sex] with women, like this. But *phu chaai* who are gay, I feel like, it is so-so [อย่างนั้นนั้น], like, it is the same as before, what we have experienced before, something like that.

For Ake, Chai, Nook and Lert, the experience of having a real *phu chaai* as their lover probably also helped to reinforce their sense of being feminine, of presumably being wanted for the sake of their feminine traits. Ironically, their *phu chaai* partners may have regarded them as a sexual outlet, and hence as an alternative to the 'bad woman', whereas the study participants would have envisioned themselves as the 'good woman' or wife. Ives, who was on a trajectory from *kathoey* to gay between interviews, also thought it was natural for a *phu chaai* boyfriend to have affairs with others; Ives was fine with it as long as he did not find out about it:

> Eh, if it is me, na, eh, in reality, I cannot accept [if my boyfriend has other partners]. But, but, if you ask me, can he have it? He can have [sex with somebody else], but like, don't let me know! Yes. Because if it happens that I know – if I know, or like, my boyfriend tells me, like, 'I went to take [fuck] this person, that person, I went to sleep with this person', like this, if he tells me that, I would not feel good anymore. Eh, yes. It is like – I don't want to 'use the same boyfriends with others' […]. If you want to have [sex], do it secretly [ถ้าคุณมี คุณก็ไปแอบมี]. Don't let me know about it […]. But I don't forbid it, like this.

In line with the *kala-thetsa* and *barami* principles described in Chapter 3, Ives was happy to be with his boyfriend as long as he kept up the appearance of faithfulness towards Ives and towards Ives's direct social environment, maintaining his and Ives's *barami* even though in his heart he understood it to be natural for a *phu chaai* to have other sexual exploits. As a matter of respect, Ives just needed to believe in his status as the 'major wife' and expected his boyfriend to hide his extramarital sexual exploits from him.

Fluk, Lert, Joe and Pong (introduced below) did not play down their own sexual desire in the way the more feminine-identified participants did. In line with stereotypical ideas about how Thai men think about sex and how it affects their moral standing, Fluk and Lert dismissed sex between *phu chaai* as something that is in and of itself intrinsically meaningless, and not something that they think should be used to judge whether somebody is a good or a bad person. They saw sex as trivial, linked to pleasure, and gave less moral meaning to it than the more feminine-identified participants. Sex can devalue good femininity, but this is not the case for good masculinity – in some instances it is rather the opposite, with womanising men commanding more respect. Thailand's iconic strongman and former prime minister, Sarit Thanarat, who was known to be a serial womaniser, was a case in point, according to some commentators:

> His mistresses did not detract from his image because he chose beautiful women. In fact, he was admired for his ability to acquire movie stars, beauty queens, night club hostesses, even young students as mistresses. His 'lady-killer' image enhanced his power, his magical virility, and conformed to a dominant model of Thai masculinity. (Chaloemtiarana 1979, 339, quoted in Van Esterik 2000, 106)

Quan and Kit, who took the insertive role during their first sexual experiences and did not see themselves as intrinsically feminine beings, did not describe their first sex in terms of passivity or something for which they needed excuses. Joe borrowed from masculine gender stereotypes in explaining his unfaithfulness to his boyfriend. He had been wooed and had had sex with a fellow factory worker a few days earlier, despite being in a long-distance relationship with his boyfriend. He explained his unfaithfulness using the Thai concept of *lan-laa*, meaning 'sexually playful', as briefly discussed above:

JOE: [interrupts] it is because I am *lan-laa. Lan-laa.*
INT: *Lan-laa?*
JOE: Yes. I don't know the word 'enough'. Maybe it could be HYSTERIA [Eng] [chuckles].
INT: HYSTERIA [Eng]? What does that mean?
JOE: The disease that you cannot live without sex [โรคขาดแบบเซ็กส์ไม่ได้].

It was a way for Joe to proffer an excuse for his unfaithfulness, and to give meaning to his inability to be with a boyfriend for very long:

I am a person like this, na, older brother Jan. I am a person who, like, stays with somebody for not a long time. I cannot date with somebody for a long time. I don't know what it is. Maybe I am too promiscuous [*jao choo*], I think that I am promiscuous.

Joe also told of a fortune teller who told him that he would meet the love of his life in two or three years' time, and also used this as an explanation for his relatively wild sexual life and his unwillingness or inability to form longer-term relationships (see the section on the role of karma in Chapter 4).

Fluk also described his own promiscuity in proud detail, especially during the second interview, when he was dating two young men at the same time, one in Bangkok and one in his hometown in the south of Thailand. Besides this, he had sex with other (one-off) partners occasionally, which he had to hide from both his boyfriends. He appeared quite proud of his sexual prowess and used the term 'Casanova' to describe himself. He did so even on his Facebook profile. Fluk's choice of the word Casanova, rather than one of the many available Thai terms denoting a womaniser, is interesting and may indicate a desire to be seen as modern and cool, not a provincial *nak leng* but a more modern and urban variety. The term is mentioned in a recent book on Thai terminology for sex and sexuality: 'To be called *Casanova*, one needs to be a young man of good background, well-known, and reportedly involved with numerous women' (Chonwilai 2012b, 44–45).

During the third interview, however, Fluk said he had changed. The relationship with the boyfriend in Bangkok had ended, but he was still in a longer-term relationship with the second boyfriend in his hometown. As a result of his settling down and abandoning his masculine promiscuity, Fluk now referred to more feminine symbols in his self-description and in his description of his relationship with his boyfriend:

INT: And between you and [your boyfriend], is it the same?

FLUK: Is it the same? I will have more [femininity]. Because I am a person who is peevish [ชอบงอน]. Eh. I am peevish.

INT: And is [he] more like a *phu chaai*?

FLUK: [He] is more like a *phu chaai*. He is in the tough team, and [likes to] go out for adventure, you know? [มันจะเป็นทีมลุยๆออกผจญภัยไง]

INT: Aha. Aha.

FLUK: Eh. To go out and travel, it is like, he is like ACTION [Eng], action [บู๊], but I am DRAMA [Eng]. I am a deep [ซึ้งๆ] and sweet DRAMA [Eng]. [chuckles]. I mean, inside, na, we are not really the same. But if you compare it, like a doll, a doll, a Blythe doll, and [he] plays Gundam [chuckles]. It is not the same.

In the above quotation, Fluk referred to popular toy dolls: the Blythe doll he compared himself to is a 'lady doll' with a big head and big eyes, whereas the Gundam doll, to which he compared his boyfriend, is a robot doll, a kind of destroyer. Hence, Fluk saw himself change from a Casanova (close to a *nak leng*) to a more sedate *chaai chatri* within the interviewing period, while also borrowing from feminine stereotypes (being 'drama').

The fluidity of Thai gender roles, and the ease with which one can move in and out of them, as Fluk had done in a timeframe of just a number of months, has previously been described by several authors, including Morris (1994), Van Esterik (2000) and Sinnott (1999). The *lan-laa, nak leng* and *chaai chatri* concepts are partly class-related, with the more 'responsible' *chaai chatri* masculinity, based on a presumably monogamous family life, more linked to the urban middle classes. The *chaai chatri* image is strongly propagated via movies, soap operas and other cultural forms linked to the urban-based higher-middle and higher classes in Bangkok. A desire to join the middle class may at least partly explain Fluk's desire to describe himself in a different way during the later interviews than he had in the beginning. It may also be age-related, with the more irresponsible and playful models of masculinity readily available for experimenting teenagers, who then get married and 'grow up' to be (more) responsible house fathers in line with the *chaai chatri* – in this sense, Fluk may also have wanted to present himself as older and wiser during the later interview.

One key element of masculinity of the *chaai chatri* type is the role of the provider, or the one who takes care, not in the sense of nurturing (which would be the feminine domain) but more in a sense of being able to provide money and protection to one's wife/partner and one's family. For unknown reasons, the English phrase 'take care' is used to describe this important aspect of Thai masculinity. Nook defined masculinity and femininity as taking care and being taken care of, respectively:

> I like to – to be a girl. I don't want to be a *phu chaai* anymore, now. I don't think about that anymore [นึกไม่ถึง]. I feel better. As a girl, one doesn't have to – one doesn't have to TAKE CARE [Eng] about anything much. I will be the person who is TAKE[N] CARE [Eng] of, more. [...] I think, like this, I feel like I can accept it. It is better, better than [if] I go against my heart [ฝืนใจ] and TAKE CARE [Eng] [of somebody else]. No, I cannot protect [my partner] [laughs]. Because I am small [laughs]. I think like this.

Masculinity is about being strong and protective, about being able to 'take care' of a partner (read woman), according to Nook. Instead, he preferred to be taken care of. He linked this partly to the smallness of his body, which helped him to naturalize his desire for a caring husband. Finding someone who would be willing to take care of him was also important for Ake, who had no ambition to make his own living but dreamed of being protected by a husband in the future. Ives also wanted his future boyfriend to provide for him: 'I don't have an education. I don't work. He will provide for me. Like that.' The roles of a wife, being taken care of, staying in the house, and providing the role of a housewife for a breadwinner are all part of the same gender concept:

> IVES: Because of the fact that he is a husband, I am the wife. I give him pleasure. I stay with him, I sit and chat with him, we hold each other's hands. I say sweet words to him [เอ่ยคำพูดที่แบบหวานๆ]: 'I love you, na' […].
> INT: Household issues, too? Like a housewife?
> IVES: Also household issues, and the issue in bed [sex].
> INT: In bed, too.
> IVES: Yes. And work in the house, too. I do it.

In brief, both the feminine-oriented men and masculine-oriented men in the study drew heavily on heterosexual masculine and feminine stereotypes in their accounts of their sexual experiences and of their romantic exploits. The young men drew on their life experience living in heterosexual families to imagine a future with a partner, and generally aimed for a division of labour that resembled that between traditional husbands and wives. There are class differences in this, with elements of the responsible, monogamous 'family man' variety of the *chaai chatri* portrayed in the mass media mixed with notions linked to the rougher, less faithful *nak leng*. Many of the men's ideas about this became less clear over the interviewing period. The imprint of sexuality-based ideas about same-sex relationships on the gender-based conceptions, and actual experiences that contradicted gender-based ideas and conceptions, caused confusion, and the actions and ideas of many of the young men started to be contradictory and in flux. This will be further discussed in Chapters 8 and 9.

Conclusion

This chapter found that Thai same-sex-attracted men can readily and easily borrow from the way Thai society understands gender and related 'good' or 'bad' masculinity and femininity. They use gendered multiple moralities and variations in making sense of their early feelings of gender nonconformity, perhaps because Thai gender is primarily body based and not sexuality based. The way the young men used differing and sometimes contradictory gender concepts and related symbols in their stories and demeanour over time confirms what several authors have found in previous studies – that there is strong fluidity and creativity (and, as a result, often contradictions) in Thai sexual subjectivity – and it also confirms how sex/sexuality and gender cannot be separated in the Thai setting.

This study has contributed the important finding that differences in forming and expressing sexual and gender identities do not only occur between groups, but that radical changes in sexual subjectivity and sense of gendered self occur within the same individual over time, sometimes within a relatively short timeframe. This fluidity itself might be linked to Buddhist ideas about impermanence, birth and rebirth, in which sexuality is a mere form of suffering and gender is subsumed by merit, and where every person is aware that he or she has most likely been all genders (and more) in the cycle of births and rebirths.

It will become clear in the following chapters that the relatively simple and straightforward gender and religious concepts the young men in this study borrowed from to define their sexuality in gendered terms were gradually destabilized and undermined by another paradigm for same-sex relationships, one that is based on sexual object choice as the basis for defining who one is sexually. One of the significant findings of the study is that it appears a significant number of rurally based, same-sex-attracted young men initially embarked on the road to become a *kathoey* for a while during their childhood, only to make a break with this trajectory in order to switch to a less effeminate, more masculine 'gay' subjectivity. In some instances, at least, the lack of awareness of the existence of forms of sexual subjectivity other than being or becoming a *kathoey* may have forced such young same-sex-attracted young men towards a disposition in which they did not feel wholly comfortable.

It is proposed that this destabilization occurred as soon as the young men in this study started putting their new-found sense of self into practice. It is in the everyday practices of dating, loving, having sex and forming and breaking relationships that new possibilities for pleasure are discovered, that the stereotypes about masculinity and femininity become undermined, and that the limitations of Buddhist explanations for homosexuality become known. This will be the topic of Chapters 8 and 9. But first, in Chapter 7, the focus is on Thai society and family, and how the young men in this study dealt with the pressures of these when they discovered that they were different from mainstream men.

Chapter 7

'ALL IN THE FAMILY': TACTICS FOR LIVING AND GROWING UP IN A HETERONORMATIVE WORLD

Because we don't just stay in the gay society, in that small group. We have to share our life with the bigger group too, hmmm. So it is an issue of sensitivity.

– Ed

Introduction

In this chapter, the focus is on how the young men positioned themselves in their family and in their social environment during the time they started to discover that there was something different about them. After a brief discussion of discrimination, stigma, acceptance and tolerance of homosexuality in Thai society, a number of tactics for fitting in to Thai society and dealing with parental expectations are presented, and the ways such tactics are applied are discussed.

During the first interview, when the young men were still living at home, I wanted to know whether they were eager to move out of their homes in order to have a freer life in terms of living their sexuality. In particular, I tried to ask the young men whether they aspired to be part of a gay community after leaving home. This question is not without public health relevance, as I will also briefly discuss: There are important implications of these findings for HIV prevention intervention strategies in Thailand, most of which are 'community based'.

Acceptance of Homosexuality in Thai Society

Most participants said that homosexuality is not accepted in Thai society. However, actual reports of acts of discrimination were virtually absent from the data that were collected. Only 3 of the 25 young men experienced something that could be called discrimination or enacted stigma. One of these men was Dee, a quiet Muslim man from the southern town of Pattalung. Dee's mother had remarried; his stepfather quite strongly objected to Dee's homosexuality. Dee said he had even considered committing suicide as a result:

> My stepfather is a person who hates this group a lot. He is the person who is paying for my studies too. He doesn't like [it]. [...] He has said, you [derogative – มึง] are a man, don't go and be *toot, taew, ying* ... [Thai slang words for 'faggot' and 'woman'].

Dee's family were Muslims; this may have contributed to his stepfather's negativity about Dee's sexuality. Ives also experienced negative societal reactions because he was a *kathoey* when he was younger. The teasing he experienced at school he considered 'normal':

> IVES: It is normal for [the third sex]. That happens, perhaps [อาจจะมีบ้าง]. Friends who tease [แซว], friends who ridicule you [ล้อ], it is normal. It is normal.
> INT: What would you do, if someone teased you?
> IVES: I didn't do anything. I kept silent [เฉยๆ]. Yes. Maybe sometimes I would answer them, like: 'Why? [ทำไมละ]. Me, what I will [or want] to be, it is my business'. Something like that.

Mint, a slightly effeminate young man from a well-to-do family in the northeastern town of Yasothon, also said he had been teased since he was a child but that he had only recently started to feel unhappy about it: 'When I was a child, I didn't really care [ไม่อะไร], but now, if someone comes to say that I am *kathoey* or *toot* [fag], I will be angry inside. But I don't do anything.'

When I asked Joe why the men in this study reported so few instances of actual discrimination or stigma, he suggested that Thai society shows its disapproval or non-acceptance of gay people in terms of principle rather than in practice:

> Eh – I don't know either. I think, I don't see them really accept it [ยินยอม], or praise it [การสรรเสริญ], that it is good. They think it is bad, like before, wrong according to tradition [ผิดตามธรรมเนียมประเพณี], something like that. [...] You cannot be open, you cannot get married, you cannot have children, things like that. So it is not – it is only like – fun, like you stay together as friends, more. [...] If it comes to the stage that there is real love, you still have to hide, like before. You have to only stay together, like

friends, to make other people view you as just friends, but in reality they are not friends [but lovers].

Joe suggested that while homosexuality is tolerated it is not accepted, mainly because it does not conform to the societal norm of getting married and having children. In line with the principles of *kala-thetsa* and the importance of maintaining a strict boundary between the private and public realms (discussed in Chapter 3), Joe implied that it is only possible to live as a same-sex-attracted person if one stays out of the public (i.e. heteronormative) purview.

Hong, who grew up in a village just outside the northeastern province of Buriram, disagreed. He said the people in his social environment generally had no negative ideas about gays and *kathoey*: 'No, there is nothing. They can accept us. It is like, they [gays and *kathoeys*] don't cause them trouble [ไม่ได้ทำให้เขาเดือดร้อน].' His choice of words here is interesting: the Thai word *deuad ron* for 'making trouble' literally means 'to bring to the boiling point'. Hence, Hong might not truly disagree with Joe; they both suggested that gay or *kathoey* people are tolerated only as long as homosexuality is kept out of the face of the other villagers, that is, as long as it is kept in private.

Some participants distinguished between gays and *kathoey* while discussing tolerance and acceptance. Mint, for example, thought *kathoey* are more accepted in Thai society than gays, but only as long as they are beautiful and adhere to the *kunlasatree* norms of 'good' feminine conduct: 'Society, usually, doesn't accept [*kathoey*]. If they are not a very beautiful *kathoey* who dresses and looks like a woman, they probably don't accept it.' Other participants said that it is easier for parents to accept a gay child than a *kathoey* child. Even if the femininity of *kathoey* is socially accepted and acknowledged, men generally disqualify *kathoey* as marriage partners because of their inability to become pregnant and have children. Therefore, most *phu chaai* tend to see them as fun sex partners and not as serious, long-term partners.

Other participants had a different view. Rather than non-acceptance, Mint suggested that in some ways villagers preferred gay people to *phu chaai*:

No, my friends like to tease like, 'Oh, those gays, such a pity, there are only very handsome ones, the ones who are not handsome they are not [gay]' [...]. Mostly gays are very handsome, they dress well, PERFECT [Eng], something like that.

Hong also saw positive attitudes towards young gay men in his northeastern village, especially among village women. He linked this to the bad behaviour of many heterosexual men in his village, many of whom he described as drunks and womanisers with no sense of responsibility. Their behaviours contrasted strongly to the contribution gay and *kathoey* villagers make to village society, especially during social events:

> But they don't do anything [against us], everybody speaks politely, because mostly they like people like me better, better than real men [ผู้ชายทั้งแท่ง]. Real men behave badly [ไม่เอาไหน]. We are better [...] Like, if there is a ceremony, we go to help them. More than [*phu chaai*], so they like it.

How can we make sense of the paradoxical finding that many young men claim Thai society does not accept but only tolerates homosexuality, whereas most participants have never come across active instances of discrimination? Andrew Matzner (2001, 90), in his research on attitudes to *kathoey* in a sample of Thai university students, proposes a model of 'spheres of familiarity' to shed light on this. He detected a certain complexity in how tolerance or acceptance of *kathoey* and, by extension, homosexuality works in Thai society. Matzner says previous authors' claims of a society that was either 'accepting' of *kathoey* (De Lind van Wijngaarden 1995) or 'tolerant but unaccepting' (Jackson 1999) were too simplistic. He found that almost all of the university students he researched accepted and tolerated *kathoey* as friends, but at the same time most of them, even those with close *kathoey* friends, would be disappointed if they happened to have a child who was *kathoey* or even reject them. When it comes to *kathoey* whom one does not personally know, Matzner found that the students generally accepted them as long as they were beautiful and lived up to the expectations of the *kunlasatree* (proper, respectable woman), in line with what Mint said above. Matzner concluded that 'appearance and public behaviour' (2001, 91) are the criteria for acceptance of *kathoey*, rather than 'gender deviancy' itself, and this also seems very applicable to the homosexuality of the participants in this study. The students' acceptance of *kathoey* in their own circle of friends was similarly influenced by factors other than their non-normative gender, Matzner found. Matzner found that only within the family circle was there 'unqualified non-acceptance' (2001, 91). This helps explain the finding in this study of much less openness about one's sexuality towards family members than towards friends (discussed later). As will be shown later in this chapter, the findings in this study concur with Matzner's conclusion that attitudes related to acceptance or tolerance 'should not be seen in singular terms, but instead need to be conceptualized as consisting of a broad spectrum of feelings that shift within the contexts of social relationships' (Matzner 2001, 91).

Next, the focus will be on the tactics the young same-sex-attracted men used to address the difference between parental and societal expectations, as well as expectations of friends, related to their gender and sexuality and their own emerging sexual subjectivity. These are self-initiated tactics, emanating from the individual, and they make use of the gendered assumptions of heteronormative society in order to blend in.

Tactic 1: Being Good

An important way of gaining and retaining the respect of parents and of one's community is being 'good', defined as being successful at school and in work, aiming for financial independence and achieving financial progress and security for one's family. There is also the cultural importance of repaying the moral debt that all children have to their parents, and the importance of impressing one's teachers and elders. As Mulder (1997, 308) put it,

> In the hierarchical setting of its experience, the child knows that it will receive, and that it has to reciprocate. In line with the fact of inequality, the resulting give-and-take will consist of unequal exchanges. Nurture is reciprocated by honour, teaching by tractability. All of these constitute obligations, of givers and receivers, that are inherent in their relative positions and roles.

Many of the young men in this study suggested that they considered being homosexual a personal defect. However, they also believed that they could compensate for this by being 'good' – or even by being 'extra good' in comparison to their siblings. By being good, the young men expected that they could retain or gain additional respect from their parents, the extended family and surrounding community. Ed, from a middle-class family in southern Thailand, linked the possibility of becoming more open about his sexuality with being financially independent and with having proven himself to be a good person:

> It is not yet the time. I am only 18 now. So, there is still a lot of time. I will prove myself, I will do my best to study, I will have a good job, and one day, they can see, I can stand on my own two feet, I have a good job, I am a good member of society, then [my parents] can probably accept [me].

Ed believed that his parents might find it easier to accept his sexuality, which he himself clearly perceived as a failure or a weak point, if it was compensated for by success of some sort. During the final interview 18 months later, his viewpoint remained remarkably similar: 'But I think, this issue, we should do well for ourselves first and when one day we are ready, then there is no reason to hide anymore.'

Nook, from a poor farmer family in the northeast, said his parents understood that he had a different gender/sexuality since he was very young; he was one of the participants who had been identified, because of his gentle behaviour, as a *kathoey* by his family even before he knew what the term meant. His father told him to 'do whatever you want', but expected Nook to make enough money to send his younger sister to school. Had Nook been a *phu chaai*, his parents would not have demanded this support for his sister, as it would have been understood that he would need to start and raise his own family. This shows that having a non-normative gender identity or non-normative sexual preference does not preclude the possibility of being a good child in the eyes of parents or others who matter. At the same time, it may raise expected standards of behaviour and achievement in other life domains, putting pressure on homosexual or transgender children that is not normally placed on heterosexual sons.

Oad, a confident young man from a well-to-do family in the northeast, told his parents he was gay shortly after he fell in love with a man when he was 16. Though his parents may have suspected something already because of Oad's history of playing with girls, he might also have felt that he could take the liberty to tell his parents because of his very strong self-confidence. This confidence was based on his excellent school results and his pride in being the school representative in a number of regional and national contests and school activities. He was frequently and publicly admired by his paternal grandmother as a shining example for the other boys in his extended family, many of whom had poor grades or had dropped out of school. Oad therefore felt he had built up enough credit to be open about his sexuality:

They say, 'You don't do anything bad.' All the time, I build fame for my family name, I progress all the time. So they don't dare to criticize me [...]. I mean, I am [gay], but I am also a good person.

In summary, if a young same-sex-attracted son is able to play the role of the good child, fulfilling or exceeding parental expectations of academic and (eventually) material progress, the private issue of his sexual preference becomes less relevant and he will become less vulnerable to rejection. Indeed, a disproportionate number of the participants in this study were class representatives, school representatives or 'activity children' [เด็กกิจกรรม] at school, supporting and helping their teachers, and most of them had better-than-average academic grades. It should be added here that this may partly be a result of selection bias during the recruitment of participants in the study, with more confident men perhaps more likely to enrol in the study than those who are less confident. Be that as it may, making your parents proud and staying out of trouble was found to be an important tactic to maintain the peace at home during the young men's high school years, whether they were successful students or not.

Tactic 2: 'Don't Ask, Don't Tell'

What does one do after finding out or privately concluding that one has a sexual preference for men? For the participants who showed traits of effeminacy this was not really an issue, as their family and others in their childhood environment would have identified them as *kathoey* from a very early age (see Chapter 5). But even among these men, when asked whether their parents knew they were gay, a surprising number of participants gave an uncertain answer. Ed, mentioned above, said: 'Because they have raised me, so they probably can see it' – however, he was not absolutely sure. In other words, he assumed his parents knew, but it had never been openly talked about. Pong, the youngest child from a large and poor family in a small village in the northeastern province of Buriram, said he was sure that his parents knew that he was gay (the parents would probably describe Pong as a *kathoey*), even though he never talked about it with them. When I asked how that was possible, he said,

> PONG: It is because sometimes I would also bring my boyfriend home, na. Really. The person whom I was dating, who was my classmate. I have brought him home.
> INT: Did they think he was just a friend, or not?
> PONG: No. They knew! [chuckles] They liked to tease me about it, for fun. But they didn't really say anything about it.

Yet Pong would not tell his family what was going on: 'They didn't ask me, you know? And if they would ask me, I would not tell them.' It was clear from the interviews that such things are not talked about between parents and children, allowing each party to cling to their own assumptions and expectations and maintaining a sense of privacy about sexual matters. Parents do not ask and children do not tell.

In contrast, the group of young men who were never overly effeminate during their childhood and who gained an awareness of being different at a much later age had to consciously deal with a discrepancy between their private feelings and knowledge and the implicit or explicit expectations of their parents and of their direct social surroundings. This would have felt quite similar to the situation of Western gay men before their coming out. As was discussed in Chapter 3, as long as social expectations are upheld by playing roles in an appropriate and respectful manner, Thai society allows significant leeway for discrepancy between the private realm and public/social presentation of the self (Jackson 2004). As discussed, this does not necessarily lead to feelings of anguish or guilt but, in order for such a situation to endure successfully, there needs to be a clear demarcation between the private issue of sexuality and one's public social role. This demarcation is upheld by all parties by adhering to a strict silence about the private issue of a person's sexuality. This silence often has to be actively negotiated, as the case of Kit illustrates. Kit was an only child from a small town in the northeast; his was a relatively well-to-do family. Kit was one of the more masculine-looking and masculine-acting of the study participants. He was always only insertive in anal sex, and girls frequently pursued him during his high school years; both these facts enhanced his sense of masculinity. Partly because of Kit's excellent study results, his mother had high expectations of him. She expressed, time and time again, her wish for Kit to marry her friend's daughter. Kit was not interested in getting married to a woman, at least not for the time being. One of his first defences was a suggestion to his mother that he is not *yet* interested in women, because of his young age:

> It is uncomfortable [or stressful] that [my] parents cannot accept it. I have encountered a problem that my mother asked: 'Why have you never taken a girlfriend home to show to your mother?' So I said, 'I don't want to have [a girlfriend] yet'. It is uncomfortable, na, that my parents cannot accept it.

His mother's continued pressure for Kit to have a girlfriend forced him to drop less and less subtle hints to her about his sexual preferences. Kit even considered telling her directly that he is gay, if she did not stop pushing him into an unwanted marriage:

> I think, sometimes I do want to tell her that I do not like girls. [...] If my mother wants to get anything, if my mother asks me anything, I have to obey. But if she was to ask me to get married I will choose to lead my own life, it is better. If she still forces me to give in [to her wishes] I prefer to find my own [way].

Kit's mother threatened to upset the harmonious balance in their relationship with her attempts to disrupt the silence between them about Kit's sexual subjectivity. Kit's second line of defence was expressing a preference to stay single throughout his life, without giving the reason why:

> I was laying down with my mother and we were chatting, and my mother said: 'I don't see you with a girlfriend!' So I said, 'No, mother, I don't really want to have [a girlfriend]. I want to stay alone.' And my mother said like, 'And when will you let me hold my grandchild?', something like that. 'I am getting old already!' [...] I was like – how to say, so I told my mother [that I preferred to stay alone], and my mother said: 'It doesn't matter. Be a good person, that is enough, son!'

Kit allowed his mother to retreat and to stop pressuring him by almost saying more than she wanted to hear. She did retreat, accepting his expressed desire to 'stay alone', saying it is okay 'as long as you are a good person'. Nevertheless, she mentioned her desire to 'hold her grandchild', enabling her to maintain the belief that Kit may one day be married to a woman and have children. By not responding, Kit allowed his mother to take her time to come to terms with this situation. This tactic requires both parties to take proper measures so that the other party is not confronted with information or situations that contradict the agreed truth. In order to do so, Kit always immediately deleted any phone messages he received from his boyfriend, who lived in another city, so that his mother would not find them. He also continuously deleted the list of outgoing calls from his phone. Kit expected that eventually his mother would come to terms with his situation and stop talking about potential girlfriends or grandchildren. Kit said that while Thai people do not talk openly about their sexuality with parents, they 'gradually let them absorb' subtle signs indicating they are gay. Another participant, Quan, also from the northeast, said about his mother: 'If it is time, she will know by herself.'

Tactic 3: Using Flexible Narratives

Another tactic is to make use of the Thai cultural fact that inner meanings and concepts can be shifted and changed over time. Van Esterik (2000, 213) described this as follows: 'It is the contexts of social life that are strictly [governed by rules] and situationally defined, not the consistency of the individual moving through these social contexts.' This means that if family members are confronted by information or behaviour that upsets the imago they have of their son/brother, this can be redressed simply by not repeating it – until it becomes conveniently 'forgotten'. Ud, from a small southern Thai town, grew up in a Christian middle-class family. One day he asked his mother to bring his Bible to church for him. While searching for the Bible in Ud's desk, his mother discovered Ud's diary in which he described a crush he had on a male schoolmate. His mother read parts of the diary, but kept quiet about it initially. Ud only found out his mother had seen his diary later, when they were quarrelling about something else:

UD: My mother scolded me, and then she said: 'Your diary, I read all of it!' At that time, if we had not been quarrelling, my mother wouldn't have spoken about the diary.
INT: How was it, at that time?
UD: I was very shocked! I thought, how can my mother know? Why didn't she say anything? [chuckles] [...] At that time, I was still, still young, I was only in ninth grade. It was like, I was not yet careful [hiding my diary]. [ยังไม่ได้ระวังอะไรเยอะ]
INT: Oh. But after that you became more careful?
UD: Much more careful! [laughs]. When I was not at home, I would take it with me, things like that.

This incident taught Ud how important it was to respect the boundaries between what is supposed to be private and what can be public, and that this is a process that entails being careful about which information is made available to whom, and at what time. Just before Ud talked about this incident, I asked him whether his mother knew that he was gay, and he summed up the point of this section nicely: 'Probably my mother knows that I liked *phu chaai* before, but right now I am not sure if she knows anything.'

Ud here indicates the possibility that the truth might change, that truths might become untrue, and shift meaning, depending on his changed performance or a move into a different circumstance. As long as Ud did not remind his mother about the diary incident and remained generally 'good' – meaning acting masculine, playing the role of a son, being good at school, being polite and respectful to his parents – the 'bad' truth that he is gay would gradually weaken and could eventually become untrue in his mother's eyes. Whereas Ud might have been outed as gay today, and his reputation damaged, this may be not be the case tomorrow, when he may become something else – this depends on his subsequent demeanour and behaviour towards his mother.

Win provided another example. Initially, he had told his mother that a male friend coming to visit him was his boyfriend. His mother was quite shocked, but when it appeared that things did not quite romantically work out, he changed the status of the visitor: 'At first I told my mother that he was my boyfriend. But after he had left I said that he was just a friend [chuckles].'

In summary, while it is of course better and less stressful to ensure parents or other family members are not confronted by information or behaviours that upset the peace and calm of the status quo, if a 'disturbing' incident happens it can be redressed, just by not repeating it. This is related to the cultural importance of *barami* or 'prestige', discussed in Chapter 3, according to which certain truths can comfortably coexist with seemingly contradictory truths, without causing anxiety or stress. To add the concept of *kala-thetsa*, also introduced in Chapter 3, if an aspect of the truth has the potential to upset a harmonious relationship it should be forgotten, or at least one should not remind others of it. Inconsistency for the sake of peace and harmony is allowed and even appreciated as part of this unspoken social contract. Jackson (2011b, 186) observed that avoiding damaged reputation and constructing positive images is a 'pervasive cultural concern', which overrides the need to have one singular truth. The ability to do this well is considered of more importance than the fact that there is inconsistency in how one behaves or what one says from one situation to the next. Jackson (2011b, 183) described two sharply demarcated phenomena at work simultaneously: one operating in public contexts, and the other in private situations 'without cultural pressure to resolve or rationalize any inconsistencies between these two domains'. This 'Thai regime of images', as Jackson called it, focuses on 'policing the social, cultural and political parameters of behaviour and speech rather than the content of deeds and words' (2011b, 183). Jackson observed that the Thai word for 'image', *phap-phot*, is derived from two Sanskrit/Pali root words meaning, approximately, 'appearance-utterance', reflecting the importance of both the image and what is or what is not allowed to be said about it to determine what is (socially) true and what is not. Westerners often see this as contradictory, hypocritical or insincere – but this is how Thai communication and the Thai concepts of power and truth are diametrically different from Western societies. Hence, Ud and Win were able to change (or restore) their mothers' perception of them by not talking (Ud) or changing the narrative (Win) about particular events that threatened to upset the status quo within the family.

Tactic 4: Non-verbal Communication and Hints

Some participants were more proactive in trying to let their parents and family know that they were not going to get married and have a family, mainly by behaving in gender-nonconforming ways and by dropping verbal hints and making jokes with a deeper meaning.

Others openly talked to their parents about their sexuality. Their revelations would, however, not have come as a surprise to their parents, because the young men who did this all described playing girls' games as children, having mainly female rather than male friends, and being tidy and proper – all signs of being a *kathoey*. Their parents must therefore have already had an inkling. Even so, they broke the negotiated silence about their sexuality between them and their parents, resulting in stress and tension. Gop, a bright and talkative man from northeastern Thailand, remembers one instance when he was 17 when his male cousin caught him checking out a dating website. His grandmother and mother were present. Tensions rose when, for the first time, Gop's sexuality suddenly became a topic of open discussion:

> My older cousin saw me [look at a gay dating website]. I don't know what he was thinking, he was standing there, and there was my grandmother, and my older brother, and he asked me, 'Are you gay?' And I said 'Hehm' – in the northeastern language, it means no. But he thought I said 'Ehm!' [meaning 'yes' in colloquial Thai]. [...] So then he asked again, 'I asked you, are you gay?' And then I said 'Ehm!' Directly. I didn't try to find an excuse. From then on, OK, I am gay. So they know, I am gay, I am not a *kathoey*.

Though his parents must already have been aware that Gop was not a *phu chaai*, it was clear that Gop found this event stressful, as it disrupted the surface calm. It left less room for any parental hopes for a change in Gop towards heterosexuality and marriage (as in Tactic 3). Even afterwards, he felt uncomfortable talking to his family about his sexuality or his romances:

> I mean, I don't dare to tell my family that I have a boyfriend. But my mother secretly, she secretly knows it, sometimes. Many people [at home] probably don't know, but my mother knows it secretly sometimes, that, eh, that this person is my boyfriend.

After the incident when his cousin 'outed' him, Gop still saw not talking about his sexuality or about his boyfriends as a sign of respect for his parents, and vice versa. This helps explain the meaning of the phrase 'secretly knowing', *aeb roo* [แอบรู้], which Gop used above when describing his mother's unspoken knowledge of his romantic entanglements. He referred to knowledge he thinks his mother had about him, but it is not knowledge that he had given her directly. Not discussing or referring to this knowledge openly is seen as a sign of mutual respect.

Dredge Kang (2011, 184) makes a useful distinction between the concepts of 'opening up' (Thai: *perd phoey* [เปิดเผย]) and 'showing oneself' (Thai: *sadaeng ork* [แสดงออก]). Opening up would mean making one's homosexuality a valid topic of discussion and talking about it with friends (or even with the family), quite similar to what a Western gay man would do during and after his coming out. This, as discussed, was rare among the participants. *Sadaeng ork* entails people around a gay/*kathoey* person determining from his behaviour (i.e. effeminacy) that the person is gay or *kathoey* without making it a topic for discussion. This links to the concept of *aeb roo* ('secretly knowing') that Gop used. This was a more common tactic.

There were a few examples where participants were much more pro-active about showing their gayness, but still without saying anything. Ud, for example, went to a wedding where his extended family was present, dressed up way beyond what was considered common for a 'normal' man, with flashy and colourful clothes, and his hair coiffed in a modern hairdo:

> Another time, there was a wedding in Hua Hin. [...] And in the bag that I had brought, it was full of powder, lotion, sun block, make-up foundation, like, many toiletries. And my mother opened my bag and she saw this. And she said, 'Do you use all these things as well?' And there was an aunt, she was an aunt-in-law, she was sitting there as well, and she said: 'He [มัน] is grown up already, whatever he is, whatever he does, it is his own business! Just to be a good person, that is enough.'

The non-verbal communication involved in Ud's performance for his family is similar to the non-verbal communication that is often involved in 'don't ask, don't tell', discussed above.

Overall, the young men were more specifically 'out' to friends and at school than to their family. In line with Matzner's (2001) findings, San suggested that sexuality was not important in deciding whether one can be friends or not. His (mainly female) friends were accepting of San's sexual preference for men. San linked this to his own capacity to be a good friend to them:

> Friends [...] would not be like, 'You, you are gay, I don't want to come near you.' [...] No. Uh, I am just being myself. I am not copying anybody. And one other thing, I am friendly, boisterous, I laugh easily. [...] I like to help my friends. So my friends say, they see that I am good. Uh, there is nothing why they should – I conduct myself, my mother taught me, that I should behave well, be focused on my studies, have friends who are good.

San suggested that a person's private sexual preference does not have anything to do with his goodness and his abilities to be a good friend, and thought it normal that friends would accept him.

Despite what San said, openness about one's sexuality might have an effect on how close friendships are. Those who had been 'out' to friends before finishing high school tended to remain in closer touch with their old high school friends. Ed was one of the few participants who had not talked to his high school friends about his sexuality during his time at school, but after moving to a new city and making new friends he had started to become more open about it. He therefore felt closer to his new friends than to his old friends at home. Ed felt that in his home environment he could not really tell the people around him that he was gay; he was one of the few participants who really needed to move to another province to achieve more freedom. San, in contrast, had always been open about his sexuality with his friends; he might not have been able to appreciate how important this was for the quality of his friendships.

Other participants did not disclose their sexuality to friends, even after completing secondary school. Asked if he had talked to his new friends about his sexuality, Kit said, 'We talk in the language of friends, I mean, but I don't know their private issues, like, do they have a partner or not – I mean, they see me and draw their own conclusions.' Kit said he would prefer to let his friends know gradually and non-verbally. He did not want to shock or embarrass his friends, but let them find out by themselves if they wanted to. The same was true for many other young men in this study. Possibly these young men's friends had already understood their interest in men, but chose not to discuss it openly, again showing respect as well as the importance of non-verbal communication in Thai society. It also shows how 'shallow' (from my personal gay Western perspective) friendships among/with Thai men often are, seemingly more focused on joint performance of ritual actions that denote friendship, such as eating, drinking, joking and getting drunk together, and not at all focused on sharing one's innermost thoughts and feelings, which would leave one vulnerable to gossip. It also shows the complexity of sexual and gender categories in Thai society, and the importance of interpreting symbols and everyday life experiences rather than only analysing discourse and language, as previous scholars of Thai homosexuality have often done.

Tactic 5: Conforming to Heteronormative Gender Roles

The final tactic was to conform to a heteronormative gender role – this tactic partly overlaps with other tactics discussed above, but in discussing it I want to focus on the importance of gender. When Gop's sexuality suddenly became a topic of discussion in his family (discussed above), he made a point of saying: 'I am gay, I am not a *kathoey*.' Many other participants mentioned this point. Perhaps being gay is bad, but it is not as bad as being a *kathoey* and at the very least, in terms of avoiding conflict and confrontation, acting in a less effeminate way is a form of fitting in. Hence, once a son's non-heterosexuality becomes known, they can use the argument of 'at least they are not a *kathoey*' to make it easier to accept because the consequence is that a son can fit in better with expectations of parents and elders as a heteronormative *phu chaai*. Ake, who still identified as *kathoey* during the first interview, acknowledged explicitly that he (at the time still 'she') thought being gay was more accepted than being *kathoey*: 'Sometimes I think the people around me would prefer me to be gay. They don't want me to have breast implants, change my sex, and wear long hair.' Acting masculine and fulfilling the social roles of a son preserves the prestige (*barami*) of the self and the family. Many participants strived to act in a normatively masculine manner in the presence of parents and family – also a sign of being 'good' (Tactic 1). Fluk was an example of this: 'I told my mother that I don't like girls, but that I will make her grandchildren.' In saying this, he informed his mother that, while he did not like girls, this would not have an effect on his duties towards her, which he thought included having children. His mother should therefore not worry about losing face before other villagers. Nook's father accepted him for who he was, but demanded that Nook 'behaved' while staying at his parental home: 'Mother accept[s] what I am. But my father doesn't really accept. My father said, "Whatever you are, I don't care. But as long as you stay with me, you have to be a *phu chaai*." '

Dee's mother had also long ago observed that he was not a *phu chaai*. She urged Dee to at least not be a *kathoey*, apparently with his best interests in mind:

> My mother said, don't be *toot*, don't be a *kathoey*! Otherwise after you finish school, you cannot find a job. […] I told her, it is normal. I am not a *toot*, I am not something, but it is, eh, how to say, I don't know how to say – I am a bit too much like a girl.

Lert's mother had encouraged him earlier to cut his hair and be masculine, since she found him unconvincing as a woman, implicitly stating her approval of him being *kathoey* if he had only been more beautiful (in a feminine way):

> LERT: Before, when I was wearing long hair, she told me to cut my hair, she said you don't look like [a girl], like that. She said, you have to be pretty, like a girl, if you want to be …
> INT: [interrupts] She said, you are not pretty, when you wore long hair?
> LERT: She said, 'Cut it like a boy, it will look much better.' My mother said that. And other family members too. So – when I came back from Bangkok, I changed, I re- established myself [เปลี่ยนลุกขึ้นมาใหม่]. Like the clothes I had worn before, they were very short, something like that, but I did not wear skirts! There were shorts, I threw them

away. I threw them away in Bangkok. And I bought new clothes to bring home with me. All men's clothes.

For similar reasons, desirable and modern potential boyfriends have to be masculine, either masculine looking or at least masculine acting. Some young men said that they would feel embarrassed before their friends if they had a boyfriend who was effeminate or more effeminate than they were. Gop, for example, worried that his friends would laugh at him if he had an effeminate boyfriend. This is not only about looks, but also about ways of acting:

If you ask 'rough'? Rough is ok. If they look rough, they will look more masculine [ดูแมนขึ้น], something like that. But if they look rough but walk in an effeminate way, then I don't want them. It does not look good.

Experimenting or flirting with girls of their own age was another tactic to fit in and to hide their same-sex attraction for a number of participants. Only Dee actually had had sex with his girlfriend. This experience helped them figure out that they were in fact attracted to men, as Ed explained:

I thought I would try it, to see what it would be like, but we just knew each other, we never even held hands. Because I wanted to try, like, the thing that we are, are we really that? So we have to try both ways, but in a way that we do not molest [ทำร้าย] either a boy or a girl, but we just see each other. I wanted to know, is my feeling real or not? Is it true? So when I went out [with my girlfriend] I knew – so, after that I will probably not go out [with girls] anymore, because I know, when I go out with a girl, it is like I discredit her [ทำร้ายเขา]. If she finds out, she would probably be sad. Better not to do it.

Fluk said he was confused about his lack of sexual feelings for girls and tried to date a girl in his class for a while. 'So I thought, let's try to date a girl. But I never had anything [sex] with her. At most, I sniffed her cheek' (referring to an innocent Thai form of kissing). Shortly after that he told his aunt, who was raising him at the time, that he was gay. Hong said he felt like he was 'cheating himself' when he was dating a girl at the age of 12–13, following the pattern of boys and girls in his classroom:

I have once liked a girl, but – no, it is not me [มันไม่ใช่ตัวเรา], it was like I was cheating [or fooling] myself [เหมือนเราหลอกตัวเองมากกว่า]. [...] There was – there was a girl who came to woo me. But, I mean, at first we chatted, but I felt, no. I didn't like it. Yes.

For the five participants who were *kathoey* at an earlier age, the tactic of adhering to heteronormative gender roles was reversed: rather than acting as 'good men', they were urged and expected to follow the ideal of 'good' femininity epitomized by the Thai term *kunlasatree*, discussed in Chapter 6. As discussed, the presumed effeminacy of these boys was established by family members and others in their proximity, because of their dislike for boys' games and toys, in their proper and tidy (Thai: *riab roi* [เรียบร้อย]) behaviour (docile, clean, tidy – all considered feminine traits) and their preference for the company of female friends. This made it easier for the young men involved, as the acceptance (or at least tolerance) of the family emerged more or less naturally during their childhood. Pong said the earlier the parents realized, the easier it was for a person to be gay or *kathoey*. For these participants, their differing gender iden-tity as *kathoey* may no longer have been a point of contention for their parents, and there was a clear set of moral norms and values that they were expected to adhere to: they had to conduct themselves as proper young women. Ake provided an example of this:

> Ehm – like my mother, my mother knows what I am, but every time when my mother opens my wardrobe and finds girls' clothes, my mother likes to tell me, 'Can you please dress a bit modestly [เบาๆหน่อย]? You could also wear trousers! Can you do that?' Something like that.

Ake's mother had accepted the fact that he was a *kathoey* at that time, but she objected to the way he dressed. His mother would like her 'daughter' to be a good girl by dressing more modestly. Roj's mother, who must have also come to terms with Roj's obvious effeminacy as a young child while he was growing up in an outer district of the northeastern province of Kalasin, also told him to behave: 'But my mother said, whatever, but don't let any bad thing spoil the reputation of our family [อย่าเสื่อมเสียตระกูล]. That is all. And that I should make sure I can establish myself [meaning: become financially independent].'

Hiding sexual relations from parents is an important way of retaining the image of a good (female) child, as Fluk indicated:

> FLUK: [My mother] knows, she knows. But – she doesn't know that I have intimate relations [มีความสัมพันธ์อะไรลึกซึ้ง] with whom or to what extent. She only knows that I am gay. I only once brought a boyfriend back home. She did not think about it much.
>
> INT: Did you tell them he was a friend?
>
> FLUK: I told them he was my boyfriend. I told them he was my boy-friend, but we slept separately, to make them feel comfortable with it. [สร้างความสบายใจให้กับเขา] Hmm.

Why Thai Same-Sex-Attracted People Do Not 'Come Out'

The insights about the importance of 'image'/*barami* combined with the principles of *kala-thetsa* discussed in Chapter 3 help explain why Thai same-sex-attracted men (and women) generally do not understand the Western concept of 'coming out' to parents and friends, and also help to put the five tactics discussed above in perspective. In the West, the open, public expression and realization of one's sexual identity is considered to be of great importance and is often even seen as a prerequisite for happiness (Seidman 2004), judging by the countless self-help books that are sold on how to 'come out'. Coming out of the closet, therefore, is a key rite of passage for gay men and lesbian women in Western countries. Being or remaining in the closet is usually derided and people who choose to do so are considered to be marginalized and socially oppressed at worst and weak and cowardly at best. Seidman (2004, 30), for example, claims that being in the closet 'will shape the psychological and social core of an individual's life [... where] secrecy and isolation are sustained by feelings of shame, guilt and fear'. Explaining this further, Seidman theorizes that for 'the closet' to even exist, society has to view homosexuality as something bad and dirty first; he calls this 'the making of a culture of homosexual pollution' by a heteronormative society. This process is essential for the creation of the closet out of which homosexuals must then liberate themselves.

For Thai homosexual men, the most important strategy for maintaining harmony and balance in their relationship with their parents is to avoid disrespecting and upsetting them by being good and retaining the *barami* of the family. Having a nonconforming gender or sexuality does – in Thailand as much as anywhere else – have the potential to upset one's parents and damage one's prestige. At the very least, it goes against parents' expectations of their children having similar life trajectories and making similar choices in life as they did, not to mention the parental disappointment if they find out their son will most likely not give them grandchildren. Since being unable to fulfil a parent's expectations is both a form of losing face and a potential threat to social harmony, the key is to leak the 'bad news' gradually. This is in itself considered a form of *kala-thetsa*, of good manners and of communication skills. Coming out experiences, in the sense of sitting one's parents down and causing shock by telling them bluntly that one is gay, are rare in Thailand and were largely absent from the stories of the young men in this study. Thai gay men, including the young men in this study, generally do not understand why Western gay men would do this. They consider it not only incomprehensibly rude but also, if they are completely frank, really stupid, as it is a sure way to destroy the calm and balance in the parent–child relationship, for no obvious gain for either side.

Western-oriented queer activists and radical feminists may interpret the decision of Thai homosexual men not to 'come out' as the forced submission to a double life or condemnation to 'the closet'. In contrast, a Thai will recognize the skill of maintaining a smooth social surface as a virtue: Thai homosexual men acquire a strong sense of self-worth from their ability to fit in and perform their expected part in social relationships, and their ability to retain and preserve their *barami*. A discrepancy between the private and public presentations of the self may not necessarily be experienced as problematic or burdensome in the same way that Western gay men usually experience this. As a result, Western men set out on a trajectory towards their 'coming out', bringing their private 'real self' in line with their public 'face' – whereas Thai homosexual men are perfectly happy living with a public performance that is different from their private sexual self.

Hence, the reason for the existence of a 'Thai closet' (if one could call it that) has more to do with the cultural importance attached to *kala-thetsa* and *barami* – proper behaviour in place and time, and the prestige that is derived from being able to fulfil expectations of elders, as well as the general lack of guilt attached to sex in Thai culture as long as it occurs away from the public eye. In other words, having a different taste, sexually, does not prevent one from participating in mainstream society and fulfilling the most important social roles, which (especially in the past) often included marriage to a woman and having children.

Expressions of Acceptance or Acknowledgement: Humour and Hints

Despite the lack of a 'coming-out' ritual, parents, caregivers and friends would occasionally express acceptance or, as Vee, a slightly effeminate young man from a large poor family in the southern province of Surat Thani called it, 'acknowledgement' [ความรับรู้] of a person's homosexuality by using humour and teasing. Joking usually involved using the 'wrong' Thai linguistic particles and adjectives towards males, that is, using feminine words, for example, calling a son pretty rather than handsome. Ek mentioned how his aunt and extended family are more open-minded these days than in the past, using their jokes as an indicator of this: 'They are open, they [are] open and accept [me] – they are more open-minded than before [เปิดรับ เปิดใจรับ มากขึ้น]. [...] Because they still tease me, for fun, like: "You are pretty!" [chuckles].'

Ud, whose gay performance at a wedding was discussed above, mentioned how he 'secretly smiled in his heart' when his mother made a joke about him to his extended family:

> But there was one time, when I came back to Trang the last time, it was like, at home there were many people. My aunts and uncles came to our house. And they asked, 'How is it, to stay in Bangkok?' [...]. And my

mother said, 'In Bangkok, he [มัน] is wearing a skirt!' [...] [chuckles]. And my aunt believed it! And my mother said, 'I was [joking]!'

Broaching this topic in relation to her own son and in a public setting, under the safe cover of a joke, was a way for Ud's mother to let him know that she was okay with his sexuality. When I asked if he felt good about it, he said,

I felt good. I felt, like, she is starting to understand me. She is starting to not, like, not forbid me [กีดกัน], but I mean, not to the extent that she would set me free [ปล่อย] for the full 100 per cent.

When I asked him how his father responds to these things, he said,

My father, he – he is indifferent [เฉยๆ] [this word (*choey choey*) can also mean 'calm' or 'normal']. Whether he knows, or doesn't know, he doesn't talk about it. I am not sure. I mean, my father is a calm [or serene] [นิ่งๆ] and quiet person.

Pong also mentioned humour spontaneously when we discussed the issue of stigma and discrimination:

Only people who tease me. For fun. But nobody has ever said anything negative. Nobody has told me, 'Stop being like that', something like that. There have only been people who teased me, 'When will there be someone asking for your hand?', like that [chuckles].

According to Thai gender etiquette, men ask for women's hand in marriage. So when the unnamed person in the fragment above asked Pong when someone would come and ask for his hand, he or she made a gentle joke in acknowledgement of Pong's supposed femininity.

There are other subtle ways for parents to acknowledge that their son is not a normal *phu chaai*. Yud, a slightly effeminate, self-confident young man from the southern province of Nakhon Sri Thammarat, remembered that his mother reminded him to watch forthcoming television programs that contained topics related to the 'third gender' or to homosexuality:

I am not a real [*phu*] *chaai*. I mean, my mother, my mother has known for a long time already, I think, na. But I mean, she like, looks at me from a distance, more [ดูเราห่างๆ มากกว่า]. It is like, when there is a report that is about the third sex/gender [เพศที่สาม], if there is an interview, like this, my mother will say, 'Did you see it or not?' Something like that.

However, when I asked Yud if he saw this as a sign of his mother's acceptance, he answered that he also saw it as a warning: 'Yes. But my mother, my mother, it is like she wants me to watch it so that it can be, can be an example for me to learn from [อุทาหรณ์], to teach me to look after myself, more.'

San explained to his parents the difference between *kathoey* and gay. He did this in a very culturally appropriate way, showing respect for his parents and their expectations of him, without elaborating how that topic may or may not be related to him personally. It must have brought the point home, also since it is quite unusual for a child to use a teaching tone towards a parent under Thai rules of *kala-thetsa*:

> Hmmmm. I tried to tell them. I told them [ท่าน], I told them that, between – I distinguished between the words 'gay' and '*kathoey*' [chuckles]. That is – I explained to them, it is like this, I am not saying that – I gave them a definition [นิยาม] of the meaning of gay, between, the different characteristics, are different. Between, it will be different. They said, hm, 'Up to you, whatever you want to be [แล้วแต่ เป็นอะไรก็เป็น], as long as you are a good person.' They said only this. So – I felt contented [สบายใจ].

Oad was one of only a few participants who brought a boyfriend home to introduce to his parents, and who felt accepted by the large family dinner that was organized while he was there:

> At first I felt excited. […] At home, they were excited, because I had never brought […] a boyfriend back home. He, he was like, he behaved well, so at home they loved him. My family liked him. So I took him to see my grandfather and grandmother […]. The first day we went, we sat and ate for a long time [chuckles], the room was full with my whole extended family, we sat there and we treated them to food, something like that. […] I felt close to them, and I felt very – it was like, how do they call it, it is like, I felt like we were a family. Yes. But he, he liked my family too. Because the people in the central plains, they will have selfish manners [นิสัย], and they don't like to share.

Note how Oad mentioned offering food to the elders after a long absence, a sign of respect and 'being good' to them, and how his boyfriend 'behaved well', meaning he paid the proper respect to Oad's elder family members. His story reminds me of the article by the Chinese scholar Wah-Shan (2001) about 'coming home', which discussed the importance and meaning of participating in family rituals, including dinners, as a silent way for Chinese parents to show at least acknowledgement, and perhaps even acceptance and approval of their homosexual children.

In the final part of this chapter, the importance of retaining good relations with one's family and, related to this, an absence of a desire to join separate gay communities will be discussed.

'We are Family'? A Sense of Belonging to a Gay Community or Society

The participants were asked whether they felt part of a gay community. Why is this an interesting question to ask? There are two reasons. First, it helps us understand to what extent the young men felt oppressed, miserable and lonely while living in their predominantly heterosexual social environment. My assumption was that, if there were a great level of suffering, I would find a strong desire to escape and to find refuge in gay communities during the interviews with the young men. The second reason why I found this an interesting question is that HIV services for gay men in Thailand are delivered with an underlying assumption that 'gay community organizations' are best placed to do this work – something which I have always questioned.

Community-based organizations themselves use the Thai term *chumchon* for 'community', but at the time of my study I was not yet aware of this term. Therefore, during data collection, I used the term *sangkhom* (more often translated as 'society' than as 'community') instead. All participants said they felt part of a gay *sangkhom*. However, after repeating this question a number of times, it became clear they had a different understanding of the word than I did. Hong illustrated this beautifully: 'Me? The gay *sangkhom*? Maybe I am. Because if you are called "gay" then you probably are in the gay *sangkhom*.'

Similarly, when asked if he feels part of gay society, Nook said: 'I have to be, because I am one of their citizens.' Whenever a participant said he felt part of gay society, it was usually linked to their patronage of particular entertainment venues. Pong also mentioned having gay friends when asked if he was part of the gay *sangkhom*. San suggested the question could only be answered if one has clarity about its definition:

But the word – a gay *sangkhom* – it has to depend on how it's defined. [...] If you ask me, am I part of it? Probably not, I think, I choose to be in the general *sangkhom*, more. I don't want to – I don't want to be like, I am in this *sangkhom*, I say, I think that I stay in the *sangkhom* of the majority, more.

The theme brought up by San – preferring to remain linked to mainstream society rather than separating from it – was common. Lert's response illustrated this: 'I think it is better to stay with general people, to blend in with other people better, with those who are *phu chaai*. To blend in is better.'

One of the questions I asked the participants was whether they would like to live in a dormitory, apartment, condo or village that was 'gay only'. I presumed that men who felt lonely, rejected and marginalized in heteronormative society would find this an appealing idea. However, for the majority, the answer was 'no'. Ake explained that it would be 'too limiting':

> It looks like an incomplete society [ดูเหมือนสังคมที่ไม่สมบูรณ์แบบ]. It is not – it, it, if suppose one lives in a society that has everything that God has created, the basis is two sexes [เพศ], and then after, we separate ourselves [...]. It is something that is colourful [สีสัน]. But if it is like that, there are only – there will be nothing that is like, when we meet a person, we meet another sex [or gender], when we talk to him, we can see his or her attitudes, we can learn something [from them]. [...] But if we go and stay like that, we will only get the ideas from gay people, we won't get anything like, like, the way I stay now [...]. It is something that is complete already, something like that. Don't force it.

Ake saw no advantages in being exposed only to people who are similar to each other. When I asked, to confirm, that it is 'not necessary to separate' gays from the mainstream, he adds, 'It is not necessary [chuckles]. Even worse, if you separate [gays], it is like we have an infection, like we are zombies, so we have to stay in that village [chuckles]. I don't want to [even] think about that!' Roj and San even suggested that a gay space like that would lead to depraved sexual behaviours and 'unlawful activities'.

About a quarter of the participants, however, did say they were interested in the idea of a predominantly gay living environment. Tam, a self-confident and ambitious northeastern young man whose father worked abroad, and Hong said it would be 'fun'. Ed, from the southern city of Pattalung, who had been depressed and lonely and who tended to see his homosexuality as a burden, thought he would be happier there:

> I would like to live there! I would like to live there, too. Because we are the same, we understand each other better. Maybe we would have more happiness. Hmmm. But in the real world, it would probably be hard to find.

Win said he would be interested in staying in a gay dormitory or condominium, if such a thing existed, but he hurried to explain: '[chuckles] But it doesn't – I mean, I want to stay there but it doesn't mean that I have to sleep around [มั่ว], like, to sleep around, something like that'. When I ask him what the advantages of living there would include, he said,

> Hmmm. I mean, it would give me – for me, there would perhaps not be many advantages, because I, perhaps, I cannot imagine, like this. But, for example, I mean, we would know – I mean, like, I would know friends who, like, are like this. And, eh, it is not necessary to look for them elsewhere. [chuckles]

Win said, however, that he would move out of this imaginary gay environment again as soon as he had found a boyfriend, worrying that his boyfriend would be stolen away from him. He clearly saw this imaginary gay space as an opportunity to find a partner at best and as a place with unlimited sexual possibilities at worst – and certainly not as a particularly safe and secure living environment or a permanent lifestyle choice.

I included a question about whether the participants would be interested in joining a gay gym. In comparison to the discussions about a gay village, apartment or neighbourhood, this question was answered rather differently. Far more of the young men would have been willing to join a gay gym instead of a general gym, in comparison to the proportion of men who were interested in living in a predominantly gay living environment. As Ives explained, he would join the gay gym: 'Because I like gays, too. And … At least, and when I go there, there will be gay people as well, and we can understand each other [คุยกันรู้เรื่อง]. Yes'. He elaborated:

> It is like, if I go there I will want to admire and watch *phu chaai* and gays, something like this. At least, when I go to do [exercise] there, it is like, 'Hu! [high voice] This guy looks good! His physique is okay!' […] Eh. If it happens that I am like, exercising next to him, like this, I probably would feel good!

Yud, however, said that he would prefer the general gym. He linked the gay gym to a potential for sex, something that he, as the only virgin in the research, felt he was not ready for. He thought he would be unable to focus if he were to join the gay gym, because he would be distracted and he would feel pressured to look his best:

> To go into a gay gym, right when we go in there, even if we don't think anything at first, but once we go in, there will be an instinct, like, 'I [กู]

have to look as good as I can'. [chuckles] […]. I have to look masculine [เข้มแข็ง] […]. It is like – it comes by itself. It is natural [เป็นธรรมชาติ].

Despite the strong economic development of Thailand in recent decades, including rapid urbanization and mass internal migration, combined with a devastating HIV epidemic among same-sex-attracted men, not a single community-based organization has spontaneously emerged in which Thai gay men are working as volunteers for the good of other gay men. This is a remarkable contrast with Western cities, where the HIV epidemic was a powerful issue to rally gay communities around. There was much anger, as the continuing and worsening HIV epidemics in Western countries were regarded as an injustice inflicted upon homosexual men by ignorant, unwilling and inherently homophobic governments, which were allowing things to go from bad to worse. No such sense of outrage and willingness to band together and act has been found among Thai homosexual men so far. In Thailand, all efforts to prevent HIV among homosexual men have been initiated and paid for by Western donor organizations and have been run by Thai organizations set up to receive and expend these donor funds.

Why has the growth of Bangkok and other cities, combined with migration, changes in family structures and social cohesion, combined with a severe and persistent HIV epidemic apparently not led to the emergence of gay communities in general, or in response to HIV in particular? There are several answers to this question. A prerequisite for 'organiz[ing] a personal life around their erotic/emotional attraction to their own sex', as D'Emilio puts it (1993, 470), is the need to do so, and this need would only exist in the face of oppression and where there is a benefit to banding together in communities and finding strength in numbers. Continuous stigma and discrimination, police intervention and harassment, strong social norms against homosexuality, and frequent arrests and humiliating 'outings' of homosexuals in the media were all part and parcel of homosexual life before the Stonewall riots in the United States (D'Emilio 1998). Oppressed homosexuals were driven together and mutual solidarity was forged. These hardships and injustices were essential elements for the process of gay community formation and the emergence of a 'gay rights movement' in Western countries. In Thai society, homophobic attitudes and oppression do not exist in the same way, and as a result there is not such a strong urge to develop safe spaces and more or less separate gay communities in Thailand. As long as they follow certain cultural rules for communication and adhere to the tactics described in this chapter, same-sex-attracted people are allowed to function normally in general society as well as, with certain constraints, within their (extended) families.

The attitudes towards gay communities found among the participants in this study were very similar to those found by Wah-Shan (2001) among homosexual men in China. He found that many same-sex-attracted men did not 'feel the need to segregate themselves from those who love the opposite sex', partly because 'sexuality is not seen as a separable category of behaviour and existence, but an integral force of life' (2001, 28). Wah-Shan explains that in China the family/kinship system (and one's position in it) is the basis of a person's identity; one only becomes a full person in the context of family and social relationships. One's sexual preferences are simply not important enough to form a social identity around. This means same-sex-attracted men in China do not usually feel the need to segregate themselves from those who love the opposite sex by coming out, by having mainly or exclusively gay friends or by demanding individual rights to be different. Indeed, Wah-Shan found that many Chinese same-sex-attracted men opposed the Western binary of homo-versus heterosexuality, seeing this as insignificant in their lives and preferring to be homosexually active with as little disruption of the harmony within their families and overall society as possible. This meant combining a private life as a homosexually active man with publicly fitting in and fulfilling the expectations of their family and community – very similar to the aspirations most of the young men in this study expressed.

For nearly all the young men in this study, participating in gay life, via entertainment, the Internet or an imaginary gay gym, sounded acceptable and even desirable, but the idea of living in a gay community, surrounded by only gay people and separated from the mainstream of heterosexual society, did not.

Conclusion

While growing up, the young men in this study made use of several tactics in order to live within a heteronormative society. The first of the five tactics was 'being good', that is, making one's parents proud and happy. Second, the young men upheld a 'don't ask, don't tell' regime about the realm of their sexuality. Third, the young men could make use of a cultural loophole that allows a strict separation of private sexual feelings and public social roles. A fourth tactic was shifting meanings and truths if necessary when the surface of smooth family and friendship relations was occasionally punctured. Finally, participants tried to adhere to heteronormative gender roles as much as possible.

The young men in this study tried to be good children – good to their parents, good to their teachers and good to their friends – so that they did not give them a reason to reject them. For the participants who saw themselves (or were seen by others) as feminine during their childhood, being a 'good woman' was seen as important. For others, acting in a way that was as masculine as possible was their tactic to fit in, aiming to disrupt parental and societal expectations as little as possible and maintaining their prestige (*barami*). In line with what was discussed in Chapter 6, concepts of gender were appropriated and strategically employed by the young men, borrowing from mainstream culture.

Separating themselves by living permanently in gay communities, based on having a shared sexual object choice or sexual/gender identity, did not make sense to the young men in this study – at least not at this stage of their psychosocial development. They preferred to engage with gay society intermittently. Their vision of gay society was limited to the entertainment sphere, very much focused on sex and romance, and did not have a political or lifestyle-related component. The participants had a strong desire to remain rooted and connected to their families and to the mainstream society in which they grew up.

This chapter has shown that, while the young men often saw their sexuality or gender identity as a burden when they were younger, they gradually acquired skills while growing up so that they could live with it in harmony with their family and social environment, making use of typically Thai tactics for (often non-verbal) communication and for positioning oneself vis-à-vis others in line with expectations of elders. They preferred to remain firmly embedded in their families and in overall society.

Existing models for HIV service provision in Thailand emphasize gay community building; this approach may be appropriate for some Thai gay men with a public gay identity. But the findings from this study among young rural same-sex-attracted men in transition calls into question the appropriateness of HIV service provision that uses the notion of a gay community as a starting point. The fact that the participants were just finishing secondary school when they were recruited and that they had mostly been living with parents in rural areas could be two reasons why these men in particular found the idea of participating in separate gay communities so alien. As a result, they may not want to or feel confident enough to access so-called community-based or community-delivered HIV services, at least not at this time in their lives.

Western donor organizations play a major role in funding HIV services for Thai men who have sex with men, a fact which has enabled certain Thai NGOs to claim a position of representation of 'the Thai LGBTI community' and to effectively monopolize HIV service provision for this group of Thai men. Without alternative, more appropriate HIV prevention approaches, many young same-sex-attracted Thai men, especially those who are (very) young and are in rural and lower-class urban settings, will become infected with HIV before they access community-based services (if they ever do) (De Lind van Wijngaarden and Ojanen 2016).

New HIV service delivery modalities for Thai same-sex-attracted men need to be introduced. Such services should take overall aspects of Thai society and culture into consideration in the way they promote safer sex, testing and treatment adherence, including the tendency towards unspoken or non-communication, especially in sexual matters, as well as the way communication and behaviours are structured along hierarchical lines. Age, gender comportment and (perceived) status or class are of utmost importance in understanding dynamics surrounding condom use and safer sex. In addition, the cultural importance of maintaining prestige and a good image, even to the detriment of the truth, will lead men to keep silent about their sexual unfaithfulness towards their permanent partners, even if these exploits may put these partners at risk of HIV infection. It is important to study further how such dynamics related to 'inner truth' and 'social truth', as well as to power and prestige, are employed in Thai sexual encounters, and use the findings to inform more effective HIV prevention approaches (De Lind van Wijngaarden and Ojanen 2016).

In the next chapters, the focus will shift to processes that created change in the way the young men in this study viewed their sexuality and gender, in particular on how they acquired understandings about homosexuality in which gender came to play a less prominent role.

Chapter 8

HOW DATING FRIENDS PLAYS A ROLE IN DESTABILIZING GENDER-BASED NOTIONS OF HOMOSEXUALITY

Introduction

In this chapter, the focus is on the practice of dating and loving. Three young men are discussed in detail – three men whose sexual life histories were particularly illustrative of personal change. The commonality in the stories of these three young men is that all three of them fell in love with friends in their social circle – a taboo in Thai society, as will be explained in the next section. They were then forced to come to terms with a discrepancy between the beliefs, norms and values they held while at high school and their actual sexual and romantic experiences over the interviewing period.

The Thai Taboo against Having Sex with Friends

Dating friends is not done in Thailand. Every participant in this study rejected the idea of dating people from within one's own group of friends. San illustrated this as follows:

> No, you know, I feel like – friends are friends. I don't expect that I want to have something [sex] with them. I, I feel that – hmmmm. I don't feel anything like that, I mean, a friend is – a friend is a friend, I am not like, something like that.

Tam explained that friends are too similar to him to be considered in a sexual or romantic manner:

> TAM: No, for [dating] friends. I say, friends who are in my group [กลุ่ม] – there are only those who are similar to me [มีแต่ที่เหมือนเรา], and – if I go to secretly like them, it, it won't fly [literally: it will not digest] [จีบไม่ลงหรอก]. I don't even think about secretly liking them [ไม่คิดที่จะแอบชอบด้วยซ้ำ].

INT: Yes. Because they are too similar to you?

TAM: They are like me. If they were not like me, they probably wouldn't befriend me. Yes.

Tam reasoned that if his friends were not like him, they would not be his friends. And because his friends were like him, they are automatically disqualified from the potential status of lover or sexual partner. This explanation is at the core of the taboo against dating friends in the gender-based model of love and sexuality: friends have to be of the same or similar gender category – this is what makes them friends. This means that more effeminate homosexual men generally befriend other effeminate homosexuals, as well as women and *kathoey*. Sexual partners or 'husbands' have to be gender opposites by definition, and are therefore recruited from outside this social circle. Friendships between gender opposites, or put another way, friendships between people who theoretically could have sex with each other, are very rare.

Friendships in Thai society are therefore homosocial, that is, they are defined by sameness, whereas love relationships are defined by gender difference. Falling in love or having a sexual relationship with a friend is therefore a taboo. A taboo is a social rule; like every social rule, the fact that it exists is also an indication that it is regularly broken. If something truly never happens there would be no reason to have a rule or a taboo about it. As we will see in the next part of this chapter, when a taboo relationship occurs, it causes shame, confusion and turmoil. It needs to be 'settled'; it demands an explanation and a repositioning of what the young men previously considered normal, possible and acceptable. In the next part of the chapter I will present the stories of each of the three young men to illustrate how each of them dealt with the shock of falling in love with a friend.

Ake's Story

Ake is Muslim and grew up in a small village in Phuket. His parents were both working as cooks in a restaurant. He had an older sister who was a lesbian; she was studying at a private university in Bangkok. Ake knew he was different since kindergarten, preferring to have girls as friends and playing girls' games rather than boys'. He was known by himself, his family and in the community where they lived as a *kathoey*. Both of his parents were accepting or at least tolerant of Ake being *kathoey*, but Ake felt closer to his mother than to his father. Ake behaved as a girl as much as he could at that time, but was not allowed to dress in a female school uniform. He (at that time 'she', using feminine particles and pronouns in the Thai language) had a good time at school, had many friends and generally felt happy. After moving from the primary village school to a high school in town, he was exposed to the term 'gay' for the first time and he became close friends with other *kathoey* and gay students.

While Ake described himself as *kathoey* or the more politically correct variety 'second type of woman' (*sao praphet song*) in the first interview, which occurred just before he earned his high school diploma, during the second interview he referred to himself as a 'gay queen'. While the word 'gay' ostensibly belongs to a new set of terms denoting same-sex attraction based on sexual object choice – that is, sexuality rather than gender based – the addition 'queen' refers to the receptive role in anal intercourse, which still has feminine connotations, especially for former *kathoey*. Ake's transformation from *kathoey* to gay queen coincided with his move from Phuket to Bangkok, where he had been accepted at a university. His transformation was similar to that of Ives, Lert, Nook and Roj, but what makes Ake's case different is that it occurred later, at 18–19 years of age, whereas the others transformed when they were two to three years younger.

Ake had been secretly in love with a fellow second type of woman at the time he (then still 'she') was about to finish high school. Ake found these feelings incomprehensible; referring to his conception both of himself and the object of his love as feminine beings, he joked that he felt that he was 'going to be a lesbian!' Ake never talked to the object of his love about how he felt. He also did not talk about this issue during the first interview, and only talked about it during the second and third interviews. The reason he gave for this was that he felt embarrassed about these feelings. In Thailand, friendships are strictly homosocial (meaning men befriend men and women befriend women), and sex between friends is therefore a taboo. Love and sexual relationships can and should occur only between a female (or *kathoey*) and a *phu chaai* who would, by definition, not be part of the same friendship circle. In hindsight, Ake sounded sentimental about this 'first love' experience: he said that if it had been possible for them to be lovers, he would have 'dumped all his current boyfriends' in order to be with that person. After moving to Bangkok, when he was back in Phuket for a visit during his holidays, he did tell some of his friends about having had these feelings:

> They were shocked. They said: 'Really?' Some people would not say a word, they would be dumbfounded [อึ้ง], for about 20 minutes. They would be shocked, like in SHOCK [Eng], like, I never told anybody and they couldn't tell [at that time] from my demeanour [ดูอาการเราไม่รู้].

His secret love feelings for his friend and fellow *kathoey* were a factor in Ake's decision to move to Bangkok – he wanted to follow the object of his love. He said he was shy to admit that the decision to go to Bangkok was formed because he wanted to 'follow a man', especially since the object of his love was, in Ake's opinion, a fellow female. However, after moving to Bangkok Ake soon lost track of this friend, who had started studying at a different university. He still had never spoken to this friend about his feelings, afraid that he would lose their friendship. When I reminded Ake of this story during the third interview, he laughed and said he had 'almost forgotten' about it – now they were 'just friends', and his feelings of love for this person had apparently disappeared.

Ake decided to move to Bangkok in the new role of gay, and not as *kathoey*. The reason he gave for this was that he was not sure what to expect there, in terms of acceptance of his feminine demeanour. He was also worried that he would not be beautiful enough as a woman to have many friends. Ake imagined Bangkok as the summit of a hierarchy of beauty and power, and as a country girl he did not feel confident enough to compete there. His love feelings for his friend may also have played a role in his decision to stop acting and seeing himself as feminine; these feelings may have led Ake to question whether he really was a second type of woman, making it easier for him to make the switch to being gay. Alternatively, it could be that he wanted to change into a more masculine role in the distant hope of becoming a lover of his second-type-of-woman friend. Before leaving, he gave away his feminine clothes, shoes and handbags by inviting his Phuket-based second-type-of-woman friends to his home and asking each of them to take their pick. Several of his friends strongly disapproved of Ake's decision and his transformation from *kathoey* to gay, and Ake lost contact with some of these friends after that.

After arriving in Bangkok, Ake was immediately very popular in his new role as gay and he was handpicked for the university cheerleading team. He lost weight and became fit, because of the physical exercise and training he had to follow. He was still taking the hormone pills he had been taking in his previous life as a second type of woman, but they were different from the ones he took before, making his skin smooth but leaving other body parts the way they were and allowing muscles to develop.

Ake looked so different between the first and the second interview that I initially did not recognize him when he walked into the coffee shop where we had agreed to meet. He changed from feminine-looking, wearing whitening face powder and other make-up as well as feminine-looking clothes (though not to the extent that he wore a dress or skirt) during the first interview to a typical trendy urban gay young man. He also talked differently, using the masculine particles and pronouns (*phom* and *khrab*) rather than the female particles and personal pronouns (*dichan, noo, kha* and *jaa*) he had used during the first interview. He also had started labelling himself as a gay queen on the Internet, changing his gender on his Facebook page from 'female' to 'male', and removed feminine-looking pictures of himself, uploading new, more masculine-looking photos instead.

His transformation was probably further encouraged by his first real sexual experience, which occurred after he had completed high school, just before he left for Bangkok. Ake had had sex before with a boyfriend of the same age whom he had dated when he was 15, but he dismissed this relationship with the English term 'puppy love'. His first serious sexual affair happened with a South American man he met in a (non-gay) sauna in Phuket. Ake described the encounter as a cat-and-mouse game of lustful and desiring gazes, smiles and gestures, and the consequent sex they had at the house of a friend made a deep impression on him. It must have been the first time that Ake felt desired and wanted by another male while he was partly (and later fully) undressed, in all his maleness. Ake spoke for a long time about this encounter, in all its detail, including the condomless penetration that occurred and how he felt about this.

During the first interview, when he was still a *kathoey*, Ake had said that he wanted to maintain his virginity for a special person, much in line with what a good woman would say (see Chapter 6). By the second interview this had radically changed. Ake had had five (sexual) boyfriends in the seven months since the first interview, and he talked about them in great detail, including the size of their penises and the kind of sex they had, and how much he enjoyed it – a strong departure from the good-woman talk. Hence, in terms of his romantic and sexual life, his transformation from *kathoey* to gay paid remarkable dividends in terms of new experiences and pleasures. His attitude towards sex changed dramatically: he no longer cared about creating an impression of himself as innocent, inexperienced and 'virginal' as he had during the first interview, but he had discovered he was actually good at sex and that he enjoyed it, and he talked about his sex life enthusiastically and with a small dose of pride. Ake even admitted that with one of his boyfriends, in a very 'un-queen' way, he had initiated sex when they woke up the morning after a wild night: 'I was the person who started it. I didn't insert him or do anything to him, he did me, I am still a QUEEN [Eng] like before. But I was the party who started to play around.' Rather than things happening to him or being done to him sexually, in accordance with the narrative of the good woman submitting to the urges of her man (in line with the language Ives used to describe his sexual exploits, in Chapter 6), now Ake was active and initiating, even though he hurried to add that 'I am still a queen'.

Ake felt proud that his sex partners had so much pleasure when they were having anal sex with him, and that they would all ejaculate inside his rectum (often without condoms being used): 'So I thought, "Oh! I am so skilled [เก่ง]." It is like a learning process, too [laughs]. Do you understand, older brother Jan? It is fun, to learn about these. things. It is something that – really challenges me.'

Despite his new-found sexual agency, during the second interview Ake still believed that same-sex behaviours and relationships are shaped by the linking of a feminine and a masculine partner, both in terms of social roles and sexual positioning. During the final interview, however, Ake told me that he had fallen in love and briefly dated a fellow 'queen' whom he very much admired. Ake had had sex with this person as the insertive partner, going 180 degrees against his previous sexual worldview in which he saw himself as the woman, and later as the queen, the feminine (read: anally receptive) partner: '[At] that time, I felt like, […] I want to try to date [this fellow queen friend], better, something like that. I can ignore this issue [that he is receptive], I was like, "I can be [insertive] too!"'

Maybe because of the turmoil this caused in his mind, going against his gendered conceptualization of homosexuality, he said he did not particularly enjoy the insertive role in anal sex, even though he did maintain his erection and reached orgasm. He also said that he was aroused to the extent that he wanted to have sex every day with this person, whereas his queen boyfriend – obviously being a 'good woman' – found sex once every two weeks enough. This, plus Ake's stated preference to be bottom rather than top, were the reasons they broke up.

In summary, partly as a result of his fear of the perceived beauty and finesse of *kathoey* in Bangkok, his love for a fellow *kathoey*, but also because of his sexual and romantic experiences with other men since the first interview, Ake changed from a second type of woman into a more and more masculine-looking and acting gay man. Several experiences were instrumental in the changes that occurred. First, there was the sex with a foreigner in a sauna when Ake felt desired for his masculine body. Second, he fell in love with fellow queen friends (twice). Third, there were his sexual experiments in taking the initiative in sex and taking the insertive role in anal intercourse while dating a feminine-oriented man. Finally, it was his move from Phuket to Bangkok that allowed a clean break with his *kathoey* past, allowing a fresh start. His previous gender-based concept of same-sex desire, in which positioning in anal sex occurs in line with each partner's feminine or masculine gender role, gradually became insufficient to account for his sexual experiences, desires and feelings. The bodily pleasures he experienced while having sex with several men drove him along in this process of reconsideration. It is not only ideas, thoughts or knowledge that drive such processes of change. As the Australian sociologist Gary W. Dowsett (2002, 414) has noted, the body cannot be discounted in importance: 'the body teaches, the body inscribes'.

To accommodate his experiences Ake had to move gradually towards an understanding of same-sex romance in which object choice – a fellow male – was the most important consideration. Despite the considerable changes, Ake probably still saw himself basically as feminine, but he had to reinvent his sexuality to accommodate and justify the pleasures he found in having sex, in being pleasured by and in pleasuring men. For Ake, becoming gay meant that he gradually appropriated a new option for living a sexually rewarding life, where feminine (anally receptive) sexual pleasure – even with multiple partners – is not frowned upon, but can be valid and good. Ake had, like other gay queen boys, scores of female friends who were attracted to this alternative world in which morally upright femininity and pleasurable sex lives are not incompatible. Ake was still in a process of change and flux when the final interview was held, and it is likely that his trajectory of change is far from over.

Roj's Story

Roj was Buddhist and was born in an outer district of a rural province in the northeast of Thailand. His father was a teacher at secondary level and his mother was a housewife. He had one older sister. Roj moved from his village to a dormitory to attend high school at the age of 13, visiting his parents only on some weekends. The first three years he was in a dormitory at the school premises; from tenth grade onwards he moved to a dormitory outside the school's supervision. After completing high school, he tried to move to a university in Bangkok, but his grades were not high enough. As a result, he went to a university closer to his home village. One of the reasons he was happy to move there was that many of his old high school friends moved there too. At his new university, Roj joined a group of cheerleaders, as Ake did, and he was busy training and performing with them, which he enjoyed a lot.

Roj knew he was different from other boys since he was very young. He described himself as a *toot* when he was still a child. The Thai word *toot* is a derogative (at worst) or joking (at best) term for *kathoey* or second type of woman, similar to the English term 'fag'. He started changing into a more masculine gay role when he was around 16 or 17 years of age. He was confused and depressed during this period, for instance when he fell in love with a *tom* (masculine-identified lesbian woman) when he was in tenth grade:

Roj: She was a tom. And my feeling changed, like I had to be a *phu chaai*.
       And she had to be a girl. It was not long ago, three or four years ago.
Int: Did you date her?
Roj: It was that period when I was wondering whether I was gay or *toot*.
       I didn't date her but we did chat and we almost were lovers [แฟน].

Roj took a long time to determine whether he was or wanted to be gay (an option he had not known about during his younger years) or to stick to the more feminine *toot* or *kathoey* identity he already had. Not long thereafter, similar to Ake, Roj settled for gay queen as a self-identifying label and stopped using the *toot* label to describe himself. His process of changing from *toot* to gay was gradual and went back and forth. His transformation was spurred along after he fell in love with what he called a 'gay *phu chaai*'. In other words, he fell in love with someone who appreciated Roj as a boy, not as a *toot* or girl. Roj wanted to be loved by this person, which pushed him further along the trajectory from a feminine to a more masculine notion of self. Roj also mentioned his parents in explaining why he embarked on this process of change, saying that it was easier for them to accept a gay son than a *kathoey* daughter.

Similar to Ake, Roj had changed remarkably between the first and the second interviews. He was taller and more muscular and fit, because of his involvement with the cheerleading team. He remarked: 'I don't take care of myself [ไม่ได้ดูแลตัวเอง], I look shabbier than before [ดูโทรมๆ ขึ้น].' 'Not taking care of oneself' is a marker of masculinity; traditionally females take care of their skin, their hair, their appearance and the way they dress, whereas men – at least lower-class men – have a more laissez-faire attitude. Roj seemed much happier than during the first interview; he said cheerleading made his life 'colourful' [มีสีสัน].

At the time of the second interview, Roj was falling in love with a fellow gay queen friend who was in the same cheerleading team. He had not acted on these feelings. Nevertheless, they were a cause of great confusion and anguish:

> It wasn't – at first it was like everything was normal. But why, one day, I started to be suspicious of myself in that – why, [when] there was somebody who came to talk to him, why did I have to feel jealous? [...] Like that, that was the point that made me think. [...] At first, I didn't think anything, but why it was getting more and more each day?

Mimicking male–female relationships, feminine-oriented gay queens are usually a few years younger than their masculine-oriented partners (often called 'gay kings'). The object of Roj's passion was younger than he was. Roj said he did not have sexual fantasies about this younger man. He referred to his feelings as 'real love', apparently in distinction to the 'unreal' love attached to sex.

Apart from the fact that this younger friend was receptive, like Roj himself, he was also part of his circle of friends, which is, as discussed above, a taboo when it comes to dating. Other people in his circle of friends started to notice something was going on, so Roj felt compelled to discuss his feelings with his younger friend, after which Roj decided to terminate their friendship. This did not work out well in practice:

[It] had been like, a very close connection [or: relationship] [ความผูกพันใกล้ชิดกัน], we would go everywhere together, so it looked like I loved him. But it was like, you can say that I was very broken hearted, at that time, I thought I was broken hearted. Because with other persons [whom I loved before], it was not a big deal. 'If you want to go away, go!' But with this person, it was like I didn't intend to love him [ไม่ได้ตั้งใจรัก], you know? It was like it was this connection that occurred. So I – I was very heartbroken [chuckles]. I shaved my head, can you imagine? [โกนหัว คิดดู] I cut my hair short!

Roj's act of cutting his hair short was an act of 'sarcasm', as he called it [ประชด]. He must have done this in emulation of monks, who do this when they are ordained, in their attempts to renounce all worldly pleasures and possessions. Young Thai men also often become ordained as monks and shave their heads when in mourning for the loss of a family member or loved one. His friends understood what was going on and they intervened, telling Roj that it was not good to break off all contact with the younger cheerleader in this abrupt manner. Then Roj and this 'younger brother' decided to 'be normal' towards each other again, in other words, to act like brothers or friends. This worked for a while, until their feelings came back, so they broke up for a second time. It was only after both Roj and this 'younger brother' had each found new boyfriends that they could act normally towards each other again.

When asked why Roj and this 'younger brother' could not be boyfriends, he gave reasons related to the way their direct social environment would have reacted:

It was because we were too close. And it was like, people already knew that we were brothers [in the sense of friends], if like, people would know, what would it be like? But, eh – we were worried that people who saw us [together] would say something, like, 'Do you have to – date each other? It is better to be brothers [or sisters]'. There were many things. I don't know how to say, it is like – it is, I had the feeling that there would be additional obligations [ข้อผูกมัด], I was afraid that I would be, like, not independent [or free], something like that.

The fact that they were 'too close' was a source of discomfort – even though they never had a sexual relationship, they were seen as close as if boyfriends and that was not appropriate considering their status as friends or brothers, a status that was known and accepted by their direct social environment.

During the first interview, Roj had expressed very negative opinions about homosexual men who call themselves 'both'. The term 'both' or 'gay both', derived from English, means that these same-sex-attracted men like to have anal sex in either the insertive or the receptive role. Roj found that such people are 'only interested in sex'. In other words, they do not care how (receptive or insertive), as long as they can have sex:

> Bi[sexuals], they are OK, it doesn't bother me [ไม่อะไรมาก], but [gays who are] 'both', I don't know. Like, they have to insert, then they have to receive – like – I don't know, I don't know what they are [ไหน ต้องมารุกแล้วต้องมารับกันแบบไม่รู้ดิ เป็นอย่างไรไม่รู้]. Just be one thing, better. My feeling is like, those who are insertive, eh I mean those who are 'both', it is like – it is not love. It is like, they are ['both'] because of sex [ที่เขาเป็นเพราะมันเป็นเรื่อง sex].
>
> INT: A-ha.
>
> ROJ: They can insert, they can receive, right? So it is like, hm, the basic factor is sex, hmm, that is it!
>
> INT: A-ha.
>
> ROJ: They are not like, one thing, one type. [ไม่ได้เป็นอย่างใดอย่างหนึ่ง]. For 'BI[sexuals]', it is like, it is okay, his is a *phu chaai*, he is caring [มีความที่จะดูแล], for either men or women, right? Because he is only insertive. He is not like 'both', like that. Hmmm.

This negative opinion is in line with what one would expect of someone adhering to a gender-based concept of homosexuality: people being both receptive and insertive are, in their eyes, both masculine and feminine at the same time, making a mockery of the separation between the genders. For Western people, it could be expected that being bisexual is somehow 'better' than being homosexual, because at least bisexuals can adhere to heteronormative expectations by dating women. But this way of thinking is based on differentiating people with different sexualities based on their object choice. For Roj and many other men, whom one has sex with is not important as long as one sticks to one's gendered sexual role of being either insertive (masculine) or receptive (feminine). It is therefore logical that Roj thought that bisexuals were okay; at least they stick to inserting (anally or vaginally) and 'taking care' (of either men and women), and therefore bisexuals still fit Roj's idea of gendered masculinity (in the role of the *phu chaai*).

This way of thinking, which is widespread, also helps explain why so many 'real men' (especially from northeastern Thailand) work in Thai gay go-go bars and take *kathoey* (or gay) lovers (always casually or temporarily) without apparent psychological discomfort about their gender or their sexuality. They view same-sex behaviour as 'gendered', so they can comfortably view themselves as 'real men', as long as they (are perceived to) stick to the penetrative role in anal sex. In other words, they do not consider sex with other males in and of itself to be an affront to their masculinity as long as they keep sexually behaving in a masculine manner, or at least as long as their direct social environment continues to assume this (De Lind van Wijngaarden 1999).

In contrast, those who call themselves 'gay both' derive their identity from the fact that they have sex with men without expressing a clear preference for inserting or receiving in anal sex and, hence, refuse to choose between a feminine or masculine gender identity. This was disturbing for Roj – as he stated it, because he 'doesn't know what they *are*' – that is, they cannot be placed in a clearly demarcated feminine or masculine category.

During the first interview, Roj was also negative about the phenomenon of more and more *kathoey* becoming gay (i.e. the 'masculinization' of *kathoey*); he also thought this could only be explained by a desire to have (more) sex, which was a bad thing according to Roj's moral views about feminine sexuality:

It is sex, the factor, 80 per cent. Because of what *kathoey* want to become gay? Because *kathoey* cannot find [sex], so they flee [หลีก] to become gay and they get it. This is one [reason]. And, and another thing. So why don't they become a *kathoey* who dresses like a women, like that? But they want to be a *phu chaai*? Do gay like *phu chaai*? So why do they change? They only change so that they like them, for sex. This is the basic factor [ปัจจัยหลัก].

During the final interview, however, Roj had, rather dramatically, changed his mind about those who were 'both'. He said he understood now, from his own experience, that at least some people were or became 'both' not because they are crazy about sex, but 'out of love'. At the time of the final interview, and after breaking up with his younger cheerleader friend, Roj had started dating a fellow 'gay queen' friend. The object of his love was a person who happened to be exclusively receptive in anal intercourse and who was unable to perform anal sex in the insertive role. Hence, Roj said he had to make a 'sacrifice' [เสียสละ] in being insertive for this person – a sacrifice out of love. To his own surprise, Roj was able to make this sacrifice and he did not dislike anal sex in the insertive role, but he said (similar to Ake) that he still considered himself to be basically receptive. Perhaps the meaning of the word receptive as Roj used it broadened from just a sexual behaviour to a statement about his feminine gender identity – or what remained of it. Roj now used the label 'both', the category he was so dismissive of during the first interview, to describe his sexual preference, meaning that he had now become versatile in anal sex.

Similar to Ake, Roj was on his way to shift away from the gender-based model of same-sex attraction towards 'object-based' same-sex attraction, in which love for a fellow male is more important than one's preference for the receptive or insertive role in anal intercourse, and – related to this – a person's femininity or masculinity. In short, the conceptual link between a person's (presumed) sexual behaviour and their heteronormative social gender role was gradually weakening, meaning that the strictly prescribed gender roles were also weakening, as Roj said himself towards the end of the final interview: 'But I think – I mean, in society nowadays, anybody can be anything [เป็นอะไรไปได้หมด]. The issue of sexuality is something that is – varied, VARIETY (Eng) [chuckles].'

Roj indicated that, whereas he found the masculine, feminine and *kathoey* gender identities easy to understand and explain, when it came to defining people based on sexuality and related aspects, the world became a whole lot more complicated to him – it is this messiness that characterizes the encounter between the paradigms of 'four sexualities' and 'three genders', to paraphrase Rosalind Morris (1994). Although Roj did not make such a strong and clean break with his past as Ake did during the interviewing period (Roj had left home at a much earlier age, and still lived near his home province), his switch from secondary school to university also led to changes in the way he saw himself sexually and in terms of his gender. Similar to Ake, falling in love and having sex with like-minded, similar-gendered friends played a crucial role in this process.

Another similarity between Ake and Roj was that both became involved in the university cheerleading team, leading them to strengthen their bodies and to learn to appreciate their own athleticism. It helped them appreciate and foster the beauty of their masculine bodies, and the newly discovered sexual pleasures that followed further strengthened a new sense of masculine-embodied, but same-sex-attracted, self. The huge popularity of cheerleading among high school and young university students in Thailand may partly be explained because of its function as a vehicle for *kathoey* and queen boys to come to terms with the perceived discrepancy of having a masculine body and a feminine disposition. Cheerleading creates a playing field for experimentation, in which there is a balance between athleticism and muscular strength (masculine) and aesthetic beauty and performance (feminine), and in so doing it may function as a bridge between the traditional gender-based and the modern 'gay' sexual paradigms.

Ek's Story

Ek was Buddhist and was born in the southern province of Trang. His grandmother in Phuket raised him since he was six months old because his

parents were unable to look after him at that time. Both his parents had
lower-middle-class jobs in the service sector. After his grandmother died he
moved to live with a younger sister of his father not far from Phuket town.
This aunt worked as an informal moneylender. She had a boyfriend but they
had no children. He mentioned several times that she scolded him again and
again, even though Ek said 'she meant well'. His real parents, meanwhile,
were raising Ek's two younger brothers. Ek, who was a close school friend
of Ake (discussed above), was always a *toot* ('sissy'). He did not participate in
boys' games and activities at school, was neat and tidy, serious and a reason-
ably good student who loved to read. In contrast to Ake, however, he never
dressed as a female or acted as a second type of woman, and he never felt that
he was or should have been a woman. Ek was very sexually inexperienced
at the time of the first interview and, similar to Ake, this changed after he
moved to Bangkok where he, like Ake, started behaving in a more masculine
manner. This coincided with his membership of a new group of exclusively
gay and *kathoey* friends, which he never had in Phuket where his group of
friends was mixed.

At the second interview Ek was in the middle of a remarkable change in
his identity. While he had been a virgin at the first interview (having had oral
sex only once with an older man when he was 13 years old), he had had three
sexual partners in the three months since moving from home, and he had a
few more between the second and the third interviews. He learned a great deal
from these experiences, both about himself and about sex and relationships
in general. Whereas Ek had always been assumed to be a *kathoey* because of
his slightly effeminate demeanour and lack of participation in boys' games,
he said that he had always been afraid of anal sex in the receptive role and
had never fantasized about it. In fact, Ek said that he realized now that he had
always felt that he liked to take care more than to be taken care of. This should
be read as follows: he always felt he was, at least when it came to his romantic
interests and needs, more masculine than feminine, since 'taking care' is seen
as a masculine trait: a man has to take care of his wife and his family ('taking
care' can also mean to protect or to defend):

EK: I felt, it [being insertive] is much better than being receptive. I feel
that I want – I want to be insertive, rather than receptive.
INT: More, right?
EK: Yes, I want to take care [ดูแล], I want to be the side who takes care,
more [อยากเป็นฝ่ายดูแลมากกว่า]. Since I met [his third boyfriend], my ideas
have changed totally, I mean, it is like I discovered myself [ค้นพบตัวเอง].

Whereas his two first boyfriends after moving away from Phuket were insertive,
Ek did not have anal sex with the first and only once with the second, an

experience he seemed hesitant to discuss and did not elaborate on – it was not pleasurable.

Ek's third boyfriend was part of his group of friends, which led to similar problems as described for Roj and Ake, that is, it was not regarded as a good thing to date friends who were supposed to be in the same gender category. Ek and his lover felt compelled to keep their relationship secret:

> [Our friend whose room we were using] had a condom in his room. But there was only one, and – we were afraid that the roommate would know, like – 'Hey! Where did that condom go?' [...] That would be bad, because the roommate is a friend in our group. I mean, the friends in my group, they will be rather ANTI [Eng], if, if it happens that we date each other, my friends would not like it.

Ek talked about how his partner expressed amazement at the contrast between Ek's masculinity in his dating and sexual practices, including during the sex they had, and his effeminate behaviour while he was among friends. Ek explained,

> I like to make my friends have fun with the things I do. So I will like, I will – I will act effeminate, like, to make my friends laugh [chuckles]. But when I – but when I stay with a person who is receptive, I mean – I tried to ask him, 'Do you feel warm, when you hug me?' [uses the masculine pronoun *phom* here] [...]. And he was like, 'Hmm!' [means: yes!]. And he said, 'You are like a different person!' When we were friends, we had to – we were friends, like, eh, we were friends like, like another person, compared with this role [or duty]. But once I fulfilled this role, it was like I was another person, something like that. I guess I did my duty well [คงทำหน้าที่ได้ดี].

Ek found the contradiction between his private explorations of a more masculine identity and his feminine social demeanour and way of acting as a 'fellow sister' in his group of mostly effeminate gay friends awkward. This may partly be because of the blurring of the boundary between his private life and his social life, as he was dating someone from his social circle. Ek also seemed to find the discrepancy between his inner sexual urges and his social performance problematic:

> Eᴋ: It was just this one person, who [penetrated me]. And – so after that, once I had the opportunity to do the role of an insertive [person], like this, I have come to think, it is more 'me' [มันใช่ตัวเรามากกว่า]. But I am

stuck with my behaviour, when I am with friends, like this, I will, like, I will be effeminate [ออกสาว]. I will be like, similar to, eh, not masculine acting [มาดแมน]. That is – it is a problem [laughs]. The group of my friends …

INT: [interrupts] Is it a problem?

EK: It is a problem. I mean, which insertive [gay] will be like, effeminate? [chuckles] It doesn't exist.

In order to bring his private trajectory towards masculinity more in line with his social environment, during the third interview Ek talked about how he had gradually started to present himself differently within his social environment, including online:

EK: There has been change. Eh – I stopped, I stopped – [thinking] I stopped to act in a very sweet way [เลิกทำตัวหวานๆ]. I mean, it is like, for example when I take a picture of myself […], I will not, like, I will not like – not look too sweet. Not sweet. [chuckles]

INT: You will take a picture like, looking masculine?

EK: To make it look, like, there is some masculinity in it [ดูมีความเป็นผู้ชาย], more.

As a further sign of his growing masculinity, Ek referred to another sexual partner he had had during the period after the second interview, as a 'wife' [เมีย]:

EK: When we had something [sex], it was like, it was [non-penetrative sex], but he played the role, like, he looked like receptive.

INT: Oh. He looked like receptive?

EK: Yes. Because he, like, he was the party, like, serving me [ปรนนิบัติ]. […] Like, he was the party who, like, gave pleasure to me. He would give me [pleasure], more, more. Like … His mood was like a wife [อารมณ์แบบ เมีย]. [chuckles]

In line with Ek's attempts to become more masculine, he also had certain characteristics in mind for the type of partner he preferred. His partner should be smaller, shorter and 'weaker' than him: 'I mean, I don't want it to be like – I feel, he shouldn't look much stronger than me, something like that'. Ek said several times that he liked his partners to be a bit effeminate or 'sissy'. However, his attempts at establishing his masculinity in bed had been unsuccessful; he had had pleasure while being fellated, but he had been unable to retain his erection for anal penetration on a number of occasions and this made him unconfident of his sexual prowess. He felt that his taking-care qualities, his masculine looks and his pleasure in being fellated needed to be complemented by the ability to penetrate – which would be the ultimate achievement in solidifying his new masculine status.

There was something else that caused him doubt: although he repeated again and again that he had always known and felt that he disliked being receptive in anal sex, and that he did not feel any desire to try it out, he was still in love with a senior student who was 'insertive'. For this person, he imagined, he would make an exception and be receptive if they happened to get together as boyfriends. When I asked why, Ek responded, 'Because he knew me before I decided to change to be insertive from now on.' Thus, despite his expressed fear of being receptive in anal sex, and despite his attempts to become more masculine, Ek would be open to the idea of experimenting with sexual behaviours that went against his developing sense of masculinity – if the outcome was right. In this case, this could land him a long-desired boyfriend.

Like Ake and Roj, Ek's looks and demeanour had changed markedly between the first and the second interview. He was less timid, still as thoughtful in his speech but more outspoken. He seemed more confident in himself. His hair was longer and dyed light brown, and he was dressed well:

[thinking] Eh, I pay more attention to it than before. I pay attention, I mean, I don't let myself look like – I mean, in the past I was like, I could wear whatever. But once I got into the university, I want myself to look a bit good [ดูดีหน่อยนึง]. Because I am also more mature [chuckles], something like that. And my taste, I – I focus on, I pay more attention to the way I dress.

Ek arrived for the final interview looking even more masculine than during the second interview, wearing very short hair in a military style, and wearing a military T-shirt. In an interesting contrast to Roj and Ake, who linked looking good and taking care of your looks to being feminine, Ek said his more masculine identity led him to take better care of himself than before. He thought it was more important to look good when you are at university. Ek, being in the environment of Bangkok, may have cultivated a different, more middle-class urban form of masculinity, in which taking care of one's appearance is important as a marker of status (see below).

Similar to the stories of Ake and Roj, Ek seemed slowly to gain a different understanding of same-sex relations in which sexual preference for males was more important than gender role. Still, gender remained important for Ek. In his growing sense of being masculine, or perhaps more precisely of not being a *kathoey* or *toot*, he wanted to take care of a partner who had to be feminine in his demeanour and manners, and smaller in terms of body size. Despite this, he had also started to conceptualize a clean break between gender and sexual behaviour:

> [My friends] probably think that I can be whatever I want. Because we are all gays together, something like that. So, it depends. Sometimes people who are very masculine [แมนมากๆ], they could be receptive. And some people who are very effeminate, they can be insertive. They think like this. They do not think like, you have to be like this or like that, if they know.

Migration and Change

Looking at the stories of these three young men, and in line with expectations and the assumptions behind the study design, it can be concluded that the participants who changed most profoundly over the 20 months of the research period were those young men who moved away from home. Weston (1995, 257) described the 'gay sexual imaginary' of the city of San Francisco and the apparent influence this imagery has on the decision of young rurally based lesbians and gay men to migrate to that city. It is clear that cities, in particular Bangkok, have been pivotal in the emergence of modern homosexualities in Thailand. They were places where sufficient numbers of like-minded men concentrated, where bars and other entertainment venues for these men developed, and where a clear division between work, school, family and entertainment emerged, associated with a certain level of anonymity and the juggling of 'two worlds' (Pachun 2008) or 'multiple identities' (Jackson 1997).

This study confirmed that the migratory transition process intensified the young men's personal trajectories of change, propelled by new experiences and the resulting contradictions and confusion. Ake and Ek moved from Phuket to Bangkok (and surroundings) and went through significant changes in the way they understood themselves. Roj moved less far away from his parental home to a regional city nearby, together with many of his high school friends. His trajectory of change had already started much earlier than Ek and Ake. Roj (like Nook and Ud) moved to a secondary school dormitory away from his parental home after the completion of his primary school. Hence, there was less of a change to a more independent lifestyle after completing high school; Roj had, if anything, already done that between the ages of 13 and 15. Nevertheless, the changes in his understanding of himself as a sexual being during the interviewing period were profound, and most changes happened during his senior high school years when he was at a private dormitory by himself and after entering university.

Curran and Saguy (2001), in their study on migration and cultural change, for which much of their data stemmed from Thailand, found that young rural women who migrated to the city for work felt pressured to choose between sets of competing rural and urban ideologies and values about womanhood. Change occurs, they write, when these women became involved in networks related to their migration, bridging rural and urban settings:

> Being involved in these networks creates and reinforces new values that are a compromise of the two initial ideologies. Although initially unsettling in their impact, networks also serve to *settle* the times by enabling such cultural compromise. These changes might normalize [...] new meanings regarding being a man or a woman in Thai society. (2001, 72, emphasis in the original)

This study certainly confirms Curran and Saguy's conclusion that the process of migrating from a parental home environment, be it after high school or at an earlier age, is an important catalyst for changes in people's concepts about gender and their sexual subjectivity, resulting from conflicting sets of ideas.

Unlike Weston's (1995) findings from his study on San Francisco, the city of Bangkok did not amount to much of a 'gay imaginary' for the young men in this study. For Ake, Bangkok seemed to hold power as a '*kathoey* imaginary', the top of a pyramid of power and beauty, but this was expressed in a negative, fearful, competitive way and not in terms of a promise of sexual liberation and freedom in the way described by Carrillo (2004). In addition, the changes that occurred for the young men in this study occurred for those who moved to Bangkok as well as those who moved to smaller, provincial cities. This suggests that the process of moving out of the parental home in and of itself, and the experience of being in a university setting with new friends with whom one shares new experiences and ideas are more important in influencing changes in sexual subjectivity than the size or characteristics of the destination city.

The Masculinity Imperative: The Need to Be '*MAN*'

This chapter has shown that existing ideas about gender and sexuality were put to the test when the young men somehow managed to fall in love with a friend of the same gender category. The feelings and passions that resulted created confusion and doubt and destabilized beliefs, norms and values that were the foundation of a gender-based concept of homosexuality, forcing the young men to come to terms with different ideas about how same-sex love and relationships can be experienced and explained. The process of migrating, as Curran and Saguy (2001) suggested above, was instrumental in helping to 'settle' this clash. It was initially settled by attempts to recreate masculine–feminine differences between them and the object of their love. Ake, Roj and Ek therefore all ended up more normatively masculine in their demeanour and way of acting than they were at the first interview.

Overall, the 23 participants with whom three interviews were completed either stayed more or less the same, or they became more masculine in their demeanour; none of them became more effeminate. Why would this be the case? Oad thought that nowadays gay people value masculinity more and suggested that it was partly related to fashion:

> They want someone who is MAN [Eng]. Masculine. Because of that, it makes that *phu chaai*, they have to be masculine first [ต้องแมนไว้ก่อน], in order to be chosen by another gay person [เพื่อที่จะเป็นตัวเลือก]. [...] It is like, it is like, you have to act masculine, because some *phu chaai* [gays] don't like effeminate [people or behaviours]. This is like – it is a culture which is like, 'forbidden to be effeminate!' Something like that. It makes that they, like, don't show [to others that they are gay] [ไม่ออกตัว]. If you don't know it already, they will not tell you, that they are gay. Some people work in an office, like this, they walk with us, some people are like, 'Eh! Eh! A *phu chaai*!' But you don't know, behind the scenes, who he dates with [...]. Because of that, it is like this, more.

Fluk said it is important to be 'MAN' [แมน], which is a new Thai word taken from English and loosely means 'masculine looking'. However, despite using this term, Fluk had not transcended the idea that there have to be elements of two differing genders to form viable and lasting love relationships, including homosexual relationships:

> [O]ne has to be MAN [Eng: masculine], you have to be both things. You have to be both, both, both the feminine side and the masculine side [ทั้งฝ่ายหญิงและฝ่ายชาย], the side who receives and the side who inserts. You have to be masculine, [couples] must [look] sufficiently masculine together. Masculine, like they won't know if you walk together with them, hey! Who is insertive, who is receptive? [It is important] not to let them know [เออ ให้เขาไม่รู้อ่ะ].

Roj suggested another reason for the masculinization of same-sex-attracted men. He said that Thai men are less and less interested in having sex with *kathoey*, so *kathoey* may have to make themselves attractive for an insertive gay audience rather than to *phu chaai*. The reason why *phu chaai* are less interested in *kathoey* is mainly because of the more relaxed sexual climate for girls and women in modern Thai society, making it easier for young men to date and have sex with unmarried girls and taking away the need to revert to the 'second type of woman' for fulfilment of their sexual needs. Ives (Chapter 9) was an example of a young *kathoey* who was unable to find a partner, but did succeed once he had changed to a more masculine incarnation of himself.

The stories of the former *kathoey* participants in the study suggest rather pragmatic and down-to-earth reasons for becoming more masculine. It was seen as beneficial for their chances of finding a good job or, in Ake's case, he feared competition with presumably more beautiful *kathoey* in Bangkok. Because of images of hyper-femininity projected in soap operas, films and the media in general, it appears that nowadays only the most beautiful *kathoey* still have a chance to woo a *phu chaai* boyfriend. As Ives will note in the next chapter, beauty can come at a considerable price for a *kathoey*, depending on how large, hairy and masculine the body that she starts out with is.

Fluk saw the process of both partners becoming more MAN as one of blending femininity and masculinity. In the light of the rise of the urban male 'metrosexual' this is an interesting interpretation. The term metrosexual emerged in 1994 to describe a softer form of heterosexual masculinity characterized by much attention to looks, fashion and cosmetics, by a drive for shopping and consumption, and possibly by the ability to communicate well and express emotions:

> The typical metrosexual is a young man with money to spend, living in or within easy reach of a metropolis – because that's where all the best shops, clubs, gyms and hairdressers are. He might be officially gay, straight or bisexual, but this is utterly immaterial because he has clearly taken himself as his own love object and pleasure as his sexual preference. (Simpson 2002, para. 7)

Fluk said it is important not to let outsiders know who is insertive or receptive, meaning that gender roles become blurred. Fluk also suggested that it does not matter anymore what happens in the bedroom. It is like playing a game that deliberately confuses one's audience, taking pleasure in creating a smokescreen. Fluk indicated that it is almost a competition among like-minded friends to look more masculine than the other, enhancing one's desirability in the eyes of potential partners.

Fluk alluded to an interesting fact, which is that a masculinizing *kathoey* or masculinizing gay man will fit into this new, softer, consumer-oriented middle-class form of urban masculinity much easier than the traditional, rougher, less fashionable and less narcissistic, lower-class form of masculinity. In order to become more masculine, you no longer need to become tough and aggressive,

start ignoring your hair, or begin practising Thai boxing. Embarking on a process of becoming more masculine has become easier and more attractive than
it might have been in the past, as this new masculinity is in certain ways more
feminine, and adopting it can be gradual, flexible and reversible in certain
circumstances.

Showing the extent to which sexuality is determined by social role and
how it is subsumed under gender performance in the eyes of many of the
participants, Fluk said that if a previously effeminate person performs a masculine role well, his sexual behaviour may follow suit and he may become
insertive:

> [M]aybe like – ah, I go to stay in a close group [หมู่], a group of gays who
> are receptive. So, I am receptive too. I have to act as masculine as pos-
> sible [*aeb man*] [แอ๊บแมนให้มากที่สุด], to make them think that I can also insert,
> or maybe let them think that I am a receptive who is MAN [Eng].
> And, those people who are receptive, some people maybe can turn into
> being insertive [ผันตัวเป็นรุก], too.

Another development is the relatively new erotic aesthetic that has swept urban
gay centres around the world, an aesthetic that glorifies and admires masculine bodies and images, even for 'bottoms'. This gym fashion prescribes that
urban men have to look strong, muscled or beefy, sometimes even unshaven
and rough, or otherwise lean and toned. The huge popularity of fitness centres
among gay men, many if not most of whom are receptive/queens, may reflect
its role as a vehicle for masculinization, at least for those who can afford it.

Peter A. Jackson (2009a) has linked these influences to Westernization
and to the ascent of capitalism, but he noted that this does not mean that
local or existing forms of identity and eroticism are being swept away and
simply replaced by these new influences. Rather, Jackson suggests, this trend
'produces hybridizations in which local agency is as important as subordin-
ation to foreign influences' (2009a, 386). The American anthropologist Megan
Sinnott (2012) found a similar hybridization of gender and sexual roles in
her research on same-sex-attracted females in Bangkok. She found a strong
influence of Korean popular culture in this process; Dredge Kang (2011)
found a similar influence on Bangkok middle-class gay men. Sinnott (2012)
described the influence of Korean popular culture and its 'soft masculinity' on
masculine-identified lesbian women in Bangkok: it confused and ultimately
weakened the gender-based notions of sexuality that these women grew up
with, resulting in more homogeneity in the way same-sex-attracted females
look and act. Although Sinnott sees 'the appropriation of explicitly sexualised
terms of identity' (2012, 456) as an important shift in the way the women

express and live their sexuality, she found that in the way her informants talked and made sense of their relationships, the gender binary between masculine-identified *toms* and feminine *dees* remained intact.

Ake is an example of the continued importance of gender in how the young men made sense of their romances. Despite his remarkable masculin-ization, which rendered him very similar in looks and behaviour to the men he was dating, he expressed a continued need for there to be some form of gendered difference between him and his partners. Although he could accept particular feminine traits in his partners, overall he wanted his boyfriend to be more masculine than he is:

> [laughs] [...] It is one of the deciding factors. If like, if he is like, does his eyebrows, like, shaves them very much like a girl, if he wears [col-oured] contact lenses, like this, I don't like that. If he wears contact lenses like – he wears foundation [make-up] powder of the wrong colour, like this – older brother Jan, it ... [...] Because [my boyfriend] has to meet my friends, and I don't want my friends to say anything negative, like, like this. Basically they like to make fun of me, so I don't want more of that [continues to speak while laughing]. No! I just ask, don't be too girly, something like that. I don't really like that. Because I think I am girly already, right, so if I have a boyfriend I have to find something who looks like, who can protect me [ปกป้องเราได้] [...]. Hmmm.

Ake's comments reveal that the processes of masculinization discussed here may be partly cosmetic and related to looks, fashion, aesthetics and the higher social acceptability of heteronormative masculinity for same-sex-attracted men, linked to urbanization and the need to fit in. Yet, gender goes deeper than clothes and behaviours: Ake still desired to be treated, in many respects, as a woman, despite the remarkable masculinization in his demeanour and way of acting.

Conclusion

For the young men discussed in this chapter, as well as for others in the study, the link between actual, preferred or supposed sexual behaviour and mas-culinity and femininity as gender categories gradually eroded the more they became involved in dating and sex. Moving away from home, coming under the influence of new ideas and trends, and falling in love with friends led to experiences that went against the gender-based concepts for understanding and interpreting same-sex sexuality with which the participants grew up.

This chapter has shown that, apart from pragmatic reasons for acting and behaving in a more masculine way (related to social acceptability on behalf of employers and parents, discussed in Chapter 7), there are also erotic and romantic reasons to present oneself as more masculine in modern urban Thailand. New forms of (heterosexual) masculinity are emerging in the cities that link to the increased importance of consumption as a marker of social status, to the increased importance of a man (regardless of his sexuality) looking good, and to the desire to be seen as modern. It might well be that, in acquiring and appropriating this new modern metrosexuality and the softer and more fashion-aware expressions of masculinity this entails, some of the young men in this study have a comparative advantage over their heterosexual male peers because of their pre-existing knowledge of fashion and cosmetics as well as their familiarity with and skills in taking care of their appearance.

When these new aesthetic, modern, consumption-related expressions of masculinity are superimposed on pre-existing gender-based concepts of homosexuality, not only does confusion result but opportunities also arise for creative exploration of new possibilities of gendered self-performance. Roj, Ake and Ek all initially struggled to explain some of the sexual experiences they had: the gender-based explanations for homosexual experience they already held could no longer fully explain the complexity of their romantic lives. They had to find new symbols and meanings to explain these experiences. Eventually, they succeeded in appropriating new concepts to define, understand and express ideas about same-sex love and romance.

Despite the emergence of these new forms and new ideas about same-sex love and romance, gender remained important as an explanatory framework for some participants in this study. Gender concepts continued to be used to create differences between themselves and their prospective boyfriends in terms of appearance as well as to define social and sexual roles and expectations within their romantic relationships. Most participants also continued to use membership of the same gender as the basis of forming friendships.

The processes of masculinization described in this chapter are indicative of a conceptual clash (and gradual merger) between a 'gay' sexual paradigm tied to modernity, progress, consumption and urbanity and a gender-based *kathoey/phu chaai* paradigm of homosexuality linked, in the minds of most participants, to backwardness and tradition. This desirability of being and acting masculine and the perceived need to hide one's femininity are signs of this clash. The emergence of metrosexuality, propagating a new, softer, more effeminate type of masculinity, may be a result as well as a cause of some of these processes. The urban setting, with conflicting messages about what is masculine and what is not, is a fruitful playground to explore new senses of self and to determine which elements of which form of masculinity are suitable and which are not. Importantly, whatever masculine identity results, in line with Thai sexual culture it remains situational and multifaceted. People generally perform a different masculinity when in the company of friends than when in the company of lovers, as Ek indicated, and yet another, likely more traditional, masculinity may be performed in the setting of one's parental family, back in the rural home.

Urban *kathoey* do their utmost to fulfil (or sometimes even surpass) heteronormative standards for feminine demeanour and beauty. Globalization, scientific progress and capitalism create opportunities for increasingly sophisticated hormone treatments and sex-change operations. At the same time, urban gay men increasingly adhere to and set standards for masculine beauty, fashion and style, both for themselves and for heterosexual men. The feminization of a subgroup of middle-class and relatively wealthy *kathoey*, the masculinization of other *kathoey* and previously effeminate homosexual men, the emergence of metrosexuality and the 'gym craze' in urban areas all combine to blur the traditional boundaries between the feminine and masculine gender domains, creating opportunities to borrow from both and to create and re-create new gendered expressions. While there is no evidence that these processes should be interpreted as 'queering' in the sense of a protest against and a deliberate subversion of sexual and gender identity norms (Blackwood and Johnson 2012), it is clear that the conceptual links between same-sex romance, gender and presumed sexual role appear to have changed dramatically in recent decades.

The reduced importance of gendered complementarity between femininity and masculinity within homosexual relationships also helps explain why most of the participants felt pessimistic about their romantic prospects and the possibility of maintaining a long-term relationship, which was discussed in Chapter 4. Because of the liberation of female Thai sexuality in recent decades, these young men felt fearful of a scenario in which both partners start to behave according to Thai masculine stereotypes, that is, sexually promiscuous, pleasure seeking, living day-by-day and unwilling to commit to a long-term partner. An alternative outcome could be that the reduced importance of complementarity between femininity and masculinity will pave the way for new and more durable relationship forms among same-sex-attracted men in the future resulting from the erosion of the 'traditional' masculine stereotype that is at the basis of their current instability – but the young men in this study seemed unable to imagine this.

This chapter has shown that, while notions of gender and Buddhism may explain the initial sexual worldview of young same-sex-attracted men in rural Thailand, as described in Chapters 4 and 5, it was through their actual dating and sexual practices and experiences that their sexual subjectivity gradually developed and changed. This process involved coming to terms with contradictions between thoughts and actions, between theory and practice, between ideals and realities, as well as contradictions within and between the cultural domains of Thai femininity and masculinity and influences from abroad.

Chapter 9

THE ROLE OF THE INTERNET IN LEARNING ABOUT AND EXPERIMENTING WITH NEW SEXUAL IDENTITIES

Introduction

This chapter will examine the way in which the Internet initially helped young same-sex-attracted men make sense of their sexual subjectivity, but also how it ended up helping to undermine some of the Buddhist- and gender-derived ideas about homosexuality discussed in Chapters 4 and 5.

Of the 25 participants 9 met their first sexual partner via the Internet, and four of these participants travelled from their home to see a boyfriend who lived in another province or district after meeting online, usually during their school holidays. In contrast to many of the feminine-oriented young men who had their first sexual affairs in the real world, with 'real' *phu chaai*, none of the first-time partners encountered via the Internet was described by the participants as *phu chaai*. This is indicative of how important the Internet is in the post-gender-based homosexuality era, especially because in the real world, because of their heteronormative demeanour, masculine-identified gay men are much harder to identify as potential mates or boyfriends than feminine-identified *kathoey* or gay queens. Therefore, the Internet is of particular importance as a mechanism for finding dates or potential boyfriends for same-sex-attracted men who do not wish to dress, act or behave in an effeminate manner.

Anonymity, Freedom and Time Lapses: The Benefits of Cyber-Dating

According to Ross (2005, 343), the Internet is a sphere where 'simulation of sex and sexual barter occur with minimal control and regulation'. Ross notes that gender, sexual and other categories that are used online can change at any time and are neither fixed nor can be controlled the same way they are in offline society. Ross observes that the Internet allows people to establish a 'surrogate body' to experiment with and to be experimented on, for example, by presenting oneself in a chat room as younger, taller or thinner than one really is, or even by representing oneself by means of a picture of someone else.

The British sociologist Anthony Giddens (1992, 46) has described how the modern notion of romantic love and intimacy is dependent on 'the process of creation of a mutual narrative biography' between two lovers. Ross notes that the Internet is precisely suited for this, as narratives are literally created on-screen, in the form of chats:

> The internet provides a missing link between fantasies, desires for intimacy, the traditional role of text in expressing these, and sexuality, and in addition provides the appropriate degree of distance, temporal and physical, to allow the combination to optimally respond to the desires and the fantasies of the partners. (Ross 2005, 344)

In the context of Thailand, with its careful consideration of comportment (*kala-thetsa*) and face (*naa*) and maintaining mutual prestige (*barami*) in real-life social conduct (discussed in Chapter 3), the Internet is a social space without agreed moral or social rules for communication. The occurrence, while chatting, of time lags between the typed communications of the chatters is important for many users, as Ross (2005, 344) explains, 'The semi-spontaneity associated with a sufficient time-lag to allow more careful construction and editing may be close to ideal for many users.'

Ake, Mint and Win confirmed how much easier it is to express one's feelings for a person while typing and chatting. They mentioned that it is easier to express feelings of love online than when speaking to people face to face, where there can be embarrassment when expressing feelings of love. As Ake explained,

> I think, typing, you will use words like – you can communicate feelings better while typing than while speaking. [...] I mean, when people type something, I observe, na, they will type like – their typing can say more [การพิมพ์ มันจะบอกได้เยอะกว่า], it will be more 'rotten' [เน่ากว่า] [Thai slang, meaning 'overly sweet']. It will be like this, more. I mean, when we meet each other in reality, we will probably be not as overly sweet [หวานจนเน่า] like when we were typing, for me. [...] Mostly, when we are chatting, suppose we are boyfriends and we are talking to our faces, he probably won't use such sweet words with me, but if suppose he is typing, he will [sighs] use sweet words with me, like this, it is something that is easier to say.

Ake suggested that in cyberspace the structured and polished ways Thai people communicate face to face are no longer in play. This gives online communications a sense of freedom that does not exist in the 'real world':

> In the online world it is like, you can say [type] anything freely [ได้ไม่ขึ้ง]. Oy! Older brother Jan, it will be like, my hands are going [automatically], my mouth will smile, it is something that is – but if we meet each other, then there will be the symptom of shyness, there will be something like this.

The Internet can therefore be particularly important for young men who are exploring their sexuality and who are still insecure about how to position themselves, as it can function, initially at least, as an 'intermediate step between private fantasy and actual behaviour' (Ross 2005, 344). What Ross calls 'a gap between thinking, doing, and being' is created because, unlike real-time and real-life communication, Internet-based communication provides the possibility of taking time out between the different lines of the script of communication in order to consider and compose a careful response. Ross suggests the space that the Internet provides was previously unavailable: in the cyber-age a person can *type* without *doing*, or *do* without *being*. It can be both a fantasy, taken to the point of acting it through with another person, or a behaviour that, through being virtual, is not actually done, and thus the person does not have to face the dissonance or (self-)stigma of actually being or having a 'spoiled identity' (Goffmann 1963, quoted in Ross 2005). This creates a new form of freedom and a new space for experimentation. The Internet can also be a special social experience, a way to sample or watch without being seen, for instance, going into a gay chatroom as a so-called lurker (Ross 2005), an act in which one belongs and does not belong at the same time.

Finding Like-Minded People

For young same-sex-attracted men in rural areas, it can be difficult to find like-minded people as friends or to approach men as (potential) sex partners, especially for those who are not open about their sexuality. The internet can be a solution. Nook explained that it is safer to approach people online than in the real world, because one can avoid the embarrassment of approaching somebody in real life who then appears to be uninterested:

> If I am chatting in Face[book], our status already indicates that I am [gay]. And in my status, I have put it up there too, that I am interested in

phu chaai. I know – he knows that I am like this, and I know that he is like this. It looks – I think, this is another thing which is good.

Gop mentioned that it is easier and less embarrassing to find out if someone is gay or not while browsing the Internet:

I think [I meet people] via the Internet more. Because if I walk around and I meet someone, I don't dare to talk to him. Right? Like just chatting with him and then going with him, that is unlikely, right? But, if I chat [online] [แช็ก] we can make an appointment, something like that.

Hong, from a small rural village in northeastern Thailand, visited Internet cafes looking for life stories of gay men, looking for recognition of his own life situation:

Mostly I would go and look at, like, people who, before they were gay [...]. Mostly I would look for, like, some people were a *phu chaai* before – I mean, I liked to read about the stories of other people, to see if it was the same as mine.

Such online endeavours can help young men get to know, understand, define and practise the use of certain terminology and identity labels. Win noted that the information he received via the Internet was sometimes quite confusing, as people seemed to contradict each other, for instance, when he tried to find out what the sexual identity category 'gay bi' meant, which he had read about. This taught him that labels for identity categories are not necessarily static or universally understood in the same way. Win and Pong both looked for online gay friends to chat with, and they talked with them about what the different terms for gay meant and how these terms worked.

Ed, after developing his very first crush on a male classmate, went online to find out if there was something wrong with him:

First I thought, am I stranger than [แปลกกว่า] others? Like, why am I like this? Because, I didn't know there were others like me. So after I read on the Internet, eh, I am not the only one who is like this, others are also [gay], so it is the same! Hmm! So it is not strange.

Win indicated that the Internet may be especially important for those who are living in more isolated situations, like him:

When I was at school I never thought about having a *faen* [แฟน, meaning either 'boyfriend' or 'girlfriend']. But once I was looking on the Internet, like on the net where gay friends are looking for each other, and I started chatting and dating them.

Online, it is much easier to find out if somebody is gay by looking at their status or profile. Often it is also possible to learn what type of gay somebody is, that is, preferring the insertive role or the receptive role in anal intercourse, or both. In Thai society there is strong cultural importance attached to determining one's social position vis-à-vis the other so that communication can be conducted in line with hierarchical rules regulated by principles of *kalathetsa* (in terms of age, gender and class, in that order of importance). Internet profiles are ideal for this, as one can skip over the awkward phase of getting to know each other to determine whether there is mutual interest in continuing communication. It can also help to determine the appropriate pronouns and particles that should be used in communication, for example, whether the pronoun 'older brother' or 'younger brother' should be used or the feminine politeness particle *kha* or the masculine particle *khrab*.

Trying Out Different Versions of Oneself

The Internet also invites role-playing, to try out different versions or presentations of oneself, and is therefore important to facilitate the trial-and-error process of gradual masculinization discussed in Chapter 8. Online, one can change the way one presents oneself to the world merely by logging into a chatroom or website as a new user, or by editing one's profile or changing one's profile pictures – something several of the participants in this study did regularly. Nook would sometimes enter a chatroom using a picture of a handsome young man he found on the Internet, and while hiding behind that person's face he would 'seduce' the person he was chatting with into showing him his penis. Doing this would be unthinkable in the offline world. It indicates how the Internet has generated new forms of conduct and new forms of morality. Nook defended his actions by pointing out that nobody can be trusted online: 'I am tricky [ขี้โกง], they have to know anyway, Internet, the extent to which you can believe [anybody]. They allow themselves to be stupid [ยอมไง], so they have to stay stupid [laughs].' Asked if he really thought they were 'stupid', Nook suggested it was more of a game, a form of role-play on both sides, in which each had their own agenda of seduction: 'No. They take [their clothes] off because they desire me [หลง] [chuckles]. I am cleverer [than they are], so I can deceive them. "What were you thinking?" I deceive them!'

Visually and virtually, the Internet can also provide an opportunity to exaggerate the masculine aspects of one's appearance, by picking particular pictures and poses and leaving others out. Ake and Ek (both discussed in Chapter 8) made optimal use of the Internet in their process of masculinization, and so did Ives (discussed in Chapter 10). For example, it is possible to choose one's gender in one's Facebook profile, and many feminine-identified, same-sex-attracted men list their gender as 'female'. In terms of language use, the Thai language's unique ability to distinguish the speaker as either masculine or feminine by the use of personal pronouns and the politeness particles *khrab* (for males) and *kha* (for females) provides another signifier and a way to play with one's desired gender. Effeminate traits (e.g. talking, walking or gesturing in a typically effeminate way) can be hidden online, and can be made invisible when preparing a Facebook (or other) Internet profile. Ake was aware of the discrepancy between his Facebook profile, with the very masculine-looking pictures he featured there, and his demeanour in the real world, where people usually easily see and understand that he is more effeminate:

> If in the real world, I will show myself [as effeminate] [แสดงตัว] more than in the ONLINE [Eng] world. Right? In the real world, I show myself as a receptive [person]. But in the ONLINE [Eng] world, I can modify [ดัดแปลง], I can do anything. I can emphasize [เน้น] my profile. We can do anything.

Keeping Options Open: The Power of Being 'Both'

The participants in this study indicated that, when online, effeminate gay men present themselves as more masculine than they are in the real world. Apart from masculine-looking pictures of themselves that they choose to post on Facebook and other social media, Fluk explained that they do this by not calling themselves 'receptive', but by using the term 'both' to indicate their sexual preference. As was briefly discussed in Chapter 8, 'both' is a word taken from English and has been given the meaning that one can (or imagine one could) be receptive as well as insertive in anal intercourse. Ake talked about an instance when he was chatting with a person whom he really liked, and who then revealed that he was receptive. Ake then told this person that he was 'both', even though Ake had at that time never been insertive in anal sex in his life. When Oad was online he also called himself 'both', although he had been mostly receptive throughout his sexual career. Being 'both' has the benefit that one's potential market for sexual partners is larger, as Oad explains: 'So people who are "both", they [can find boyfriends easier]. Because this time, this era, they don't like to, like, SET [Eng] [means: fix, stick to one role], they like to take turns [สลับกัน], like this.'

He commented that the label 'both' is increasingly popular. This suggests that it is more desirable for the inserting person to have sex with a masculine-looking and acting person than with a feminine-acting person: 'A lot, yes.

Because people who are "both", they are like – insertive gays [รุก] like to date with people who are "both" '.

Fluk, however, had his doubts about whether people who said they were 'both' could live up to the expectations. He said most of them were lying about their presumed masculinity:

> Most of them. Not most of them; it is exactly everybody [เป็นทุกคนเลย]. Ah, suppose there are 30 people that I talk to, I ask 30 people via the Internet what type they are, they say 'both', all 30 of them! [But] about 28 will be [in reality be] receptive!

Fluk suggested that persons describing themselves as 'both' often have a preference to be receptive, but they use the term 'both' to ensure that their chat partner will not immediately be turned off and reject them: 'Sometimes if it happens that the person who comes to talk to me is receptive too, then he will not chat with me anymore.' He explained later during the interview:

> It is like, people who are not confident in themselves that, if they say they are receptive, they may be rejected. Maybe we are both receptive, like, receptive meets with receptive: 'What type are you?' [แบบไหน] 'I am "both" '. And then, they can start talking. But once you ask, 'What are you like?' 'I am receptive'. 'Oh, I am also receptive – I won't talk any further! Bye!'

Saying that you are receptive may also give the impression that you are effeminate in your demeanour, something Fluk suggested should be avoided these days:

> Or maybe, [they think] this guy says he is receptive, will he be effeminate? [ออกสาว] 'Probably he is effeminate for sure'. Something like that. 'Maybe he is a *toot* or a *kathoey* or a sissy [ตุ๊ด กะเทย แต๋ว], and he will deceive me by saying he is [masculine looking and] receptive [แล้วเอามาอ้างว่าเป็นรับนะ]'. So my friends, they will refer to themselves as 'both', all of them.

The fear of being seen as effeminate and therefore undesirable ensures that the receptive person presenting himself as 'both' maintains his stated preference, even if the person with whom he is chatting has already indicated that he is insertive, making a potential match. Even if the partner is exclusively insertive, it is considered more desirable to have sex with someone who is 'both' than with someone who is receptive. Using 'both' to describe oneself rather than choosing *ruk* (insertive, with masculine connotations) or *rab* (receptive, with feminine connotations) is, at face value, a strategy to become acquainted with each other at a safe distance, to play one's cards close to one's chest, so that the newly established contact can evolve in many possible ways. Is the chat moving towards a potential friendship (for those who consider themselves sexually incompatible); is it moving towards a possible sexual encounter or even towards a longer-term romantic relationship? But choosing 'both' is also a sign of the increasing value attached to a masculine demeanour. It is as if the more masculine one is, looks or behaves, the more value one has in the sexual marketplace.

The introduction and use of the word 'both' is an important departure point from the gender-based ideas about homosexuality many of the young men in this study grew up with, where gender roles were seen as fixed and sexual behaviour (insertive or receptive) was closely linked to being either masculine or effeminate. The weakening divisions between the feminine and masculine domains could be facilitated by the ascent of metrosexuality, a softer, more cultivated and feminine form of masculinity discussed in Chapter 8. Being and acting masculine or 'gay' rather than acting in a strongly effeminate manner may therefore increasingly be perceived as a sign of being urban, progressive and modern, and therefore more valuable and desirable.

Not everybody is happy with the introduction and recent popularity of the term 'both'. Much like Roj, in Chapter 8, Nook disliked the ambiguity of the word 'both':

> Maybe [if someone is 'both'] we can only be friends. Because I don't like people who change from this to that all the time [เปลี่ยนพลิกกลับไปกลับมา]. Really. If I suppose you are KING [Eng, meaning 'anally insertive'], you should be KING continually. I mean, if about love, if I will get a partner, I want that person to really be gay. Not someone who changed from *kathoey* into gay. I don't like that. I don't want it. He has to really be gay, I mean, a *phu chaai* who, like, who likes *phu chaai* who are like me. I mean, they have to be able to accept it, they shouldn't tell me like: 'Behave a bit more masculine, please! [ทำตัวแมนๆหน่อยซิ] You have to change into a new person, don't you show effeminacy and girliness' [เธอต้องเปลี่ยนตัวใหม่ เธออย่ามาแตกสาวตุ้งติ้ง]. I don't want that.

Nook showed some conceptual confusion in his use of 'gay', '*kathoey*' and *phu chaai* in the above quotation. Nook wanted a partner who was 'really gay', by which he meant a person who was not receptive in anal intercourse and who was not inclined to adhere to feminine mannerisms or demeanour: in fact, Nook wanted a *phu chaai*, someone who is MAN (masculine). Nook's choice of the word 'real gay' is interesting here, as he seemed to perceive the word 'real gay' as similar or equal to the term *phu chaai*, implying that there were also 'fake gays' who were in fact feminine entities like Nook himself. Indeed, that is exactly what Nook perceived the word 'both' to be about. The reason for his distaste for such men would be that when such a man acts in a masculine way, from Nook's perspective that man is lying:

> I don't like it [if he is effeminate]. I mean, that is like me, already. Something like that. I mean, he lies. But if suppose he can accept me, then it is another issue. Yes. There is a set of things to consider [ดูหลายๆอย่าง ประกอบกัน]. But it is not that I will always choose [a person like that]. I just – just want somebody who understands me, that is enough.

Nook preferred it if people stayed with just one role, insertive or receptive. He introduced himself online as receptive and he said he would immediately stop talking to people who said they were 'both' because, similar to Fluk, Nook thought that many people who labelled themselves as 'both' had been *kathoey* in an earlier period of their life, just like Nook himself. This indicates how deeply ingrained Nook's feminine gender identity was. Even though he now no longer dressed as a female and had adopted masculine dress, speech and demeanour, Nook continued to see himself as a feminine entity and he wanted a 'real' man as his partner. The idea of having sex with someone who was, in Nook's mind, in reality a fellow woman abhorred him. The term 'both' was for Nook a symbol of a new and scary ambiguity, in which the boundaries between the masculine and the feminine have become blurred. Nook also rejected the pressure to act more masculine than he felt he really was. Hence, not everybody tends to masculinize when they are online. Fluk explained that for receptive people who were very good looking it would not matter if they said or admitted that they were receptive, because they were in demand anyway.

The masculinization of same-sex romance is not limited only to receptive people appropriating the word 'both' to make themselves look more desirable. Fluk explained that he was one of a small group of people who are really 'both', that is, he really had sexual experience with and could derive pleasure from both the insertive and the receptive role in anal sex. Even so, Fluk sometimes picked just one of the two gendered roles, insertive or receptive, when he was chatting with an interesting prospect for sex or romance:

> And if one person has said he is receptive already, and I say 'Oh! He is so handsome! Even though he is receptive!' I can do both, you know. So if he asks me, I will say: 'Oh, I am insertive.'

So, according to Fluk, a person who really is 'both' will sometimes say he is strictly insertive when communicating with a person who is a declared bottom, hence presenting himself as more masculine and more desirable. A person who is receptive will present himself as 'both', also making himself more masculine and hence more desirable.

The shift from receptive to 'both' (and from 'both' to insertive) may not be only linked to the increased desirability of a superficially more masculine performance in terms of dress, fashion or demeanour. There probably are underlying forces at work – forces that are changing the gender division of insertives and receptives towards a concept of gay in which anything goes, sexually, and where sex object choice (a man rather than a woman) becomes the defining principle for same-sex romance, rather than gender performances as discussed in the previous chapters. On the Internet, sexual attraction for the same gender is becoming the most important criterion to approach or date somebody, whereas one's feminine or masculine gender orientation (which in this case means 'being receptive' or 'being insertive') is becoming less an issue as long as one looks and acts in a masculine way. This is similar to Sinnott's (2012) findings among a group of Bangkok-based young same-sex-attracted females.

As briefly discussed in Chapter 8, Fluk also mentioned the social aspect of boyfriend relationships, in that he would feel embarrassed taking a partner to meet his friends if this partner was effeminate in his demeanour or appearance. This may point to something else: that adhering to a feminine–masculine model of same-sex relationships is increasingly being seen as outdated (*ban nok*), whereas couples with two masculine-identified men may be conceived as modern, urban and advanced.

The variety of viewpoints on the concept of 'both' found among the participants in this study is an indication of the confusion and anxiety that arises from the destabilization of gender-based homosexuality. The young men in this study dealt with this confusion differently, based on personal experiences and viewpoints.

'Both-*ruk*' and '*Bai-ruk*': Reinstating Gender in Identity Labels

Along with the conceptual clash between gender-based and post-gender-based understandings of homosexuality that is described in this book, new words are being coined or creatively combined in hybrids to describe the diversity of meanings that are emerging. Fluk presented an example of this. He used a recently coined term to describe himself: 'both-insertive', or in Thai, 'both-*ruk*'. This term makes use of the new word 'both', which seemed designed to transcend the gendered terms insertive (masculine) and receptive (feminine), but is followed by '*ruk*' (insertive), one of the very gendered terms the word 'both' purports to reject or transcend. Asked what the word stood for, Fluk said, 'Both-*ruk* means they have a propensity [ถนัด] to insert, but they can receive too, still they are more inclined to insert.' The term 'both-*ruk*' may have emerged to distinguish those who are girly 'would-be-both' from the masculine-looking and acting 'real both'. As a result, a gender distinction is reinstated among those who are 'both', and people again express a gendered preference for what they eventually might want to do in bed.

Oad noted that some men who like to be insertive have now started calling themselves something even more masculine sounding than 'both-*ruk*': *bai-ruk*, which means 'bi-insertive':

OAD: People who are insertive, they like to say that they are bi-insertive [*bai-ruk*], something like that. [...] I mean, I mean, they may have been a *phu chaai* in the past, with a girlfriend [...].

INT: This they call bi-insertive [*bai-ruk*], right?

OAD: Yes. Yes.

INT: So they have become gay recently?

OAD: Maybe they have been for a long time, but they use the word 'bi-insertive'. Some people are insertive, and they are very MAN [Eng, meaning 'masculine'] [แมนๆ]! They are very masculine, they don't allow anybody to enter their back [anus], like this. Yes.

With the term *bai-ruk*, the preference for insertive anal sex is enhanced by the qualification that one can have (or has had) sex with a woman, increasing one's masculinity and therefore one's desirability. By avoiding the word 'both' the word *bai-ruk* also indicates that such men are absolutely not engaging in receptive anal sex, another marker of their masculinity.

As a result of the trend to present oneself in the most masculine way possible while operating in the more public settings of the Internet (e.g. on Facebook) or while going out to meet a date, some of the participants mentioned that they acted effeminate only within their group of like-minded friends. As Gop explained: 'Many people ask me whether I am effeminate. I said, "Am I effeminate?" Mostly I am not quite effeminate. I am effeminate only in the words [I use] when I speak with my friends.'

Quan, even though he preferred the insertive role in sex and generally acted as a masculine person, mentioned a similar pattern of behaviour: '[When I am with friends,] my femininity breaks out [แตกสาว] [laughs]. I am not afraid, when I work, I am myself [เป็นตัวของตัวเอง], it is the best. I don't see why I should act masculine [แอ๊บมองแอ๊บแมน], I speak out.' Quan said that his friends knew that he was insertive, but they did not find it problematic or strange that he sometimes acted in an effeminate manner, and in contrast to Ek (discussed in Chapter 8), Quan did not see it as problematic either:

> [It is] not strange. It is not that I, like, am totally effeminate, like, dressing as a woman. Eh, eh, I am like this. I dress like this. I don't consider it too effeminate. I think the way I speak, we all know, what you are like. So we tease each other for fun, sometimes.

The banishing of feminine demeanour to the intimate sphere of friends re-establishes, in a way, the division of the outside masculine domain (which is now taking the form of the Internet) and the feminine home domain (the 'real' world of close friends), as described by Mulder (2000) (discussed in Chapters 3 and 5).

The gradual process of inscribing non-gender-stratified homosexuality on pre-existing gender-based understandings of homosexuality should be understood, to return to Van Esterik's metaphor introduced earlier, as a palimpsest. This process creates a force for change in both paradigms and leads to hybrid concepts and new, often conflicting meanings. Previous meanings can also make a comeback, as is the case with the re-inscription of gender labels on the word 'both'. The Internet seems extraordinarily well suited for this process, as expressions of identity can be tried out in different settings online and can easily be forgotten or altered on another occasion. Since there are time lapses while chatting online that are not present in real-life communication, written responses can be thought about first, allowing for a more contemplated and convincing presentation of the self.

The Role of Pornography

Pornography played an important role in the emerging and changing sexual subjectivity of the participants in this study. The Internet was the main channel through which the study participants gained access to pornography. Many participants watched porn clips and images, often stored in their mobile phones, as Oad illustrated:

> Probably it was in eighth grade [at the age of 13–14], because then I had my first mobile phone, and one could watch videos on it. So I started, started to have [clips] in my phone. I started to look for places to download. I would find places to load. Mostly, I would keep them in my computer, more [than in my phone]. [...] And if I wanted to watch

them, I would load them [from the computer] on my phone, and then I would watch them, and delete them. And then I would put new ones on [laughs].

Yud, who had his own room at home, ordered porn DVDs via the Internet, which were delivered via the mail. He described an irresistible pleasure while watching them for the first time:

I can remember when I watched [porn videos] for the first time, it – it came [ejaculated] by itself. Yes. [...] [chuckles] I was secretly shocked [แอบตกใจ] at that time [laughs]. But it was like, once I started watching, it was like a learning process [เหมือนกับการเรียนรู้], from watching that type of film.

The actors in these movies are often masculine looking, without there being a clearly masculine 'gay king' and a feminine 'gay queen'. Muscled, masculine-looking porn actors are regularly anally penetrated. In this sense, pornography can help promote a new awareness and concept of same-sex love occurring without a clear division in gender roles. Quan was inspired by pornography: he watched both gay and straight porn while in junior high school, and he gained a measure of popularity in his class because of his ability to find porn of all types, earning the nickname 'godfather of clips':

Clips of men and women, my friends would order them, and I would load them, like – I was a person who liked to play the Internet anyway, since I was a child. I knew every web [page], this one has downloads, I put them in my phone, and I gave them to my friends. My friends asked me to.

Having one's first mobile phone to store pornographic images or clips could be important in this regard: one can use one's phone to create a personal and private space, since many of the participants lived with families and had shared rooms with siblings or other family members. Quan mentioned that he gained a measure of privacy by password-protecting his laptop computer.

Sometimes porn was used quite literally as a learning tool. San's female friend let him watch a pornographic clip, after San had indicated that he was not sure whether he was gay or not:

SAN: [W]hen I was in tenth grade [at age 16] a friend showed me a clip of men and women. And she asked, 'Which person do you like?' [มึงชอบคนไหน] [chuckles].

INT: Really?

SAN: Really! She asked me that! [...] Oi. And I said, I like this one [แก ฉันชอบอันนี้แหละ]. So she said, That means, you are [gay]. [ก็แสดงว่าแกใช่แล้วแหล่ะ].

Kit met his first partner during a special study camp during the school holidays, and when they had made a date to have sex for the first time they looked at pornographic clips downloaded from the Internet to find out how to proceed:

KIT: Eh, at first I didn't dare, didn't dare to have sex [laughs].

INT: Had [your partner] had [sex] before? Did he know? Did he have experience?

KIT: He eh, but, this, I don't know. But he said, he had never. So – before we had [sex], we watched a movie. A – porn movie. And then we had sex.

INT: You watched what you had to do?

KIT: [laughs] Yes.

A recent Thai movie, *Bangkok Love Story*, is an example of the increased desirability and erotic power of physical masculinity and the emergence, at least in certain circles in Bangkok, of a new sexual compatibility between men that is not grounded in the idea of complementarity between a feminine and a masculine partner. The movie depicts a love affair between two very masculine-looking Thai men, who are shown in many slow shots zooming in on their torsos and six-packs (see Unaldi 2011). Although no research exists on this issue, pornography depicting masculine-looking men who are anally penetrated by other masculine-looking men (or, in some specialized niche products, by *kathoey*) probably plays an important role in the process of the masculinization and destabilization of gender-based concepts of homosexuality. Such pornographic imagery creates an awareness of hitherto unthinkable possibilities of the body and of masculine sexual pleasure, and, more importantly, these movies prove that acting and dressing masculine and having a muscled, athletic man's body no longer preclude the pleasure of being anally penetrated. The Australian sociologist Gary W. Dowsett et al. (2008, 122) pointed out that the Internet, including the Internet's function in distributing and sharing pornography, is not merely 'reflective' of sexual cultures but that it plays a productive role in itself: 'These productive energies are changing sexual relations between gay men and thereby affecting the gender order more broadly.'

How the Internet Blurs the Moral Foundations of Feminine and Masculine Sexuality

Following Mulder's (2000) take on Thai society discussed in Chapter 3, in Buddhism there is a distinction between pure and compassionate love and love based on attachment and suffering, which includes love and sexual relationships. The former is associated strongly with moral goodness, the home and the mother, who guards the home and raises the children. The latter type is the domain of the Thai male who, as a father, is the protector of the family, the person who is in the wild sphere of the outside world characterized by chaos, danger and immorality. In the age of globalization, including the rise of the Internet, Mulder's domain of the outside world has advanced and intruded into the home domain. Through the Internet, there are now more ways of communicating and interacting with the outside world, including people in different environments and provinces, blurring the boundary between the two gendered domains and their related moralities. In other words, the feminine-oriented young men in the study now have similar access to the outside world as do the masculine-oriented young men. Norms about what is appropriate or permissible behaviour in dating for feminine-oriented men are shifting. This is exacerbated by the tendency of Thai society to prioritize surface and presentation over the 'inner truth'. This makes it easy for a feminine-oriented man to combine one or multiple concurrent sex or love relationships online in different locations, while maintaining an image of a respectable (read: chaste or monogamous) woman in the parental home and community.

As a result, there is little trust in relationships established over the Internet. This is because people cannot directly assess and evaluate, in terms of social position, whom they are dealing with when they approach or are approached by someone online. There is also little control over a partner's behaviour, especially in long-distance relationships. Fluk said that 'everybody is cheating' on the Internet – this is no longer only the realm of the masculine men in their out-of-home domain. Gop admitted that he was chatting with several people at the same time, and that his friends laugh at him for his 'collections' of men or boyfriends. Oad admitted that, even when he had a boyfriend, he would still talk to others online:

> Just if this person comes to chat with you, and if you feel good about him, you put him on hold [ติดไว้ก่อน], to chat with him at a later moment – They are all just people I know, but I chat, chat, I chat with them first. [chuckles]. Whoever is good, I will take [ใครดีใครได้] [as my boyfriend] [laughs].

Fluk lamented how difficult it is to know whether a person one meets online is 'good':

> We don't know, whose child is he? [...] Because we have never talked to him before, never seen his face. So how can we know whether he really is a good person or not? It cannot [be better than meeting a] person who comes walking past, and whom I meet, [so] I can see his face, I can see his personality [บุคลิก] and his way of acting [ท่าทาง].

Trusting somebody is difficult in the time of the Internet, where it is so easy to strike up a conversation with strangers, and potential sexual encounters are everywhere. In this sense, having little experience on the Internet is a good sign for some participants. Win once met someone online who did not yet know much about the Internet. He saw that as a desirable trait – a kind of 'digital virginity':

> How to say, he had just started to play the Internet, but he didn't know how to use Face[book], he couldn't do anything. I think, maybe it is a good point that he is unable to chat with other people, so he cannot be promiscuous [...] He didn't have M[essenger], he didn't have Face[book], he didn't have anything. So he registered, he wanted to see what it was like, so he registered, like this. He was unable to use any of those. Maybe it is a good thing [ข้อดี].

On the Internet, relationships can easily be started with men from all over the country, rather than just from a smaller pool of men in and around one's village. Due to the ease with which one can find a date on the Internet, conduct a dating process or break up with a boyfriend, and the speed at which this can happen, the meaning of the word *faen* (boyfriend/girlfriend) in Thai may be changing. The emergence, less than ten years ago, of its more playful and fleeting new linguistic cousin *gig* may be a sign of this, as Gop explained:

> Hmmm, it is like, we are talking, like, we are tricks [*gig*], or something like that. Like, if we are going to say that we are boyfriends, [...] it feels at first like we are going to be boyfriends, but he doesn't break up with me, and I secretly have another person. Like, dating with this one, but this other one is still there, I didn't break up. [...] So my friends said that I have a lot of COLLECTIONS [Eng].

Laphimon (2012, 182) noted that the word *gig* is very ambiguous: it has a meaning between friend and sexual partner as well as between a one-off sexual event and a longer-term sexual relationship: 'While the relationship type itself is not new in Thailand, the emergence of a cute term that is not predominantly negative for casual sexual relationships is a recent phenomenon that has elicited many attempts to define it.'

The word *faen* (boyfriend, girlfriend) is acquiring a less serious meaning, less than a supposedly permanent love relationship, due to the ascent of Internet dating. The breakdown of the gendered spheres of the feminine world of the home and the masculine outside world is largely responsible for this. Some men in the study clearly differentiated between the Internet and the real world and tended to see them as separate moral domains. When participants were asked to compare a boyfriend whom one dates via the Internet with a person whom one dates in real life, most said it was different, with an Internet boyfriend being taken less seriously, as Ed illustrated: 'Hmmm. It is different, because, a boyfriend, if we only talk in the world of the Internet, like, it is like we never really know each other. We could lie to each other about anything.'

Yud, who had never had an 'offline' boyfriend, similarly thought a cyberboyfriend and a real-life boyfriend are not the same:

> It is not the same. It is completely different. A boyfriend who one dates – I mean, a boyfriend in the real life, at least, one can learn from his outside in person. It is like, we see each other, face to face. But a boyfriend via the Internet, one cannot know who he is, where he is from – you can only chat.

Conclusion

The Internet provides new and previously unheard-of opportunities and possibilities for same-sex-attracted young Thai men to form, experiment with and alter their sexuality, as well as to find friends, sex partners and boyfriends. The Internet also helped the young men in this study come to terms with the growing inadequacy of gender-based homosexuality to explain their increasingly complex sexual and dating experiences, as discussed in Chapter 8. Many participants in the study used the Internet to find information about homosexuality in an attempt to acquire or alter their sexual subjectivity, experimenting, exploring and pondering their options. It also played an important role in the process of masculinization that many of the men went through, facilitating the spread of new concepts to describe aspects of the participants' changing sexual subjectivity, such as 'both', 'both-*ruk*' and '*bai-ruk*'.

The Internet involves a new form of communication. It provides anonymity, a freedom to enter or exit communications easily, and the creation of scripts that can easily be altered and changed on another occasion, as well as time lapses between chats. The freedom that the internet provides in communicating and in creating and altering personal space for experimental and innovative presentations of the self is in sharp contrast to the way Thai society organizes communication in real life. Real-life communication is governed by hierarchy and is underpinned by the principles of *kala-thetsa* and *barami*, which provide strict formats for how to handle and conduct surface interactions. These principles are taught to ensure smooth interactions with others and to keep hierarchical relationships in place, avoiding loss of face.

Both real-life communication and Internet-based communication allow for a multifaceted concept of truth, based on 'power prestige' rather than 'power truth' (see Chapters 3 and 5). In this context, the impact of the Internet on dating and romance practices could ultimately be the experience of what I would like to call 'cyber-geographic monogamy': neatly managed and compartmentalized multiple and concurrent relationships in which a person has a 'monogamous' relationship in one area, and another (or several other) concurrent 'monogamous' relationships in other areas, cities, provinces or Internet sites.

Enhanced by processes of masculinization in the way same-sex-attracted people present themselves and behave towards each other, the Internet erodes the moral distinction between the sexuality of men and women and, as a consequence, between the sexuality of two same-sex-attracted partners in terms of their presumed feminine or masculine, monogamous or promiscuous, virtuous or flirtatious attributes. Everybody, regardless of gender, can initiate a date and can be promiscuous. The Internet, as a culmination of broader socio-economic processes in Thai society, directly undermines the traditional separation of the feminine sphere of the home and the masculine sphere of the outside world. The domain of the Internet has no clearly defined sexual or dating morality. Participants are free to define and redefine their sexuality, their dating practices and their sexual market value and to play around with their definitions.

The advent of the Internet and the trust issues it generates will only function to reinforce the existing negativity of the young men about the possibility of finding long-lasting love and romance for same-sex-attracted people, based on ideas about karma and traditional notions of Thai masculinity (discussed in Chapter 4). This will especially be the case when this negativity is placed in the context of parallel societal narratives and anxieties about the decline of Thai morality, the 'badness' of youth and the corrupting influences of the media and the Internet on sexual norms and values as a whole, and about the HIV epidemic in particular (Fordham 2006).

From another perspective, the growth of the Internet and the breakdown of the feminine home sphere have led to more sexual freedom for Thai females, including feminine-oriented same-sex-attracted men. Women's sexual needs and demands were generally ignored or even denied in the dominant Thai sexual culture that emerged at the beginning of the twentieth century and which has since been propagated as 'traditionally Thai' by the Bangkok-based elites (see Sinnott 2009). There is an intriguing parallel between these changes in attitudes, practices and ideas about Thai female sexuality and the emancipation and empowerment of women in Western societies starting in the 1960s – changes that were also set in motion during a period of rapid socio-economic changes in society (Weeks 1985). Jackson (2011a, 37) observed that *kathoey* (as well as effeminate gay men) have played 'pivotal roles in the redefinition of masculinity and femininity', and as a result in the definition of a modern, liberalized and free sexuality for women. An example is Ake (discussed in Chapter 8), who used his diverse array of sexual experiences, combined with newly acquired knowledge and ideas obtained in the new symbolic universe he entered after leaving home, to define a modern and new sexuality that suited his new situation. He combined a masculine gender role with feminine desires, including the expectation that he would depend on a man and be taken care of, romantically and sexually. Morally, he shed his earlier desire to remain a virgin and preserve himself for a future partner, and rid himself of his previous negative judgements about enjoying sex, or about having many sexual experiences, talking openly about his pleasures and sexual exploits.

This sexual liberation process is not necessarily welcomed by everybody. Since it produces countless new options for forming ever-changing sexual subjectivities and gender roles; it also leads to less clarity about what to choose and how to act. Whereas this freedom was handled well by Ake, who was brave and creative enough to grasp the opportunities it provided; for people like Nook, who was more conservative and traditional in his outlook and aspirations, this new situation constituted an over-abundance of options and possibilities, which he found disturbing.

Chapter 10

'NO MONEY, NO HONEY': LOVE AND SEX IN PURSUIT OF A BETTER LIFE

In my heart, I want somebody who takes care of my whole family.
I mean, who can lift my family up higher, increase their status.

– Ives

Introduction

Several of the young men in this study, especially those from poor families in the northeast, used their youth and beauty and the promise of the pleasure provided by their bodies as a means to try to improve their lives and that of their families. Many of them tried to find a wealthy boyfriend who could help them and their families financially.

Many of the young men held the perception that viable love relationships are based on complementarity between two differing partners. Implied in this is that for a relationship to work, the partners need to have something to exchange with each other. In the case of many of the men discussed in this chapter, this involved an exchange of their beauty and youth for financial security and stability. Often this complementarity was also gendered in the imagination of the men in the study, with the desired boyfriend seen in the role of the providing husband, and they themselves in the role of the housewife.

Five out of the twenty-five participants in the study had some experience in sex work; four of them worked for brief periods of time in male sex work establishments in Pattaya, Bangkok and Phuket, and one of the five still occasionally engaged in sex work via the Internet at the time of the final interview. Sex work is usually seen as being purely about casual sex-for-money encounters, and it seems to have little to do with longer-term love and romance. However, the young men in this chapter downplayed the importance of payment and money in the stories they told about their sex work experiences. Their most important motive for engaging in it, at least at the beginning, was to find a long-term partner who could 'take care' of them and their families.

The chapter will start with an overview of studies on male sex work in Thailand, followed by a description of three study participants' experiences with it. Young men who started off as effeminate during their childhood years were more aware of, and driven by, the value of their bodies and of their sexuality than the masculine-oriented men who discovered their same-sex desire later. This is linked to the different value attached to feminine and masculine sexuality in Thai society. I will also show how Thai cultural constructs of masculinity as well as the physical distance between the moral sphere of the home and the outside world help to facilitate sex work.

The Study of Male Sex Work in Thailand

Thai studies on sex work have mainly focused on female sex work. Jeffrey (2002) suggests that this may be because the female sex worker as the archetypical 'bad woman' provides a powerful image in the cultural definition of womanhood, and is the topic of frequent political and societal angst about the supposed decline of gender norms and sexual values. Despite these moral panics about declining norms and values, Peter Jackson (2009a) found evidence of the existence of male sex work in Thai newspapers and magazines dating back to many decades.

At the end of the 1990s, in the context of growing concern about the HIV epidemic in Thailand, a number of authors conducted social research into male sex work in order to shed light on how culture, society and communications are linked to HIV risk and vulnerability. McCamish (2002) described social support systems between male sex workers in the seaside resort town of Pattaya and found that their relationships were characterized by distrust and competition, a low level of mutual solidarity and no sense of being a member of a sex work or same-sex-attracted community. He found important differences between sex work in so-called 'go-go bars' and freelance sex work; bars provided a certain security, both for sex workers and clients, and bar-based sex workers appeared to have a higher status than street- or beach-based sex workers. McCamish noted that most male sex workers did not tell their parents about the work they were doing, hiding behind a facade of restaurant or other service-oriented work. He also noted the appeal of finding a long-term foreign partner as a possible result of sex work, securing a materially better future for oneself or one's family – something that was also an important motivation for the men discussed in this chapter.

Some of my own early work focused on the economic aspects of male sex work in the northern Thai city of Chiang Mai (De Lind van Wijngaarden

1999). My research described how bar-based sex work was organized in Chiang Mai – especially how the word 'bar' served as a euphemism to hide the sex work function that such places fulfilled. The study revealed a relaxed atmosphere towards sex work as an option for earning money among Thai young men, even those who did not identify as homosexual. I linked the emergence of male sex work to changes in Thai society during the 1990s, in which money and earning power were becoming more prominent markers of social status. Another factor in the emergence of bar-based male sex work was the growth of (initially primarily Western) gay tourism to Thailand. The study explained how many men who said they were not sexually attracted to other men rationalized and justified working in these venues. As has been explained in previous chapters, same-sex relationships are strongly gendered in Thai culture. Masculinity, from a sexual viewpoint, is largely defined by the act of penetration, and not so much by the object of penetration. This means that if a man penetrates another man, he is not, as would be the case in Western societies, automatically classified as 'gay' or homosexual. Beyond this, sexual behaviours can be rationalized in the context of hierarchical power relationships. While shameful, a 'real' Thai man could, privately, justify being anally penetrated if this happened in a context where he was with an older, richer, wiser or otherwise more powerful partner; a client of a male sex worker would usually qualify on several counts. Self-reported motives of the male sex workers in the sample ($N = 131$) for involvement in sex work included the possibility of earning much more money than in other professions (66 per cent), the fact that it was easy and light work (51 per cent) and that it had flexible working hours (36 per cent).

Graeme Storer (1999a, 1999b) conducted research on male sex workers in Bangkok and focused on the manner in which the Thai language positions different actors in sexual exchange in terms of their gender and age. He noted how Thai constructions of gender and sexuality allow for a fluidity that is not apparent in Western societies, but also drew attention to the power relations implicit in the positioning of the two parties involved in a sex work transaction through the Thai language terms used to refer to each of them.

The PhD candidate Rory Gallagher (2005, 7) conducted a study on sex tourism in Phuket and noted that the sex industry is 'diversifying and as a result its spatial organization and structures are being reconfigured'. He quoted Eric Cohen (2003), who found that Thai forms of sex work were less 'contractual' and the exchange of goods or money for sex was more hidden and subtle, which served the self-concepts and values of both sex worker and client, neither of whom usually like to be seen or labelled this way.

Another PhD candidate, Thomas Shulich (2006), conducted research on the long-term relationships between younger Thai men and older retired

Western gay men in Chiang Mai. These relationships often evolved from initial contacts made in the context of male sex work. He showed how several of the young local men, by entering into long-term erotic relationships with older Western men, managed to achieve a significant upgrade in their, and their families', material living conditions and financial security.

The findings reported in this chapter are quite different from the studies above, mainly because this study did not set out and was not designed to study experiences around sex work per se. The stories about sex work were an unexpected side product of this study. In a way, this study has therefore unexpectedly helped to make sense of male sex work in the broader context of the sexual subjectivities of same-sex-attracted men in modern Thailand. In the next part of this chapter, the stories of three research participants with experience in sex work will be discussed in detail.

Ives' Story

Ives grew up in a relatively poor family in a rural province of the northeast of Thailand. His father was a gardener and his mother made some money looking after neighbours' children. He had a happy childhood and his relationship with his parents was very good. His older sister was studying in a university near Bangkok and Ives really wanted to study as well, but for financial reasons he had to wait until his sister completed her studies, which would be two years after he finished high school. Ives was a *kathoey* or 'second type of woman' (*sao praphet song*) in his early secondary school years, dressing as a girl outside school hours and taking contraceptive pills in order to become more feminine. This desire to put brakes on his growth towards masculine adulthood was linked to his relatively large and hairy body. This was in contrast to the other feminine young men in this study who were *kathoey* during their younger years, who, with their petite and slim bodies, would have had an easier time passing as a girl.

In senior high school, Ives witnessed his classmates getting boyfriends and girlfriends and starting to have sex, but he was still a virgin at age 17. Then, one of his fellow *kathoey* friends decided to cut his long hair and posted a picture of himself on a gay website, calling himself a 'gay queen' in his profile rather than a *kathoey*, and found a boyfriend soon after. Ives decided to do the same. Ives had dreamed of being a beautiful woman, a *sao praphet song*, but this status was unattainable for him, because of the large size and masculine features of his body and, more importantly, his lack of money for hormone treatment and surgery to achieve a convincing transition. But the rural *kathoey* role (often derogatively denoted as *kathoey khwaai*, or 'buffalo *kathoey*'), with its connotations of backwardness and poverty, was also not an option for him, because Ives wanted to move ahead and pull himself and his family out of poverty. He deemed this task impossible in the role of (unattractive) *kathoey*.

Hence, Ives cut his hair, changed his dress, and posted pictures of his new masculine self on the website his friend had shown him. Soon after his transition into the gay role Ives found his first-ever boyfriend, who also became his first sexual partner. This short-lived relationship was followed by another short relationship. This second man, a few years older, was very interested in Ives and wanted to settle down with him, promising to take care of him. He wanted Ives to move to his area and finish his high school there so that they could work and live together. Ives decided against it. One of the reasons for this was that this man was not wealthy enough to help pull his family out of poverty:

> Eh, [laughs]. When I stayed with him, I got the feeling that he could take care of me, at a certain level. But speaking about, in my heart, I want somebody who takes care of my whole family. I mean, who can lift my family up higher, increase their status.

After finishing high school, Ives moved to stay and work with his sister near Bangkok. However, the factory job his sister had found for him there did not materialize. During the first two interviews Ives mentioned that he had thought about moving to Phuket to work in a gay bar. He had also been invited by someone he met online to work in a gay spa as a masseur in Bangkok ('massage parlour', 'bar' and 'karaoke' are all used as covers for sex work venues in Thailand). But at that time he had no money to move out of his sister's place. To my initial shock, his mother was strongly in favour of Ives's working in sex work, hoping that he would find a foreign boyfriend:

> IVES: My mother told me to go to work like that. To meet a lover, a life partner, a foreigner, who can take care of me. Who can take care of our whole family.
> INT: Your mother, your mother told you that?
> IVES: Yes. Yes. I talked to my mother, like, what shall I do? Like – how can I say – we have debts. And something else, I was born like this. If you want to make it right, one has to find a foreign boyfriend, let him take care of us. Something like that.

For a Western observer it may seem strange or even cruel to imagine a mother telling her 17-year-old son to prostitute himself in order to alleviate the debts that she and the rest of the family had accrued. However, from Ives's perspective, his mother provided him with a way to make himself of use to the family – a route to a sense of pride and importance for his family, a chance to be 'good'. He may also have appreciated his mother's implicit acceptance of Ives's feminine concept of self, as a 'dutiful daughter'; a parent would never ask a 'real' son to work in prostitution. His mother's encouragement indicates a more relaxed attitude towards sex work in certain areas of northeastern Thailand, which are important sources for the female and male sex industry in Thailand's main entertainment cities. Many, if not all, of the young north-eastern men interviewed had relatives who had married a foreigner and settled either in Thailand or abroad, often with significant improvements in the financial status of the extended family. Although this is rarely discussed in the open, the majority of these relationships are initiated while the Thai partner was working in a sex work establishment in Pattaya, Bangkok or Phuket. For most foreign men looking for a Thai wife, these establishments are the easiest way to get into contact with Thai women. It is likely that Ives's mother witnessed some of these phenomena first-hand and envied the prosperity these marriages brought to families in her neighbourhood, and she was therefore not opposed to Ives's plans to work in sex work in one of these cities.

Between the second and third interviews, Ives was invited by a female family member to go to the southern tourist resort of Phuket to work in a gay bar, which was again strongly encouraged by his mother who told him that this was 'better than that you stay here and do nothing'. Ives spoke extensively about his two months working in a gay go-go bar in Phuket. One of his new colleagues coupled him with one of the bar's steady customers during his first night there. The customer asked Ives why he had come to work at the bar:

> Because, 'I don't have money. So I came to work here, in order to MAKE MONEY [Eng], and I have to send it home.' Ah. So I said, 'In reality, I don't like to work like this' [...]. Ehm. 'But it is necessary. Because I just finished HIGH SCHOOL [Eng], that is all.' Something like that. And I told him that our [financial] status at home was not good [...]. Hmmm. So he was like, 'Oh, oh', like this.

Note the discrepancy between what Ives told his first customer ('I don't like to work like this') and his stated desire to work in sex work during the three interviews I had with him. Ives wanted to be seen as desirable and innocent by his customers. He thought he would be less desirable if he presented himself as a 'happy hooker'; his comment that he 'just finished high school' fits this presentation of himself as a fresh, innocent, just-arrived-from-the-countryside boy. Focusing on the poverty of his family as a justification for doing sex work also enhances the well-rehearsed narrative of the selfless, hard-working, dutiful daughter.

Ives saved around 40,000 baht in the two months that he stayed in Phuket, of which he was very proud (the Thai minimum wage is currently 300 baht a day, hence less than 9,000 baht per month). Most of the money he received came from one European man who had started to behave more and more like a boyfriend rather than like a customer, and of whom Ives had high hopes. This man had taken Ives out on day trips and bought him gifts and a cake for his birthday. He also promised to send Ives to university by sending him 20,000 baht per month. After returning from Phuket, Ives gave half of his earnings to his parents to pay off some of their debts, and the rest he used to register for a university, in expectation of monthly support from this de-facto boyfriend. However, this support did not materialize, partly because the man appeared to already have a (Thai) boyfriend who intervened in the planned arrangements.

In the end, Ives did not succeed in his aim of finding a permanent foreign boyfriend. Despite this, Ives looked back on his experience in Phuket in a positive way. He enjoyed the freedom of the work in Phuket and had a lot of fun while dating his foreign client, although he said he did not want to go back to work there again. The reason he gave for this was related to the wickedness of the 'society' in which the sex work occurs, a society which Ives called 'fake': '[It is] like a society that cheats you. […] It is like, they don't have any honesty with each other.' Whereas Ives saw the experience in sex work as an opportunity to find a long-term partner, he did not see it as a good environment to work in and make money for an extended period of time, possibly partly because of a fear of losing his status as a 'good woman'.

After returning from Phuket, Ives once again based himself at his sister's place near Bangkok, but he continued to have sex for money, meeting his partners online. Whereas in Phuket he would occasionally have sex with people he fancied without asking for money, he had stopped doing this now. He elaborated on this a bit later:

> They have to – because I – how to say, I cannot find money otherwise. If it happens that I – and if I miss the chance [to ask for money], uh, I don't know where I will find [money]. I don't know who I will ask for it.

He linked the fact that he asked for money in exchange for sex to his unemployment but also to his receptive role in sex – in other words, to the value of his feminine sexuality and the pleasures it can provide:

> I am receptive, you know? I don't want to 'lose my body' [เสียตัว, means 'to have sex'] for free. I am like, I will tell them, I will tell them, I want at least 500 [baht]. 500. […] Ehm. It is not too much [for them]. And I,

> I am also willing. It is not like, I go to see him and I just want money, it is not like that. I hope for [good] sex [too].

In an attempt to distinguish himself from the archetypical bad woman, the prostitute, Ives introduced a new moral distinction. Although he received money for sex, he also wanted and enjoyed sex. Thus, he did not have sex *only* for money, with entirely unattractive partners. Ives had a sense that sex should provide him with a reward, since he gave away some of his femininity, his beauty, his virginity, his body. Ives saw it as a waste to have sex for free, or perhaps as a luxury he could not afford. In a further attempt to distance himself from sex workers, Ives talked with disdain about how his fellow bar boys in Phuket were addicted to drugs and gambled away their earnings, and how they were unable to save any money despite the many customers some of them had. In combination with stories about how he 'knew his place' in his behaviour towards his more experienced and older colleagues, and how he would respect the elder bar boys and the manager, Ives regarded himself as better than the average bar boy. Since he had only had a relatively brief exposure to sex work and urban society, Ives saw himself as having maintained his pure and innocent (read: morally superior) rural manners and habits. More importantly, he used the money he earned to help his family and to invest in his educational development, not for personal enjoyment or consumption as was the case with many of his colleagues.

Ives's experiences in Phuket did wonders for his self-esteem. During the second interview, he felt useless, staying at his elder sister's house, doing nothing. Now, he had gained the respect and appreciation of his mother, who was very pleased with the support he had provided to her. In addition, for the first time he discovered that there were people who desired him for his masculine, rather than feminine, beauty, and he had almost managed to find a steady foreign boyfriend of good status. He had discovered a way to put his newly acquired masculine desirability to good use while, interestingly, still acting from a frame of mind in which he considered himself to have a feminine nature. While firmly rejecting the label of sex worker, the experience of working in the gay bar opened up new opportunities for him to play out his feminine characteristics combined with the desirability of his relatively large and masculine body – which had been such an obstacle to becoming a successful female, but was now an advantage. Above all, the experience opened a window to a better future.

Lert's Story

Lert grew up with his family in a rural area in the northeastern province of Sri Sa Ket. His father had died long ago and his mother had remarried. He lived with his mother, stepfather, a 'naughty' younger brother who had already dropped out of school before completing ninth grade, a cousin and his grandmother. His mother and stepfather worked in the fields. Most of Lert's junior high school peers were already married and had children and they had started working after ninth grade. Lert was the only one who had completed senior high school and was continuing his studies at the higher vocational level.

Lert, like Ives, was a *kathoey* in his early teenage years and grew long hair, although he did not feel the need to use feminizing hormones because his body was small and hairless. He did not dress as a female all the time but only on special occasions, often with friends. Lert left home to work in a go-go bar in Bangkok at age 15 or 16. He said he went for less than two weeks, during the summer break (April) before he began the second year of vocational education (equivalent to 11th grade). Friends from the neighbourhood introduced him to this work. Lert did not elaborate on his sexual experiences while at the bar. His period there was life-changing, however, because he became aware that he was not in demand with his long hair and girly demeanour:

> Before, I was going to be a *kathoey* too. I was going to grow my hair. But when I went to Bangkok, when I tried to find a job, I didn't get anything. They hardly ever employ *kathoey*. If you go to work in a bar, one has to take medicines [hormones], have breasts, things like that – I was afraid to do that. So I thought, better to be gay. So I worked, I went to apply for a job, I cut my hair short, and then I went to apply for a job and they took me. So I think, being gay is better than being *kathoey*, I think, in many ways.

When Lert entered the sexual marketplace he was able to rapidly adjust to the tastes of his prospective customers. In contrast to Ives, his entrance into sex work was not directly motivated by the desire to find a boyfriend; it was a kind of an experiment linked to a desire to earn money, a desire to explore a new sexual identity, and the result of encouragement by his friends. A Thai customer took him out of the bar the first night he worked at Patpong. The money he received for his virginity was disappointing:

> I was the new kid. The first day, I was taken out by a Thai person. In fact I didn't want to go. He gave me only 1500 [baht]. Eh. I didn't like it. I was, I had never done it before. I wanted to try it, many things. So I did it, but not again.

Apart from this, he had a customer from Singapore, after which he went back home to the northeast. In contrast to Ives, Lert never told his mother about his experiences in Bangkok, and he also did not tell the Thai boyfriend whom he was dating at the time. When he first talked about selling his body, during the first interview, Lert felt ashamed and did not go into much detail. He may have felt a bit embarrassed as the story about his experience in Patpong contradicted his otherwise flawless self-presentation as an inexperienced, pure, innocent and 'good' rural person.

While Lert had said during the first interview that he did not want to do sex work again, between the second and the third interviews he changed his mind and went to work in Pattaya for six weeks. He was convinced to do so by two friends he knew from school, both of whom worked at a well-known northeastern Thai restaurant in Pattaya. This restaurant opened all night and it was known as a place where many young men and women who worked in the sex industry (and their partners/customers) went to party after their establishments had closed. It was open until the early morning, and it was widely known that all waiters were, in principle, 'available' for a fee. While working at the restaurant, Lert was taken out by customers three times in two weeks. One only wanted his company, and two of these men Lert ended up having sex with in exchange for money.

After two weeks working there, Lert and his two friends left the restaurant to work in a go-go bar in Pattaya, again invited by a friend. Lert was quite nervous about it. His first client was a Russian with whom he went 'long time' – meaning 'all night' in go-go boy vernacular. When asked about his other customers and experiences, he hesitated and then quickly focused on the financial gains he made, skipping over the details of his encounters, quite similar to Ives:

> And there was – it – there was a foreigner, he was from Germany. And I went LONG TIME [Eng] with him, too. I worked for a week, [and] I got money, about 5000–6000 [baht]. But I didn't really save anything, I went to buy clothes and I bought – things to eat, like this.

During his initial weeks in Pattaya, his friends taught him how to use the website GayRomeo (also known as 'PlanetRomeo'). Whereas the GayRomeo website is sometimes used as a site to facilitate sex work, it is also known as a venue to find 'free' casual sex or to search for a more serious long-term partner. Lert said that between 500 and 600 people looked at his new profile within hours after he created it and that he received many messages and requests to hook up for sex. Lert gradually became motivated by the desire to find a long-term boyfriend. He had problems communicating, however, but he used Google Translate to understand the many messages as well as to respond to some of them.

Not long after he had started using GayRomeo he met a *farang* (Caucasian) boyfriend, a retired French man in his sixties. The man had a condominium in Pattaya, a housekeeper, a speedboat and many other possessions, so he seemed a good catch. Before meeting him, Lert had appointments with a Chinese and a Russian man, but he could not communicate with them. Lert chose the French man specifically because he could speak Thai. Asked about his feelings for this man, Lert said:

> LERT: I respected him, but if you ask me if I loved him – I didn't. [...]
> He was very old already. I just stayed with him, and he paid for me
> and took care of me.
> INT: [Was it] like he was a long-term customer?
> LERT: Yes. Yes.

Lert said he had sex with the French man 'not often, maybe once every 3 or 4 days' and, upon asking, he said he experienced 'happiness' while having sex. However, during the final interview, when the experience was revisited, he was less positive about it.

In line with Lert's expectations, his French boyfriend supported his living expenses. Lert did not do anything while staying at the man's condominium, and hung out on the beach with his friends from the bar and the restaurant he had worked in. While he was staying with the French man, Lert was still looking around for opportunities to find someone better by chatting and playing with other potential suitors on Facebook. This unfaithfulness may partly be explained by the fact that Lert was becoming aware that he was not the first one who had stayed at the French man's home; there had been many young men before him.

After having dated each other for two weeks, the French man visited Lert's home, staying in a hotel in a town 10 kilometres from Lert's parental home. He took the French man to his mother's house and introduced him to her. Similar to other countries, introducing a partner to one's parents has a symbolic meaning in Thai culture, and usually is seen as a sign of taking a relationship to the next level. It is likely that Lert hoped to use the event as a way to strengthen his claim on his boyfriend, as well as a token of his commitment. His parents were, however, not particularly enthusiastic about the visit:

> My mother, she – she didn't say anything, she said: 'Why did you bring
> him, I am ashamed for the neighbours!' [laughs] [...] She was afraid
> that the people around our home would say something, like, 'Your son
> has a *farang* boyfriend', something like that. That they would say some-
> thing (bad) about it, gossip about it a little bit.

The French man left after a few days, and Lert did not want to go back to Pattaya after their trip, planning to enrol in his new vocational school, and this meant the relationship ended. Since then, Lert has stayed at home and continued his studies, not too far from his parental home.

When I went to meet him for the third and final interview, Lert had completely changed. He had gained considerable weight, looked unkempt and dressed shabbily, and was even sporting a beard of a number of days. All of these attributes can be interpreted as a rejection of his previous attempts at femininity and his later adoption of elements of 'gay metrosexuality'. Lert was subdued and seemed depressed, a big change from the first two interviews, when he had been outgoing and happy. He said that he had decided that it was time to be 'serious' with his life. His mother played a major role in keeping him grounded, in stark contrast to the role Ives's mother played in encouraging him to explore possibilities in sex work. When asked if he had plans to go back to Pattaya to work, Lert said:

> LERT: [My mother] wants me to stay at home.
> INT: Because of what?
> LERT: Eh – when I go there, she is worried that I go with – that I sleep around [or: be wild], to go – [do things] like that. She doesn't let me go. She wants me to stay at home.

Having failed to find a long-term foreign boyfriend while in Pattaya, Lert had embarked on a radically different track over the several months before the final interview. He had started to fulfil his mother's and other family members' expectations of him as a son by fulfilling a number of typically Thai masculine duties. First, he became a monk for a few weeks, earning his mother important karma points; furthermore, he was planning to (and eventually did) embark on a military career, in line with family tradition. Rather than going his own way, Lert had chosen to follow his family and their heteronormative expectations of their son. When I noted how much he had changed over the past three to four years – from *kathoey* to gay receptive to (possibly) gay insertive, and from an effeminate person into a soldier/monk (both very masculine roles) – he responded,

> I think it is best to change myself. I will change continuously, I will – I like to change, like, like this, I have been this and that already, right? It is better to change myself continuously. Which one WORKS [Eng] the best for me, which one WORKS [Eng] the best, I will change into that one, better.

Joe's Story

Joe was an only child. His mother and stepfather were farmers, living in the countryside outside the northeastern province of Buriram. His parents were unable to support Joe to enrol at university after he finished high school because of financial hardship. During the second interview, Joe had found work at a pig farm around sixty kilometres from his hometown. He was planning to continue his education at a vocational college focusing on veterinary studies, paid for by his employer. He liked his job and the people around him, and the labour conditions were good. Asked whether he had ever considered working in a gay bar, like Ives (whom he knew personally) had done, Joe said he had considered it but that he did not have the courage to do so:

> I don't think it is bad work, [I think]. It is also a kind of work, it is honest, or not? It likely is. [...] Maybe it is because of necessity that they have to go and work like that. [...] But I want to do it, but I am not brave enough yet to do it. Or maybe it is because I am still too young to work there. One has to get more experience first before you can work there.

Joe was impressed with the people who were brave enough to work in a go-go bar in Pattaya. He said, 'If I have an opportunity, I will go.' Joe linked working in a go-go bar with the opportunity to meet foreign men, and mentioned that he wanted to have a foreign boyfriend, someone who was rich:

> If you have a foreign boyfriend, they are saying, that women go to find a foreign boyfriend, a foreign husband [...], and their family life is very comfortable. They have a house, a car, things like that. I want that too, you know? For what, if you ask me, why do you want that? At my home, nowadays, I mean, life is quite difficult [...]. If I have [a foreign boyfriend], then I will be like, a wealthy person. My family will be more comfortable. So, I want – I want my mother to have a better life [...]. I don't want my mother to suffer, I want to have a house for my mother, something like that.

He had also discussed this with his mother who, similar to Ives's mother, was favourable to the idea: 'My mother said, "That would be good! We will have a house, and so on. You will be rich! [...] If you can get [a *farang* boyfriend], it [would be] good." [chuckles]. I would have money, then.'

Everything seemed to be going well at his job in the pig farm, but when I tried to contact Joe to meet for the third and final interview, he had unexpectedly left his job. Invited by a friend, he had gathered his courage and started working at a gay bar in a well-known sex work area in Pattaya. A man from Sweden became his first customer at the bar. He referred to this man as 'the generation of my father'. He described his second customer, an Englishman, in very unfavourable terms: '[H]e was very fat. He was like a balloon, like, do you know a frog when it has swollen itself up? When he laid down, his belly went up against me'. He felt pressured to go with this ugly man, noting that if he did not, he would have no money that day. He went only a 'short time' with his customers; in other words, he did not stay overnight, which is an indication that he did not try to stay with them as long as he could in order to get to know them in a longer-term relationship.

Joe had been working in the go-go bar for only three days when he was picked up by a German man, who said he wanted Joe to be his boyfriend. Joe agreed and immediately moved into the German man's house. Asked why Joe chose this German as his boyfriend and not any of the other men that had been interested in him, he said,

> He chose me. In reality I didn't want to stay with him. [...] I thought, to stay with him, that it would be good, like – that I wouldn't have to work, that I could just stay at [his] home. At his home – in reality I did not just stay at home. I went to the [gay] BEACH [Eng], the BEACH [Eng] [...]. So I walked around there. [...] It was close to Dong Tan beach. So I went to walk on the beach every day. Every day. [...] We went to lay there for fun [นอนเล่น], there was nothing to do, I laid down and read, and – we did like that every day. [silent] It was boring. Boring.

While he was staying at the German man's home, he had a lot of time to use the computer, and was on the chat platform CamFrog all the time, looking for excitement and sexual encounters. He also got secretly involved with the Thai boyfriend of another German man, who was a friend of his then boy-friend. He then decided it had become too complicated, and one day he ran away. An important reason for leaving was his disappointment with the money he received from the German man: 3,000 baht (around US$ 90–100) per week: 'He was very stingy.' When justifying himself, he started by focusing on the German man's age:

> JOE: He was the generation of my father, my mother, my grandfather, grandmother, great-grandmother, great-grandfather.
> INT: [chuckles] How is it, suppose he had been better? Suppose he had given you 10,000 per week …
> JOE: It would have worked out. I would have [stayed with him].

By talking about his small earnings and linking this to the fact that the man was old, Joe made the case for leaving clear: it was not worth it. Joe felt his sexuality and his beauty were not sufficiently valued by his German boyfriend, and that he should be able to make more money, to get a better deal. That left him no alternative but to leave. In Joe's view, a person as old as this boyfriend should take care of a young person like him better, especially if the young person was as good looking as Joe.

If Joe were sexually attracted to older persons and enjoyed having sex with them, the situation would have been different. While Joe said that he had an attraction for *farang*, he also said he generally dated people because of their looks. Hence, he preferred younger, fitter men. Joe said that the fact that he found most customers unattractive was a key reason for leaving the go-go bar after just three days: 'I couldn't really do it. That is probably why I didn't stay for long. I couldn't stay long, it is like this.' While walking around Dong Tan beach, Joe would gaze at the many handsome and young *farang* who were enjoying their holiday there, and he would wonder why these handsome men would not come out to his bar to be his customers. Unlike Ives, Joe had no good memories of his very short period in sex work: 'If I knew it was like this [...], I wouldn't have done it. I wouldn't have.'

At the time of the final interview, Joe was about to start working at an electronics factory in Chonburi Province and was dating a Thai property broker. Even so, he said that last night he had spoken to a *farang* online, as he said he was still interested in finding a *farang* boyfriend who could provide for him and his family:

> [I said to the *farang*] 'If you will bring me to do something [sex], if you take me and provide for me, it will be good, I mean, I cannot be good by myself, I also have to make my family good too.' Something like that.

Asked if he had ever thought, after Pattaya, about going back to work at the pig farm – after all, it had looked promising, he was quite happy there and had his studies paid for by his employer – Joe said,

> I have never thought about it. I never think about walking backwards. I only think about walking forwards. [...] If you walk forward you will be successful, you know? To walk backwards, who would want to walk backwards? Nobody has eyes on their back. Maybe we would fall, maybe we bump into something, there are many obstacles if one walks backward. It isn't like (walking) forward. There are eyes in the front to look with, so you can walk better.

Note how Joe used the language of developing, of progressing, to describe his life, his dating experiences and his aspirations; his experiments in Pattaya's sex industry and his short-lived relationship with the German man can also be explained as attempts to progress towards a better life. He was clearly not yet at the end of the road, and had hoped to find a partner he could stay with for the longer term, something a fortune teller had told him was going to happen in two years' time.

Multiple Moral Aspects of Exchanging Love for Money

In all three cases described above, the young men presented their experience of working in the gay bars as attempts to find longer-term partners and have a better life, financially, for themselves and their families. There was no stated motivation to earn quick money, except perhaps for Lert during his first stint of sex work. This finding is different from the study I conducted on male sex work in Chiang Mai in the mid-1990s (De Lind van Wijngaarden 1999), and also different from the findings of McCamish's (2002) research in Pattaya. In both those studies, money, either to use for personal consumption or to send to the family, was the most important consideration for engaging in sex work, and there was no or little mention of finding a long-term partner. McCamish linked the importance of making money to the cultural expectation of parents in northeastern Thailand that children, including sons, especially unmarried sons, should provide financial support to their parents. McCamish may not have picked up on the gender dimension of this phenomenon, that is, that the 'sons' he described would in reality see themselves as dutiful daughters, similar to Ives in this study. The expectation that they would take care of ageing parents was definitely part of the narratives of many of the young men in this study; more for those who were from the northeast than for those from the wealthier south.

What explains this difference in findings? The first factor may be age. The research participants in the two earlier studies were up to 10 years older than the participants in this study. The expectations of men engaged in sex work might therefore shift throughout their career. The aim of a typical Thai male sex worker may initially be to find a long-term relationship, but after a number of experiences (mainly disappointments) in their attempts at long-term romance with foreigners, expectations may shift to be shorter-term, and become more pragmatic and money-oriented. After embarking on a career as a 'bar boy', gradually increasing peer pressure from fellow sex workers may also lead young men to become more oriented towards short-term gain and towards consumption and spending their earnings on entertainment, including gambling. Ives indicated that camaraderie between 'bar boys' establishes a pattern of joint entertainment, drinking, drug use and gambling for which a continuous stream of income is needed; I also found this in my earlier study in Chiang Mai. A gradual refocusing on short-term gain rather than on long-term romance is also in line with the general pessimism, which may be growing over time, about same-sex love and romance that many young men expressed in this study.

A new 'Thai theory of prostitution', to paraphrase ten Brummelhuis's influential paper (1993) would do well to add a temporal perspective to the motivations and expectations of men (and possibly women) in sex work, and investigate whether younger men are motivated more by hopes and aspirations for a long-term relationship than their more experienced and older peers. This is important, since such aspirations are likely to have a significant effect on HIV vulnerability. It has been shown that the perception of a sex partner as a (potential) boyfriend decreases the likelihood that condoms are used; young men, in their desire to land a boyfriend, are therefore probably at increased risk of HIV infection when they are at the start of their sex work careers (Mansergh et al. 2006; Sirivongrangson et al. 2012).

In terms of morality, many of the young men in the study found that sex work is an acceptable option as long as it is applied for a 'good' purpose, such as supporting one's family or paying off debts. Chai, for example, seemed to approve of sex work as long as it was applied for a goal he would agree with: supporting one's family. Similarly, Roj said that whether sex work is morally acceptable or not depends on whether the younger person 'really needs' the money or not:

> To do it for money, then we have to see first, the money that he gets – what is it for? One has to look at the situation [กาะ] of that person who does it, is he in trouble, is he like this, really?

Win, a Muslim from the south of Thailand, lamented that many young people seemed to be willing to have sex with paying strangers in order to purchase what he saw as unnecessary luxury goods:

> Some people want to get money [...] and have sex, because some people don't have enough [money] to use. But I think, 'Why do you do that, if you don't have enough money, why don't you look for a different type of work?' Some people post, like, 'I want an iPhone, I want to get a Blackberry' – so I am like, Oh! Why don't you save money for yourself?

Ek, who had a more conservative and middle-class background, firmly rejected the idea of exchanging sex and love for money:

> It is desperate. They don't think far enough. Because, we still have certain skills, we have arms and legs, something like that. Work, if you don't think too much, if you are not too picky, one can do anything, older brother. There are many ways to make a living [ช่องทางทำกิน], I don't see it as necessary to ask for somebody's help. [...] There is more pride/dignity [น่าภูมิใจมากกว่า] to that.

If he was in trouble, Ed said he would ask his mother for money rather than his boyfriend. He linked that to the fact that his boyfriend and Ed had not been together for that long, suggesting that he had not earned the right to be financially reliant on his boyfriend yet. Hence, the duration of a relationship in which exchange occurs is important: the longer the relationship lasts, the more acceptable it is for money to change hands – usually from the older/richer to the younger partner.

In short, participants in the study found exchanging sex for money in love relationships morally acceptable if the exchange occurs in the context of a relationship in which there is a significant difference in wealth between the two partners as well as a difference in age and perceived beauty. Similar to the negative and positive poles of a battery, there has to be difference before exchange can occur. Second, the money that changes hands must have a higher purpose, for example, to assist a poor family or to help a person in his studies, rather than be squandered on consumer goods or on gambling. Finally, the exchange should occur in the context of a longer-term relationship, not a one-off sexual encounter, although many of the young men from the northeast had no problems with the concept of one-off sexual encounters for money, especially if the second condition (helping one's family) had been met.

Selecting a Boyfriend: The 'Take-Care' Imperative

When asked about the criteria for selecting a boyfriend, most of the men referred to good looks or being handsome. Over half (14 out of 23 participants, including the 3 young men described in this chapter) mentioned that their preferred boyfriend should be older or better educated or more mature, implying their desire for somebody who takes care of them, which often meant somebody who would take responsibility for the young man's material needs or financial support. Indeed, 11 out of 24 participants had a first partner who was at least two years older than they were, and none reported a younger person as their first-ever male partner. This confirms the common idea found among most men in the study that relationships should be based on difference, not sameness. If there is sameness, there is nothing that can be exchanged, and hence, there is no long-term interest or reason for the partners to stay together. This idea is rooted in the only viable long-term living arrangement many of the young men in the study could really draw inspiration from: heterosexual marriage.

Oad saw many younger guys in his environment who preferred to date older men. In explaining this, Oad focused on the element of exchange:

[A] younger person wants love and attention [and] cannot yet make money himself. […] A *phu yai* [means adult, or 'rich or powerful person'], he can find money, the older he is, he will make a lot of money. And he, it is like, he wants happiness in life. […] The person who is the younger guy he is like – he can love anybody, he doesn't FIX [Eng] whether it has to be an old person or a mature person. He only asks to – have someone who loves him, that is enough. […] But […] the issue of money, of wealth, it is an issue that is related to it.

Oad thought that young men can love men of their own age as well as older men; for the young men age does not matter, and hence they might as well choose a person who comes with financial benefits. This is slightly contradictory, because if age does not matter for a young person, why does it start to matter for an old person? Oad linked age discrepancy to wealth discrepancy and saw these relationships as first and foremost based on a model of exchange.

Nook admitted that a boyfriend with money would attract him, saying he could not survive on love alone:

[B]ut if he loves me really, but if he doesn't have anything to give me to rely on, then it is ridiculous. These days, probably there is nobody around who will agree to 'eat pure salt' [กัดก้อนเกลือกันกิน] [Thai saying for people who are willing to suffer for love]. What I say is true. I speak frankly. It is like this.

He added a bit later:

If like me, I still think it, like, if I had a rich boyfriend – he probably would dare to buy me an iPhone! He would probably dare to buy this and that for me […]. It is just hope/ desire [ความอยากหวัง], something like that. But if you ask me: Do you want to have a rich boyfriend? Of course. I really want to have [a rich boyfriend]. I am not joking, too. I want to have. He can help me with everything.

Nook had had experience with both older and younger men, and said, resolutely,

> But if you ask me, I don't like young boys [เด็ก]. They are too similar to me. Their way of thinking is like mine, right? And they are probably, they are boys, they say: What is up with you? When I don't pick up the phone, they will be angry, like that. They are not reasonable. Not like adults, they are more reasonable. I can talk to them [คุยกันรู้เรื่องกว่า]. I like grown-ups [ผู้ใหญ่] better.

In the case of Joe and Ives, there was strong support from their mothers for the idea of finding a rich *farang* boyfriend. Note that Ives's and Joe's mothers did not necessarily like or condone working in a gay bar selling one's body; they were attracted to the idea of a long-term partner for their 'daughters', and saw the work at the gay bar as a vehicle to achieve this.

In regard to the element of exchange in relationships, Morris (2002, 51) noted that it invites the question of 'where the limits of prostitution are to be drawn in Thailand, and whether these limits should encompass relations between (foreign) men and (Thai) women'; the same could be said for relations between foreign and Thai men. Morris (2002, 51) described these relationships as follows:

> [R]elations in which foreign men and Thai women agree to a long-term performance of domestic intimacy, for which performance the foreign man agrees to provide money and support while the Thai woman agrees to provide pleasure, nurturance, and translational abilities.

One can wonder to what extent the example Morris draws on is applicable only to relationships between Thais and Westerners or to males and females. In all marriages there may be similar considerations, although in most instances the discrepancy in wealth and age may be less pronounced than in the case Morris discusses. Among the more feminine-identified participants, there seemed to be a definite desire to provide pleasure and nurturance in exchange for material benefits in order to progress and to help their family progress as well.

Not only young men who were involved in sex work had a preference for foreign boyfriends. Thirteen out of the 25 participants in the study expressed a preference for foreigners as potential partners. Two (Win and Pong) preferred foreigners who were Asian, and the rest had a liking for Caucasian foreigners (*farang*). Tam said he wanted to go to the gay beach in Pattaya, which he had heard about but had never been to: 'I want to have [a *farang* boyfriend]! I want someone to provide for me [chuckles].' The desire for foreigners as partners is, as discussed above, often conflated with the ability to 'take care' (financially), and foreigners in Thailand are often perceived to be wealthy. Second, feminine-oriented men tended to have a preference for partners who look or act masculine (see Chapters 8 and 9), and foreign bodies are often perceived as more masculine (read: taller, bigger, hairier, 'rougher looking') than Thai bodies. Third, some participants believed that foreigners are more serious and more willing to settle down in a monogamous relationship than Thai men. This belief, linked to stereotypes about Thai masculinity (see Chapter 6), is widespread among certain circles of Thai heterosexual women as well (Esara 2009). Ives illustrated this:

> Thai boyfriends are only interested in fun. Another thing, they may be able to take care of me in terms of certain things. But they would take care of us, like, not fully, not in the way I want them to take care of me/us. Yes. [...] I wanted to find a person who could pay off the debts for my family. [...] And then, I would give him my love, in return. [...] I will take care TAKE CARE [Eng] of him [...].

Part of the reason for this belief could be the fact that many foreign men settling down in Thailand with local women are already retired, have often had a marriage and children before, and are much older than their new wives, leading them perhaps to be less 'wild' and philandering than the younger Thai husbands whom these foreign men are compared with.

In the northeast of Thailand the phenomenon of *farang* men marrying local women is common, and the financial benefits this produces for the families of the women can be clearly seen. This is an important reason for the desirability of *farang* partners among certain segments of the population (Cohen 2003). Since dating *farang* has become closely associated with 'money boys', middle- and higher-class urban Thai gay men have started to prefer East-Asian foreigners (Japanese and Koreans, in particular), where money is presumably of less consideration (Kang 2011). Among young rural same-sex-attracted men, however, dating *farang* is still important as a strategy for upward mobility.

In choosing a boyfriend, most young men in this study did not consider sex or sexual attraction to be important, as Fluk illustrated:

> The issue of sex, for me, it is not important. Because we are all human beings, when you have a partner [แฟน], then you have to have sex anyway, it is normal. But I am not SERIOUS [Eng] about that.

Sex was, however, probably implied indirectly in some of the other criteria for desirable boyfriends that were mentioned. When the young men mentioned the need for a 'masculine looking and acting' boyfriend, they were implying that, apart from social desirability, this is what they found sexually appealing (i.e. someone who is masculine and insertive, making for a match). Another way in which sex was implied was in preferred body type (mentioned by over a third of the participants) and skin colour (mentioned by a quarter).

Discussion and Conclusion

What are the deeper reasons for the relative importance of upward mobility as a criterion for partner selection, the importance of complementarity and exchange in preferred romantic relationships, and the high moral acceptability of sex work that was found among the young men in this study? The different value attached to masculine and feminine sexuality in Asian societies provides part of the answer. In traditional Thai sexual culture, unspoilt masculine sexuality does not carry the same moral value as unspoilt feminine sexuality and is therefore less guarded and protected by the family. Using your sexuality in order to progress or gain an advantage is therefore less an issue for men/masculine bodies than it would be for women/feminine bodies. Masculine bodies involved in sex are not seen as being subject to pollution and loss of virginity. 'Nothing is lost' was a comment often heard when participants were asked about their feelings about losing their virginity at an early age, under circumstances that could in some cases (Win, Ek) be called deceitful or exploitative. These young men did not see the loss of their virginity as a big deal. Still, it is interesting to note that the more effeminate young men in this study would downplay the number of sexual experiences they had, worrying that it may affect their moral standing as 'good women'. This shows that they viewed their sexuality as something of value, and implicitly they felt that they were gradually 'devalued' by having more and more sexual partners and experiences.

The second reason why there was little objection among some participants to the idea of sex work or to tying oneself to a partner longer-term with an implicit or explicit monetary objective is the cultural idea that a child has to repay a moral debt towards the parents, especially the mother (Mulder 2000). Making money to help one's family is considered good, even if it is through sex work.

A third reason is linked to the gendered spheres that Niels Mulder describes as governing the Thai moral world and how these play a role in creating different moral universes (discussed in Chapter 6). The force of power (*decha*) rules the outside world and is associated with danger, struggle, amorality and the father as a protector; a different set of rules, norms and values govern the home, the sphere of moral goodness (*khuna*), associated with morality, goodness, and the mother (as a nurturer). This strongly gendered system creates a 'firewall' between the *decha* worlds of go-go bars in Pattaya, Bangkok and Phuket, on the one hand, and the quiet and traditional *khuna* village world, on the other. As long as somebody engaging in sex work does so outside the home sphere, while at the same time maintaining a proper demeanour and behaviour in relation to the family while at home, in line with the skills of knowing how to act in time and space (discussed in Chapter 3), there will be no questioning on the part of people nearby. There will also definitely be no sense of introspection, shame or guilt on the part of the person engaging in sex work, because he can uphold his personal morality in relation to the sphere of *khuna* and derive a sense of self-worth and satisfaction from this.

A fourth reason is economic and manifests itself in the sheer difference in the amounts of money that young men and women can make in sex work. This must be placed in the context of the increased importance of money in Thai society as a marker of social status. During the high season in a go-go bar in Pattaya, earnings can easily reach 30,000 to 40,000 baht a month (US$ 1,000–1,250), and there are plenty of stories of particularly attractive or skilful young men (and women) who are making much more than that. Compared with the current minimum wage for manual labour, which stands at 9,000 baht per month, these amounts are huge. The work in go-go bars is physically relatively light, with short working hours. As discussed, there often is a certain camaraderie among colleagues in bars, and they enjoy some freedom to start or end working early or late, and to skip work whenever they want (De Lind van Wijngaarden 1999). If one compares it with the eight-hour shifts in factories or convenience stores, for a salary that is usually less than a third of what can be earned in sex work, the appeal of sex work is not so hard to understand. In addition, sex work is flexible: one is able to work for a few weeks or months at the time, as Joe did, whereas in other jobs people often have to sign longer-term contracts in order to be eligible for work.

The fifth explanation for why love relationships with financial benefits are relatively well accepted among many research participants is more philosophical. The idea at the bedrock of heterosexual love relationships in the Thai worldview is that two different partners come together to form a couple, exchanging what they have to offer to one another. There must be difference; otherwise, there is nothing to exchange, nothing to complement. Without difference, most participants were certain that relationships would be unable to survive. This also explains why so few of the men in this study dreamed about or strived to have egalitarian gay relationships in the Western sense of the word. Egalitarian relationships were not seen as feasible, let alone durable.

Modern gay relationships can be compared with what Giddens has described as a 'pure relationship' (1992, 58), which

> refers to a situation where a social relation is entered into for its own sake, for what can be derived by each person from a sustained association with another, and which is continued only in so far as it is thought by both parties to deliver enough satisfactions for each individual to stay within it.

Giddens saw the emergence of this pure relationship as a culmination of a process of female emancipation, delinking sex from reproduction and delinking sexual pleasure from marriage. The stories of the young men in this study increasingly described this state of affairs in modern gay romantic life but, rather than appreciating the freedom and equality this brings, the young men in this study lamented the lack of structure and sustainability that pure relationships brought. The key reason for this pessimism was that the young men in this study felt that there must be substantive difference in successful relationships: either femininity complementing masculinity or a richer provider complementing a poorer person in need or an older person complementing a younger person or, in most cases, a combination of these factors.

The distinctions between the feminine and masculine domains and the different forms of love this entails, as noted by Mulder (2000), and the Buddhist distinction between pure love and worldly love parallel and mirror each other. In both forms of love, there is this element of exchange between the male and the female partner, and the two forms complement each other. In the home sphere, children are expected to repay the moral goodness bestowed upon them by their parents, especially their mother. Outside, there is a different set of exchange rates at play; sex and sexuality are commodities that should not be squandered but offered and exchanged (for money, security, long-term support) to the highest bidder. Due to the lack of importance placed on virginity for men, they can play this out again and again. Commodification and exchange have become even more pronounced since, as described in the previous chapters, masculinity and its gendered values and symbols have slowly overruled the need to protect and be careful with one's feminine identity, (presumed) virginity and sexuality among many of the young men in this study who made a transition from being *kathoey* to a more masculine sense of self.

Finally, the Internet, discussed in the previous chapter, makes engaging in sex for money even easier, as anonymity is easier to achieve, bypassing the moral spheres of the home versus the outside world even further. Taking the increased importance of consumption and possessions as markers of status in Thai society into consideration, it is unlikely that the phenomenon of exchanging sex for money or the importance of upward mobility as a criterion for choosing a partner are going to decrease in importance anytime soon.

Chapter 11

CONCLUSIONS AND IMPLICATIONS FOR HIV SERVICE PROVISION AND SEXUALITY EDUCATION

In this final chapter, the findings of this research project are summarized and discussed, including what the study has contributed to the field of sexuality research in Thailand. Implications for HIV prevention among young same-sex-attracted Thai men are also discussed, including comments about some concepts and assumptions that currently underpin HIV prevention programming for gay men in Thailand. Some remarks are offered on the theoretic approach of the study, on the research design and experience, as well as on the need for further research in the future.

Summary of Key Findings

In summary, most aspects of the young men's personalities and sense of self were found to be unrelated to their gender or sexuality, but were derived from overarching aspects of Thai culture and society. Thai personhood is strongly embedded in the family and is more defined by the social and the relational, rather than by individual traits. Hierarchy, and knowing one's place in it, is of utmost importance in forms of communication and in social behaviours, with clearly defined linguistic and behavioural rules in place about what can or should (or should not) be said or done vis-à-vis people who are placed in a higher or lower position than the actor/speaker. One's place in the hierarchy is determined, above all, by age and position in the family. Apart from this, profession and class, as reflections of presumed power and influence, are important.

Maintaining harmony in social relationships, in both equal and unequal ones, is an important cultural concern. This is done by maintaining principles of *kala-thetsa*, a cultural concept aimed at maintaining relationships by preserving peace and calm at the surface of communications, which is characterized by saving face (*naa*) and mutual prestige (*barami*) when dealing with family and social surroundings. Being a good child towards one's parents, to whom one is morally indebted for life, and the importance of being seen as a good Thai citizen and loving one's nation are also important in this regard. In Thai culture, maintaining the prestige of the nation, the self, one's partner, parents and other important people in one's life often overrules the need to be factually truthful. This can allow for a multiplicity of truths, depending on the context and position of the speaker. The higher importance placed on image and prestige in comparison with factual truth has important considerations for living a gendered or sexual life in Thai society.

A useful concept for understanding contradictions in the way Thai society operates is the division between the two gendered moral spheres of the household and surrounding community, which falls under the feminine sphere of the mother, and the outside world, which is governed by the masculine sphere of the father. Different sexual norms and values operate in these spheres.

This study has discovered two patterns in the way sexual subjectivity emerges and unfolds among young rural same-sex-attracted Thai men. Most of the participants had a sense of gender nonconformity from a very early age, and were identified by their parents and other people in their social environment as effeminate (*kathoey*). A smaller group of participants discovered their attraction to other men at a later stage, after they had reached a level of sexual maturity and after falling in love with another man.

Besides culturally determined aspects of how Thai personhood functions, gender was of overriding importance in how sexual subjectivity emerged and unfolded among the young men in this study. Philosophically and conceptually, the men initially considered homosexual relationships in terms of the coming together of a feminine and a masculine partner, in line with presumed sexual behaviours (a masculine 'top' referring to insertive anal sex, with a feminine 'bottom' being receptive) and social roles (the masculine partner being the care taker responsible for making money, and the feminine partner being in charge of the household). Sexually, at least in principle, there was a strict conceptual separation of behaviours according to gender.

This gendered understanding of homosexuality is initially shared with parents, friends and others in rural communities; this is part of the reason why so many of the young rural same-sex-attracted men had experienced being *kathoey* (rather than gay) for a while during their early teenage years. They were assuming, at the time, that their inability or unwillingness to fulfil typically masculine social roles meant that they in fact were – or should become – women. While a plethora of studies has emerged in the past decade focusing on sexual subjectivity and the presumed 'queering' of same-sex experience in Thailand, this study has pointed out that, for rural same-sex-attracted young men, gender remains the most important structuring framework for same-sex behaviours, relationships and experiences, at least during their younger years.

Buddhist explanations also played a role in the way the young men understood and explained their homosexuality. According to such explanations, being born with homosexual preferences is a punishment for unethical or immoral sexual behaviour in a previous life. Homosexuality itself is therefore not seen as a sin, in contrast to many other religions, but is understood as a form of suffering. This negative view held by most of the young men in this study paralleled their general pessimism about the likelihood of finding a fulfilling and durable same-sex relationship. This pessimism about the possibility of 'real love' between men was also explained by pointing to the natural and inherent philandering characteristics ascribed to Thai masculinity. The men in the study also considered the absence of children in same-sex relationships as a key reason for their inherent instability.

Overall, sexuality appeared to be relatively unimportant in the way the young men viewed themselves and the way they positioned themselves in society. In other words, their sexuality was mostly seen as a preference in behaviour and not as the basis for a social identity. The idea of a more or less separate gay community did not appeal to them. The assumption that rural gay Thai men move to the city in order to escape oppression and be free, which was part of the design of this study, can safely be refuted. On the contrary, many of the young men had strong and warm relationships with their families and objected to the idea of moving far away from home if there were no obvious reasons for this, such as work or study. The young men in this study attached great importance to remaining part of their families and of mainstream society. Most had many friends who were heterosexual (often girls), and none aspired to have a more or less exclusive circle of fellow-minded same-sex-attracted friends, which they considered too limiting. This is an important finding, because current approaches to HIV prevention among same-sex-attracted men harbour important assumptions about the existence and importance of gay communities in Thailand (see below).

One important phenomenon that undermined the young men's early gendered understandings of homosexuality was falling in love with presumably same-gendered friends. In Thailand, friendships are generally homosocial, and sexual partners are recruited from outside one's group of close or intimate friends. Falling in love with someone in one's inner circle is taboo and is considered problematic, partly because both partners would be presumed to be feminine and receptive in anal intercourse, making intercourse impossible. Despite this, a number of participants experienced feelings of love, sexual desire or actual sexual experiences with a friend, and in all instances this was an important cause for confusion and searching for answers, and a reason to form new concepts about the possibilities and potentialities of same-sex romance. In some cases, the experience of falling in love with friends resulted in distancing from a feminine concept of self, and led to a process of masculinization, including experimenting with the insertive role in anal intercourse. It generally also resulted in less importance being attached to one's presumed role in anal intercourse in determining one's sense of self, with the choice of object rather than gender role becoming more prominent in defining and understanding same-sex romance.

Another important force for change was the Internet. This study has shown the important role that the Internet plays during the emerging and evolving sexual subjectivity of rural same-sex-attracted men. The Internet helped in creating shared understandings of concepts related to homosexuality and gender, despite many contradictions. In later stages, in particular during chatting and dating, and in combination with processes of 'loving friends', the Internet helped further undermine gender-based understandings of homosexuality. Partly under the influence of pornographic videos and images as well as global gay culture, the Internet also played a role in the growing importance and popularity of more masculine images in same-sex relationships.

A number of previously more effeminate participants in the study started presenting themselves as more masculine on the Internet, gradually gaining experience and confidence in this new social role, encouraged by the positive responses received by actual or potential romantic partners. Under the influence of this new aesthetic, a masculine comportment was increasingly seen as fashionable and cool, while acting masculine no longer precluded the pleasure of being anally penetrated. The Internet therefore provided the encouragement to experiment with multiple gendered presentations of the self. In supporting this fluid, previously unattainable freedom of experimentation (without consequences for one's direct social surroundings), the Internet further complicated the moral, sexual, geographic and social links between sex, gender and love. Whereas some participants enjoyed this freedom to experiment, others were confused by it and tried to resist the gradual blurring of clear boundaries between the masculine and the feminine.

An important linguistic concept that helped downplay the importance of sexual role (and, linked to this, gender) in understanding same-sex relations is the term 'both' in same-sex chatting discourse. 'Both', taken from the English language, refers to someone who can take both the insertive as well as the receptive role in anal intercourse. Several of the young men initially had strong reservations about this term, indicative of how difficult it was for them to move beyond a gendered concept of same-sex attraction. Initially, they understood 'both' to refer to someone who was part of the masculine and the feminine domains at the same time, refusing to choose. The word 'both' functions to undermine the link between position in anal sex and actual or presumed feminine or masculine identity. While the labels *rab* ('bottom') and *ruk* ('top') remained important for the Thai same-sex-attracted young men in this study, who presented themselves in gendered ways, a growing number of hybrid variations on these terms were found. These hybrid terms seem to reflect a person's presumed level of masculinity on an axis with two poles (masculine–feminine), as Jackson (2000) observed. With practice and experience, considerable variation emerged in possibilities for self-presentation and social role (or surface), and as a result sexual practices among the young men in this study started to become more varied.

In general, the young men perceived love relationships to be viable only if both partners had something to contribute or exchange, something that the other did not have. In this sense, old complements young, feminine complements masculine, top complements bottom, rich and ugly complements poor and beautiful. The Western gay idea of egalitarian, more or less equal relationships was alien to most of the participants, indicating the continually important role of difference and exchange in love relationships. The importance of the concept of 'taking care' in the young men's criteria for selecting a boyfriend also points to the underlying view of a viable relationship as being based on exchange and complementarity rather than similarity, and also points at a continued importance of gender in defining and interpreting male–male relationships in Thai society.

The same chapter focused on how important it was for many young men, especially those from poorer families, to use their youthful beauty and the promise of pleasure provided by their bodies to move higher in society and help themselves and their families attain better status. These young men were looking for a partner who was of higher status (and therefore often considerably older) than them, in the hope that such a partner could 'take care' of them. Related to this, several of the participants were involved for shorter or longer periods in sex work, with the main goal being to meet a foreign partner to help them and their family escape a life of poverty. Several of the participants were strongly encouraged by their families – especially their mothers – in their quest to find a wealthy partner. The young men acted partly out of a sense of moral duty to help their family, especially their parents. In other cases, a more experienced and presumably wiser partner was preferred out of a perceived need for guidance, and social and mental support, and less for material reasons.

Not surprisingly, those who moved to another part of the country to further their education or to find work gained more freedom, and hence experienced greater changes to their sexual subjectivity than the few participants who stayed at home after completing high school. This was not only the case for men who moved to Bangkok and surroundings but also for those who moved to smaller cities closer to home. After they moved away from their parental home, changes in the young men's sense of self often resulted from their exposure to a new living environment, new friends and the chance to make changes to the way they presented themselves in this new context.

This study has shown that it is impossible to gain an understanding of the sexual subjectivity of young, rurally based, same-sex-attracted Thai men without a deep understanding of Thai culture and society. The young men borrow symbols and meanings from overall Thai culture and society in order to construct and reconstruct their sexual and gender identity. Important cultural constructs that help interpret Thai sexual subjectivities include the concept of face (naa) and the importance of keeping it; the concept of kala-thetsa (comportment, proper communication in line with one's position in the social hierarchy) and barami (maintaining prestige). Two other important cultural constructs are the importance of the family and the related moral obligations of children towards their parents (especially the mother) and the Buddhist concept of karma. Furthermore, Thai sexual subjectivities cannot be understood without understanding the concepts of gender, including the gendered division of the (feminine) home versus the (masculine) outside world. At the same time, relatively new cultural concepts are absorbed and new understandings merge with or partly replace older understandings, for which the study used the metaphor of the palimpsest. Examples of this are new ideas about gender and sexual possibilities influenced by the availability of pornography, leading to new terms and words such as 'both', both-ruk and bai-ruk that can be used to describe oneself and others. The introduction of masculine looks and attire as aesthetic and fashionable rather than as an expression of a deeper intrinsic gender identity is another example.

At the beginning of this study I assumed that asking questions about sexual experiences would lead to a greater understanding of the young men's sexual subjectivity. Generally, the young men did not have experience talking explicitly about sex, especially not with a stranger. Even for those who during later interviews became more comfortable talking about their sexual experiences, it was striking to note how little this yielded in terms of understanding sexual subjectivity. Perhaps this was because so little symbolic meaning could be derived from describing physical sexual acts. Much more could be learned about sexual subjectivity without talking directly about sexual behaviours, but by talking about social aspects and understandings related to sex, gender and relationships. This points to the merit of a symbolic-interactionist approach to studying sexuality in Thailand. Interpreting indirect references to sex, or interpreting the reasons why sex was not mentioned or discussed more explicitly than it was, led to many of the key findings and insights presented in this study.

Implications for HIV Service Provision and Sexuality Education for Young Same-Sex-Attracted Men

One important rationale for this study was the ongoing HIV epidemic among young same-sex-attracted men in Thailand. The study had a selection bias towards those who can be considered exemplary or 'good': several reported being leaders of their class or representatives of their schools, and all had at least the self-confidence to enrol as participants in this study. Despite this, the young men reported considerable HIV risk and vulnerability. In line with the finding that most of the rural young men's initial understanding of homosexuality was gender-based, in which they explained their attraction to men in terms of their own feminine identity, 17 out of 24 men had receptive anal sex as their first sexual experience, and a quarter of the young men in this study had their first sex with someone whom they described not as gay, but as a *phu chaai* ('real' man). Whereas at first sight the dominance of anally receptive young men in the study may point to selection bias, it is important to consider the changes that occurred during the research period. During the first interview, 19 out of 25 participants in this study considered themselves to be 'receptive', but only 10 out of those 18 remaining men (i.e. 10 out of 23) considered themselves to be exclusively receptive during the final interview (two men were lost to follow-up). Over time, many of the first-time receptive males therefore gained experience being insertive as well, either as a one-off experience, in a series of experiences, or permanently. This study suggests that this process is linked to the young men gradually coming to terms with experiences and feelings that contradicted their initial gender-based understanding of homosexuality, such as exposure to pornography on the Internet and falling in love with friends.

The finding that a shift in sexual behaviour occurs, from exclusively receptive to versatile, has important epidemiological consequences, as sexual versatility has been linked with higher HIV vulnerability in several countries (Lyons et al. 2013). I suggest that the Thai HIV epidemic among gay men is exacerbated by the fact that the youngest same-sex-attracted men are initially having unprotected receptive anal intercourse with men who are older (and therefore more likely to be infected with HIV), whereas later in their sexual career they learn to insert and potentially transmit their early HIV infection to people who are of their age or younger.

What can the study findings tell us about improving the provision of HIV prevention, testing, treatment and support services for young Thai men who have sex with men? One striking finding in the study is the low priority the young men gave to HIV. Despite the study being advertised as related to sexual health and HIV prevention, the topic came up spontaneously during 87 hours of interviews only once or twice, and when I raised it the participants usually had little to say about it. The young men had heard about HIV but did not consider it relevant to their lives; almost none of the participants knew anyone with HIV, and they had received little to no HIV prevention education in their lives. If they did receive any HIV information, it was usually linked to heterosexual transmission. There is a need to find ways to make young same-sex-attracted men more aware of and interested in HIV, starting with making them aware of the fact that so many of them are becoming infected during the first few years of their sexual careers. If the high HIV incidence among 15- to 22-year-olds found in Bangkok-based cohort studies (van Griensven et al. 2013) is projected onto the participants in this study, two to possibly four of them would have become infected over the period in which this study took place. It is important not to be misled by the low HIV prevalence in rural areas compared with Bangkok, Pattaya, Phuket and Chiang Mai, since young same-sex-attracted men from rural areas are more likely than not at some stage to have sex in these cities. HIV prevention and sexuality education efforts should therefore start in rural areas with a focus on young men who are close to their sexual debut, and not be entirely concentrated on the 'hot spots' of the epidemic.

Another finding that is relevant to understanding the HIV epidemic among young same-sex-attracted Thai men is that they start being sexually active at an early age. Some of these instances of early sex are abusive; in this study, two of the 25 participants' first sexual experiences can be described as such. The study has shown that efforts to prevent abuse and improve sexual health outcomes have to start much earlier than is currently the case. Since most participants became sexually active at the age of 13 to 15, and given the high enrolment rate of Thai youth in secondary schools (> 95 per cent), the school should be considered as a potential vehicle to reach young same-sex-attracted men with sexuality education. It is imperative to pilot specific HIV prevention and sexuality education programs in lower secondary schools. There is a need to be innovative and use new media (Instagram, Twitter, Facebook, GayRomeo/PlanetRomeo, Hornet, Jack'D, Grindr, CamFrog and other Internet platforms) as channels for increased awareness of sexual abuse, as well as about HIV and other sexual health issues. It is also important that sexual health services, including HIV counselling and testing facilities, should be allowed to test people under the age of 15 without the need for parental consent. The staff working in such facilities need to be trained to deal with the needs of young same-sex-attracted men in an understanding and non-judgemental manner.

Furthermore, HIV prevention and sexuality education for young same-sex-attracted men should address the finding in this study that many young men (especially from the northeast) go for short stints of sex work in Bangkok and Pattaya during their school holidays, often with the open or tacit approval of mothers hopeful for their son to land a wealthy foreign partner, and discuss the specific health and other risks involved in sex work.

Most importantly, HIV interventions need to incorporate the finding in this study that young Thai same-sex-attracted men, at least those in rural areas, do not consider themselves to be part of Western-style gay communities. Despite decades of efforts by the Thai government and Western donor agencies to create and strengthen gay community-based organizations to address the HIV prevention needs of Thai same-sex-attracted men, this study indicates there is little sense of belonging to a gay community in Thailand in the same way as that exists in the West – at least not among the young men in this study. This could be an important reason for the failure to reduce HIV incidence and prevalence in recent years, and may also help explain the lack of urgency, outrage or anger found among Thai gay men about the HIV epidemic in their midst, at least in comparison with the days of 'ActUp' and other gay-led initiatives in Western cities in the 1980s and early 1990s.

Instead of trying to copy HIV prevention efforts that have been successful in Western settings, HIV services for Thai same-sex-attracted men should adopt messages and approaches that take overall aspects of Thai society and culture into consideration, including its tendency towards unspoken communication, especially in sexual matters, as well as the way communication and behaviours are structured along hierarchical lines. The cultural importance of maintaining prestige and a good image, even at the detriment of the factual truth, is an important cultural aspect that will lead men to keep silent about their 'extramarital' sexual exploits, even if these exploits put their partners at risk of HIV infection. It is important to study further how such dynamics related to power and prestige are employed in Thai sexual encounters (see Kippax and Smith 2001).

Indeed, this study found how age, gender comportment and (perceived) status or class are of utmost importance in understanding the dynamics surrounding condom use and safe sex. Usually an older or wealthier partner takes the lead in a sexual encounter and decides (without verbal discussion) whether condoms are used or not. Several of the young men in the study tended to leave the use of condoms to the discretion of their older (and presumably wiser) partners, especially the feminine-oriented or anally receptive men, who, in line with their 'good woman' image, presented themselves as sexually innocent and not knowledgeable. They also aspired, often quite naively, for their often older and wealthier partners to 'take care' of them in the future in a long-term romantic relationship, further diminishing the like-lihood that they would discuss or insist on condom use. In this regard, the development of a freer and more 'liberated' sexuality of certain groups of Thai women, mirrored by changes in the gender/sexual identities of some participants, offers some hope that these power inequalities can be challenged.

Finally, Western-inspired programs for peer education are unlikely to work in a context where friends feel it could look bad or arrogant to 'teach' people who are the same age as them. To deal with this, a level of hierarchy needs to be introduced in such programs: one possible approach would be to mobilize 'older brothers/sisters' as '*phi* educators' (*phi* meaning 'older brother/sister') for HIV prevention with younger people rather than same-aged peers, as suggested by McCamish (2000) and Borthwick (1999). At the time of writing this book (2020) I have worked on the development of such an age-segregated peer education program with a group of researchers aiming to pilot such a program in three Thai provinces and linking first- and second-year uni-versity students (*phi*) with younger same-sex-attracted high school students (*nong*) recruited from their previous schools. There are significant barriers to overcome, not the least of which is the ongoing Covid epidemic, but also in terms of resistance by policymakers and teachers. Significant support for the proposed project concept has been received from young people themselves, which has been heartening.

Deconstructing Categories: Redefining the Building Blocks of Social and Health Services

The findings of this study put the use of some categories for studying aspects of, or phenomena in, Thai society in question. One of these is the term 'com-munity'. The Thai language does not appear to have a popular term to dis-tinguish clearly between society and community, and this study suggests they may not need a word for community, as the young men in this study want to be part of mainstream society. The idea of a separate community even had mor-ally negative connotations for some of the young men in the study. Another English term that appears problematic to translate into Thai is 'identity' with its individualistic connotation; this study has therefore avoided using this word, preferring the term 'sexual subjectivity' and, for matters not related to sexu-ality, 'personhood'. 'Identity' also has connotations of a static, permanent situ-ation; however, this study has found the Thai sense of sexual/gender identity to be highly fluid. Thai personhood is defined by gender comportment, age, status and position in one's family and neighbourhood, as well as nationalist elements. For behaviour change programs, such as those currently working to reduce the incidence of unsafe sex, it is important to reassess the extent to which social context, sexual and gender fluidity and Thai culture of communication are sufficiently taken into consideration in its 'model of change'. Individuals should never be assumed to be fully rational decision makers when it comes to HIV risk behaviours – even less so if these individuals are young, Thai, feminine-oriented same-sex-attracted men.

Related to this, the study found that identity labels used in human rights and sexual health programming, such as 'LGBT' ('lesbian, gay, bisexual and transgender') and even the term 'gay men' should be used with care in the Thai context, since for many people social identity formation on the basis of sexual orientation or preference makes about as much sense as identity formation on the basis of preferred car brand or sports activities. As discussed, the Thai word *phet* can be translated as sex, sexuality or gender, which is in itself indicative of the linguistic and cultural oddity of defining people solely by their sexual preference. Similarly and related to this, homophobia is a term that the study shows has no place in the study of Thai sexualities and genders. There is no deep-seated hatred of homosexuality in Thai society and it is generally not seen as evil, a sin or a crime; homosexuality is instead seen as karmic punishment or a social deficiency. This does not make growing up 'different' any easier in Thailand, as there are no cultural blueprints, no role models and no clear life trajectories available for young same-sex-attracted Thai men, except for *kathoey*. The word 'heteronormativity', describing how the needs of non-heterosexuals are routinely ignored or made invisible by Thai society, is therefore suggested as a more appropriate term (see Yep 2002).

The basic concepts of HIV prevention and human rights interventions in Thailand need to be restudied and redefined, ensuring that the social realities of young Thai same-sex-attracted men are in line with the basic principles and foundations of interventions attempting to address their needs. Interventions should be grounded in Thai values related to family/parents, nationality, harmony, face saving, the importance of maintaining *barami* and prestige, karma, and knowing one's place in time and space (*kala-thetsa*).

This book has shown that understanding how and according to which logic(s) vulnerable people interpret and fulfil their social and sexual needs is a prerequisite for designing effective HIV prevention and sexual health strategies. I hope the lessons of this book will be picked up and implemented; only then will it have reached its ultimate aim of contributing to the improved sexual health and well-being of young Thai same-sex-attracted men.

APPENDIX

Glossary of Thai Terms Used in this Book

Aeb roo [แอบรู้]   'Secretly knowing', referring to knowledge one has without being directly told about it.

Bai-ruk [ไบรุก]   Someone who is 'bisexual-insertive' and is only insertive in either anal, oral or vaginal sex.

Barami [บารมี]   Charisma, charm or prestige.

Both [โบท]   From the English word 'both', meaning someone who can either be receptive or insertive in anal intercourse.

Both-*ruk* [โบทรุก]   Someone who can in principle be either receptive or insertive in anal intercourse, but prefers the insertive role.

Both-*rab* [โบทรับ]   Someone who can in principle be either receptive or insertive in anal intercourse, but prefers the receptive role.

Chaai chatri [ชายชาตรี]   A man who is loyal, honest and strong.

Faen [แฟน]   Boyfriend/girlfriend; this word is gender neutral and usually (but not always) implies a sexual relationship.

Farang [ฝรั่ง]   Foreigner/Westerner, usually denoting a white-skinned Caucasian.

Gig [กิ๊ก]   Casual sex partner or potential casual partner or boyfriend.

Jao choo [เจ้าชู้]   Meaning 'owns multiple lovers': flirtatious, womanising.

Kala-thetsa [กาลเทศะ]   Thai cultural concept of knowing how to behave and conduct oneself properly in every situation.

Kathoey [กะเทย]   Gender label referring to a feminized man, also often translated as 'third gender', 'transgender', 'transvestite' or 'hermaphrodite'.

Kathoey khwaai [กะเทยควาย]   Derogative term ('Buffalo kathoey') to denote an unfeminine or unsophisticated *kathoey*.

Kunlasatree [กุลสตรี]   A stereotypical good woman, defined as 'proficient and sophisticated in household duties; graceful, pleasant, yet unassuming in her appearance and social manners; and conservative in her sexuality' (Taywaditep et al. 2003, 1023).

Lan-laa [ลั้นลา]   Sexually playful, flirtatious.

Mathayom [มัธยม]   High school, divided into three years of junior high school (*mathayom ton* [มัธยมต้น], grades 7–9) and three years of senior high school (*mathayom plaai* [มัธยมปลาย], grades 10–12).

Mia noi [เมียน้อย]   Minor wife, meaning a second (or third or fourth) woman who is taken care of by a man in a more or less permanent arrangement.

Naa [หน้า]   Face (in the sense of one's reputation, as in 'losing face').

Nak leng [นักเลง]   A rough, tough, womanising, heavy-drinking man, sometimes associated with mafia practices.

Perd phey [เปิดเผย]   Opening up, similar to 'coming out'.

Phet [เพศ]   Gender, sex, sexuality.

Phu chaai [ผู้ชาย]   Man.

Phu yai [ผู้ใหญ่]   Adult, but can also refer to a richer or more powerful person.

Phu ying [ผู้หญิง]   Woman.

Por Wor Chor [ปวช.]   Abbreviation, from *Prakasaniyabat Wichacheep* [ประกาศนียบัตรวิชาชีพ]. Vocational training school (lower equivalent of *Mathayom plaai*, grades 10–12).

Por Wor Sor [ปวส.]   Abbreviation, from *Prakasaniyabat Wichacheep Soong* [ประกาศนียบัตรวิชาชีพชั้นสูง]. Higher vocational training, equivalent to an academy or college (post-grade 12).

Rab [รับ]   Literally 'receive'. Someone who prefers the receptive role in anal intercourse. Usually this has connotations with being effeminate in one's demeanour and social role.

Riab roi [เรียบร้อย]   Neat, tidy, traits somewhat associated with femininity.

Ror dor [รด.]	Abbreviation from *raksa dindaeng* [รักษาดินแดน], 'to take care of/defend the land'. Pseudo-military training that boys can choose to follow while studying in senior high school. If they do so, they are exempt from military conscription.
Ruk [รุก]	Literally insert. Someone who prefers the insertive role in anal intercourse. Usually this has connotations with being masculine acting in one's demeanour and social role.
Sangkhom [สังคม]	Society, community or something in between.
Sadaeng ork [แสดงออก]	'Showing oneself'; dropping hints about one's gender nonconformity via behaviour or language use.
Sao praphet song [สาวประเภทสอง]	Second type of woman, respectful word for *kathoey.*
Toot [ตุ๊ด]	Derogative term for *kathoey* or effeminate gay, sometimes translated as 'fag', but in some contexts it is perceived as merely teasing or playful.

REFERENCES

Barmé, S. 2006. *Woman, Man, Bangkok: Love, Sex, and Popular Culture in Thailand*. Chiang Mai, Thailand: Silkworm Books.

Beyrer, C., S. D. Baral, F. van Griensven, S. M. Goodreau, S. Chariyalertsak, A. L. Wirtz and R. Brookmeyer. 2012. 'Global Epidemiology of HIV Infection in Men Who Have Sex With Men'. *Lancet* 380, no. 9839: 367–77.

Blackwood, E., and M. Johnson. 2012. 'Queer Asian Subjects: Transgressive Sexualities and Hetero-Normative Meanings'. *Asian Studies Review* 36, no. 4: 441–51.

Borthwick, P. 1999. 'HIV/AIDS Projects with and for Gay Men in Northern Thailand'. *Journal of Gay & Lesbian Social Services* 9, no. 2–3: 61–79.

Bun, C. K., and T. C. Kiong. 1993. 'Rethinking Assimilation and Ethnicity: The Chinese in Thailand'. *International Migration Review* 27, no. 10: 140–68.

Carrillo, H. 2004. 'Sexual Migration, Cross-Cultural Sexual Encounters, and Sexual Health'. *Sexuality Research and Social Policy* 1, no. 3: 58–70.

Chaloemtiarana, T. 1979. *Thailand: The Politics of Despotic Paternalism*. Bangkok: Social Science Association of Thailand, Thammasat University.

Chonwilai, S. 2012a. 'Chai Rak Chai: Men Loving Men'. In *Thai Sex Talk: The Language of Sex and Sexuality in Thailand*, edited by P. Boonmongkhon and P. A. Jackson, 125–33. Chiang Mai, Thailand: Mekong Press.

————. 2012b. 'Khun Phaen: A Womanizer'. In *Thai Sex Talk: The Language of Sex and Sexuality in Thailand*, edited by P. Boonmongkhon and P. A. Jackson, 43–49. Chiang Mai, Thailand: Mekong Press.

————. 2012c. 'Kathoey (กะเทย): Male-to-Female Transgenders or Transsexuals'. In *Thai Sex Talk: The Language of Sex and Sexuality in Thailand*, edited by P. Boonmongkhon and P. A. Jackson, 109–17. Chiang Mai, Thailand: Mekong Press.

Cohen, A. 2009. 'Dek Inter and the "Other": Thai Youth Subcultures in Urban Chiang Mai'. *Sojourn: Journal of Social Issues in Southeast Asia* 24, no. 2: 161–85.

Cohen, E. 2003. 'Transnational Marriage in Thailand: The Dynamics of Extreme Heterogamy'. In *Sex and Tourism: Journeys of Romance, Love and Lust*, edited by K. Sung Chon, T. Bauer and B. McKercher, 57–84. New York: Routledge.

Connors, M. 2005. 'Hegemony and the Politics of Culture and Identity in Thailand'. *Critical Asian Studies* 37, no. 4: 523–51.

Cook, N. M. 2002. 'Thai Identity in the Astrological Tradition'. In *National Identity and Its Defenders: Thailand Today*, edited by C. J. Reynolds, 189–211. Chiang Mai, Thailand: Silkworm. (Reprinted from 1993.)

Curran, S. R., and A. C. Saguy. 2001. 'Migration and Cultural Change: A Role for Gender and Social Networks?' *Journal of International Women's Studies* 2, no. 3: 54–77.

Danthamrongkul, W., and W. Posayajinda. 2004. เครือข่ายสังคมและเพศสัมพันธ์กลุ่มชายชอบชาย [Social Networks and Sexual Relations of the Group of Men Who Like Men]. Bangkok: Department of Research on Drugs and Abuse, Research Institute of Medical Science, Chulalongkorn University.

De Lind van Wijngaarden, J. W. 1995. 'A Social Geography of Male Homosexual Desire: Individuals, Locations and Networks in the Context of the HIV Epidemic in Chiang Mai, Northern Thailand'. MA thesis, University of Chiang Mai, Chiang Mai, Thailand.

———. 1999. 'Between Money, Morality and Masculinity: Bar-Based Male Sex Work in Chiang Mai'. *Journal of Gay & Lesbian Social Services* 9: 193–218.

De Lind van Wijngaarden, J. W., T. Brown, P. Girault, S. Sarkar and F. van Griensven. 2009. 'The Epidemiology of Human Immunodeficiency Virus Infection, Sexually Transmitted Infections, and Associated Risk Behaviors Among Men Who Have Sex with Men in the Mekong Subregion and China: Implications for Policy and Programming'. *Sexually Transmitted Diseases* 36, no. 5: 319–24.

De Lind van Wijngaarden, J. W., and T. T. Ojanen. 2016. 'Identity Management and Sense of Belonging to a Gay Community among Young Rural Thai Same-Sex Attracted Men: Implications for HIV Service Delivery'. *Culture, Health and Sexuality* 18, no. 4: 377–90.

D'Emilio, J. 1993. 'Capitalism and Gay Identity'. In *The Lesbian and Gay Studies Reader*, edited by H. Abelove, M. A. Barale and D. M. Halperin, 467–76. New York: Routledge.

———. 1998. *Sexual Politics, Sexual Communities: The Making of a Homosexual Minority in the United States, 1940–1970*. Chicago: University of Chicago Press.

Diamond, L. M. 2008. *Sexual Fluidity: Understanding Women's Love and Desire*. Cambridge, MA: Harvard University Press.

———. 2016. 'Sexual Fluidity in Male and Females'. *Current Sexual Health Reports* 8, no. 4: 249–56.

Dowsett, G. W. 2002. 'Bodyplay: Corporeality in a Discursive Silence'. In *Sexualities: Critical Concepts in Sociology*, edited by K. Plummer, 408–22. London: Routledge.

Dowsett, G. W., H. Williams, A. Ventuneac and A. Carballo-Dieguez. 2008. '"Taking It Like a Man": Masculinity and Barebacking Online'. *Sexualities* 11, no. 1–2: 121–41.

Embree, J. 1950. 'Thailand: A Loosely Structured Social System'. *American Anthropologist* 52, no. 2: 181–93.

Esara, P. 2009. 'Imagining the Western Husband: Thai Women's Desires for Matrimony, Status and Beauty'. *Ethnos* 74, no. 3: 403–26.

Fabian, J. 1991. *Time and the Work of Anthropology: Critical Essays 1971–1991*. New York: Routledge.

Fongkaew, W. 2002. 'Gender Socialization and Female Sexuality in Northern Thailand'. In *Coming of Age in South and Southeast Asia: Youth, Courtship and Sexuality*, edited by L. Manderson and P. Liamputtong, 147–65. Richmond, UK: Curzon.

Fongkaew, K, A. Khruataeng, S. Khamphirathasana, M. Jongwsan and O. Arlunaek. 2017. *Media as a Tool for Change: Enhancement of Positive Media Engagement and Advocacy on Issues Relating to Sexual Orientation, Gender Identity and Gender Expression (SOGIE) and Intersex Issues: SOGI and Intersex in the Media Study*. Chonburi, Thailand: Burapha University.

Ford, N., and S. Kittisuksathit. 1994. 'Destinations Unknown: The Gender Construction and Changing Nature of the Sexual Expressions of Thai Youth'. *AIDS Care* 6, no. 5: 517–31.

Fordham, G. 1995. 'Whisky, Women and Song: Men, Alcohol and AIDS in Northern Thailand'. *Australian Journal of Anthropology* 6, no. 1–2: 154–77.

————. 2006. *A New Look at Thai AIDS: Perspectives from the Margin*, Vol. 4. New York: Berghahn Books.

Foucault, M. 1979. *History of Sexuality Volume 1: An Introduction*. Translated by R. Hurley. New York: Vintage Books.

Fuller, T. D., J. N. Edwards, S. Sermsri and S. Vorakitphokatorn. 1993. 'Gender and Health: Some Asian Evidence'. *Journal of Health and Social Behavior* 34, no. 3: 252–71.

Gallagher, R. 2005. 'Shifting Markets, Shifting Risks: HIV/AIDS Prevention and the Geographies of Male and Transgender Tourist-Orientated Sex Work in Phuket, Thailand'. Paper presented at the Sexualities, Genders and Rights in Asia: 1st International Conference of Asian Queer Studies, Bangkok, Thailand, 7–9 July.

Giddens, A. 1992. *The Transformation of Intimacy: Sexuality, Love & Eroticism in Modern Societies*. Stanford, CA: Stanford University Press.

Goffmann, E. 1963. *Stigma: Notes on the Management of Spoilt Identity*. New York: Touchstone.

Hanks, L. M. 1962. 'Merit and Power in the Thai Social Order'. *American Anthropologist* 64, no. 6: 1247–61.

Hanks, J. 1964. 'Reflections on the Ontology of Rice'. In *Primitive Views of the World*, edited by S. Diamond, 151–54. New York: Columbia University Press.

Harrison, R. 1999. 'The Madonna and the Whore: Self/"Other" Tensions in the Characterization of the Prostitute by Thai Female Authors'. In *Genders & Sexualities in Modern Thailand*, edited by P. Jackson and N. M. Cook, 168–90. Chiang Mai, Thailand: Silkworm Books.

Jackson, P. A. 1995a. *Dear Uncle Go: Male Homosexuality in Thailand*. Bangkok: Bua Luang Books.

————. 1995b. 'Thai Buddhist Accounts of Male Homosexuality and AIDS in the 1980s'. *Australian Journal of Anthropology* 6, no. 1: 140–53.

————. 1997. 'Kathoey > < Gay > < Man: The Historical Emergence of Gay Male Identity in Thailand'. In *Sites of Desire, Economies of Pleasure: Sexualities in Asia and the Pacific*, edited by L. Manderson and M. Jolly, 166–90. Chicago: University of Chicago Press.

————. 1999. 'Tolerant but Unaccepting: The Myth of a Thai "Gay Paradise" '. In *Genders and Sexualities in Modern Thailand*, edited by Peter A. Jackson and N. M. Cook, 226–42. Chiang Mai, Thailand: Silkworm Books.

————. 2000. 'An Explosion of Thai Identities: Global Queering and Re-Imagining Queer Theory'. *Culture, Health & Sexuality* 2, no. 4: 405–24.

————. 2004. 'Gay Adaptation, Tom-Dee Resistance, and Kathoey Indifference: Thailand's Gender/Sex Minorities and the Episodic Allure of Queer English'. In *Speaking in Queer Tongues: Globalization and Gay Language*, edited by W. L. Leap and T. Boellstorff, 202–30. Chicago: University of Illinois Press.

————. 2009a. 'Capitalism and Global Queering: National Markets, Parallels among Sexual Cultures, and Multiple Queer Modernities'. *GLQ: A Journal of Lesbian and Gay Studies* 15, no. 3: 257–394.

————. 2009b. 'Global Queering and Global Queer Theory: Thai [Trans]genders and [Homo]sexualities in World History'. *Autrepart* 49: 15–30.

————. 2011a. 'Bangkok's Early Twenty-First-Century Queer Boom'. In *Queer Bangkok: 21st Century Markets, Media and Rights*, edited by Peter A. Jackson, 1–42. Hong Kong: Hong Kong University Press.

————. 2011b. 'The Thai Regime of Images'. *Soujourn (Journal of Social Issues in Southeast Asia)* 19, no. 2: 181–218.

————. 2012. 'Introduction to the English Edition'. In *Thai Sex Talk*, edited by P. Boonmongkhon and Peter A. Jackson, 5–14. Chiang Mai, Thailand: Mekong Books.

Jeffrey, L. A. 2002. *Sex and Borders: Gender, National Identity, and Prostitution Policy in Thailand*. Chiang Mai, Thailand: Silkworm Books.

Kang, D. 2011. 'Queer Media Loci in Bangkok: Paradise Lost and Found in Translation'. *GLQ: A Journal of Lesbian and Gay Studies* 17, no. 1: 169–91.

Keyes, C. F. 1984. 'Mother or Mistress but Never a Monk: Buddhist Notions of Female Gender in Rural Thailand'. *American Ethnologist* 11, no. 2: 223–41.

Kippax, S., and G. Smith. 2001. 'Anal Intercourse and Power in Sex between Men'. *Sexualities* 4, no. 4: 413–34.

Kirsch, A. T. 1977. 'Complexity in the Thai Religious System: An Interpretation'. *Journal of Asian Studies* 36, no. 2: 241–66.

Klima, A. 2004. 'Thai Love Thai: Financing Emotion in Post-Crash Thailand'. *Ethnos* 69, no. 4: 445–64.

Knodel, J., M. VanLandingham, C. Saengtienchai and A. Pramualratana. 1996. 'Thai Views of Sexuality and Sexual Behaviour'. *Health Transition Review* 6, no. 2: 179–201.

Laphimon, M. 2012. 'Kik (กิ๊ก): A Casual Partner'. In *Thai Sex Talk: The Language of Sex and Sexuality in Thailand*, edited by P. Boonmongkhon and P. A. Jackson, 180–87. Chiang Mai, Thailand: Mekong Press.

Lyons, A., M. Pitts and J. Grierson. 2013. 'Versatility and HIV Vulnerability: Patterns of Insertive and Receptive Anal Sex in a National Sample of Older Australian Gay Men'. *AIDS and Behavior* 17, no. 4: 1370–77.

Manderson, L. 1992. 'Public Sex Performances in Patpong and Explorations of the Edges of Imagination'. *Journal of Sex Research* 29, no. 4: 451–75.

Mansergh, G., S. Naorat, R. Jommaroeng, R. A. Jenkins, R. Stall, S. Jeeyapant, … F. van Griensven. 2006. 'Inconsistent Condom Use with Steady and Casual Partners and Associated Factors Among Sexually-Active Men Who Have Sex With Men in Bangkok, Thailand'. *AIDS and Behavior* 10, no. 6: 743–51.

Matzner, A. 2001. 'The Complexities of Acceptance: Thai Student Attitudes towards Kathoey'. *Crossroads: An Interdisciplinary Journal of Southeast Asian Studies* 15, no. 2: 71–93.

McCamish, M. 2002. 'The Structural Relationships of Support from Male Sex Workers in Pattaya to Rural Parents in Thailand'. *Culture, Health & Sexuality* 4, no. 3: 297–315.

McCamish, M., G. Storer and G. Carl. 2000. 'Refocusing HIV/AIDS Interventions in Thailand: The Case for Male Sex Workers and Other Homosexually Active Men'. *Culture, Health and Sexuality* 2, no. 2: 167–82.

McCargo, D. 2009. *Tearing Apart the Land: Islam and Legitimacy in Southern Thailand*. Singapore: NUS Press.

Mills, M. B. 1995. 'Attack of the Widow Ghosts: Gender, Death, and Modernity in Northeast Thailand'. In *Bewitching Women, Pious Men*, edited by A. Ong and M. G. Peletz, 244–73. Berkeley: University of California Press.

Morris, R. 1994. 'Three Sexes and Four Sexualities: Redressing the Discourses on Gender and Sexuality in Contemporary Thailand'. *Positions: East Asia Cultures Critique* 2, no. 1: 15–43.

————. 2002. 'Failures of Domestication: Speculations on Globality, Economy, and the Sex of Excess in Thailand'. *Differences: A Journal of Feminist Cultural Studies* 13, no. 1: 45–76.

Mounier, A., and P. Tangchuang, eds. 2010. *Education & Knowledge in Thailand: The Quality Controversy*. Chiang Mai, Thailand: Silkworm Books.

Mulder, N. 1997. *Thai Images: The Culture of the Public World*. Chiang Mai, Thailand: Silkworm Books.

———. 2000. *Inside Thai Society: Religion, Everyday Life, Change*. Chiang Mai, Thailand: Silkworm Books.

———. 2011. 'The Crux is the Skin: Reflections on Southeast Asian Personhood'. *Journal of Current Southeast Asian Affairs* 30, no. 1: 95–116.

Murray, D. A. 2009. 'Introduction'. In *Homophobias: Lust and Loathing Across Time and Space*, edited by D. A. Murray, 1–15. London: Duke University Press.

Ojanen, T. 2010. 'Mental Health Services and Sexual-Gender Minority Clients in Bangkok, Thailand: Views by Service Users and Service Providers'. Masters thesis, Assumption University, Bangkok.

Pachun, T. 2008. ' "Life in Two Worlds": A Qualitative Study of Identity Conflict Management among Male Homosexual Medical Students in Bangkok'. Masters thesis, Mahidol University, Bangkok.

Rabibhadana, A. 1984. 'Kinship, Marriage, and the Thai Social System'. In *Perspectives on Thai Marriage*, edited by A. Chamrathrithirong, 1–27. Bangkok: Sri Ananta Press.

Reynolds, C. J. 2002. 'Thai Identity in the Age of Globalization'. In *National Identity and Its Defenders: Thailand Today*, edited by C. J. Reynolds, 308–38. Chiang Mai, Thailand: Silkworm Books.

Ross, M. W. 2005. 'Typing, Doing, and Being: Sexuality and the Internet'. *Journal of Sex Research* 42, no. 4: 342–52.

Saengtienchai, C., J. Knodel, M. VanLandingham and A. Pramualratana. 1999. ' "Prostitutes Are Better Than Lovers": Wives' Views on the Extramarital Sexual Behavior of Thai Men'. In *Genders and Sexualities in Modern Thailand*, edited by P. Jackson and N. M. Cook, 78–92. Chiang Mai, Thailand: Silkworm Books.

Seidman, S. 2004. *Beyond the Closet: The Transformation of Gay and Lesbian Life*. New York: Routledge.

Shulich, T. 2006. 'Love in the Time of Money: Intimate and Economic Affiliations between Men in Chiangmai, Thailand'. PhD thesis, Brandeis University.

Simpson, M. 2002. 'Meet the Metrosexual: He's Well Dressed, Narcissistic and Obsessed with Butts. But Don't Call Him Gay'. *Salon*, 22 July. http://www.salon.com/2002/07/22/metrosexual/. Accessed 12 July 2019.

Sinnott, M. 1999. 'Masculinity and Tom Identity in Thailand'. *Journal of Gay & Lesbian Social Services* 9, no. 2: 97–119.

———. 2004. *Toms and Dees: Transgender Identity and Female Same-Sex Relationships in Thailand*. Honolulu, HI: University of Hawaii Press.

———. 2009. 'Public Sex: The Geography of Female Homoeroticism and the (In)Visibility of Female Sexualities'. In *Out in Public: Reinventing Lesbian/Gay Anthropology in a Globalizing World*, edited by E. Lewin and W. Leap, 225–39. Oxford: Wiley-Blackwell.

———. 2012. 'Korean-Pop, Tom Gay Kings, Les Queens and the Capitalist Transformation of Sex/Gender Categories in Thailand'. *Asian Studies Review* 36, no. 4: 453–74.

Sirivongrangson, P., R. Lolekha, A. Charoenwatanachokchai, U. Siangphoe, K. K. Fox, N. Jirarojwattana, … O. Suksripanich. 2012. 'HIV Risk Behavior among HIV-Infected Men Who Have Sex with Men in Bangkok, Thailand'. *AIDS and Behavior* 16, no. 3: 618–25.

Sivaraksa, S. 2002. 'The Crisis of Siamese Identity'. In *National Identity and Its Defenders: Thailand Today*, edited by C. J. Reynolds, 33–48. Chiang Mai, Thailand: Silkworm Books.

Storer, G. 1999a. 'Performing Sexual Identity: Naming and Resisting "Gayness" in Modern Thailand'. *Intersections: Gender, History and Culture in the Asian Context* 2. http://intersections.anu.edu.au/issue2/Storer.html. Accessed 12 July 2019.

———. 1999b. 'Rehearsing Gender and Sexuality in Modern Thailand'. *Journal of Gay & Lesbian Social Services* 9, no. 2: 141–59.

Taywaditep, K. J., E. Coleman and P. Dumronggittigule. 2003. 'Thailand'. In *The Continuum Complete International Encyclopedia of Sexuality*, edited by Robert T. Francoeur and Raymond J. Noonan, 1021–53. New York: Continuum.

ten Brummelhuis, H. 1993. 'Do We Need a Thai Theory of Prostitution?' Paper presented at the 5th International Conference on Thai Studies, London, July 1993.

———. 1999. 'Transformations of Transgender'. *Journal of Gay & Lesbian Social Services* 9, no. 2: 121–39.

Thianthai, C. 2004. 'Gender and Class Differences in Young People's Sexuality and HIV/AIDS Risk-Taking Behaviours in Thailand'. *Culture, Health & Sexuality* 6, no. 3: 189–203.

Unaldi, S. 2011. 'Back in the Spotlight: The Cinematic Regime of Representation of *Kathoeys* and Gay Men in Thailand'. In *Queer Bangkok: 21st Century Markets, Media, and Rights*, edited by Peter A. Jackson, 81–98. Hong Kong: Hong Kong University Press.

Van Esterik, J. 1982. 'Women Meditation Teachers in Thailand'. In *Women of Southeast Asia*, edited by P. Van Esterik, Vol. 9, 42–54. DeKalb, IL: Center for Southeast Asian Studies, Northern Illinois University.

Van Esterik, P. 2000. *Materializing Thailand*. Oxford: Berg.

van Griensven, F., P. H. Kilmarx, S. Jeeyapant, C. Manopaiboon, S. Korattana, R. A. Jenkins, … T. D. Mastro. 2004. 'The Prevalence of Bisexual and Homosexual Orientation and Related Health Risks among Adolescents in Northern Thailand'. *Archives of Sexual Behavior* 33, no. 2: 137–47.

van Griensven, F., J. W. de Lind van Wijngaarden, S. Baral and A. Grulich. 2009. 'The Global Epidemic of HIV Infection among Men Who Have Sex with Men'. *Current Opinion in HIV/AIDS* 4, no. 4: 300–7.

Van Griensven, F., A. Varangrat, W. Wimonsate, S. Tanpradech, K. Kladsawad, … K. Kanggarnrua. 2010. 'Trends in HIV Prevalence, Estimated HIV Incidence, and Risk Behavior among Men Who Have Sex with Men in Bangkok, Thailand, 2003–2007'. *JAIDS: Journal of Acquired Immune Deficiency Syndromes* 53, no. 2: 234–39.

van Griensven, F., W. Thienkrua, J. McNicholl, W. Wimonsate, S. W. Chaikummao, … P. Akarasewi. 2013. 'Evidence of an Explosive Epidemic of HIV Infection in a Cohort of Men Who Have Sex with Men in Thailand'. *AIDS* 27, no. 5: 825–32.

Wah-Shan, C. 2001. 'Homosexuality and the Cultural Politics of Tongzhi in Chinese Societies'. *Journal of Homosexuality* 40, no. 3–4: 27–46.

Walker, A. 2008. 'The Rural Constitution and the Everyday Politics of Elections in Northern Thailand'. *Journal of Contemporary Asia* 38, no. 1: 84–105.

Weeks, J. 1985. *Sexuality and Its Discontents: Meanings, Myths, and Modern Sexualities*. New York: Routledge.

Weston, K. 1995. 'Get Thee to a Big City: Sexual Imaginary and the Great Gay Migration'. *GLQ: A Journal of Lesbian and Gay Studies* 2, no. 3: 253–77.

Winichakul, T. 1997. *Siam Mapped: A History of the Geo-body of a Nation*. Honolulu: University of Hawaii Press.

Winter, S. 2006a. 'Thai Transgenders in Focus: Their Beliefs about Attitudes Towards and Origins of Transgender'. *International Journal of Transgenderism* 9, no. 2: 47–62.

―――. 2006b. 'Thai Transgenders in Focus: Demographics, Transitions and Identities'. *International Journal of Transgenderism* 9, no. 1: 15–27.

Wyatt, D. K. 2003. *Thailand: A Short History*, 2nd ed. Chiang Mai: Silkworm Books.

Yep, G. A. 2002. 'From Homophobia and Heterosexism to Heteronormativity: Toward the Development of a Model of Queer Interventions in the University Classroom'. *Journal of Lesbian Studies* 6, no. 3–4: 163–76.

INDEX

www.ingramcontent.com/pod-product-compliance
Lightning Source LLC
Chambersburg PA
CBHW030649270326
41929CB00007B/277